Maroons in Guyane

Race in the Atlantic World, 1700–1900

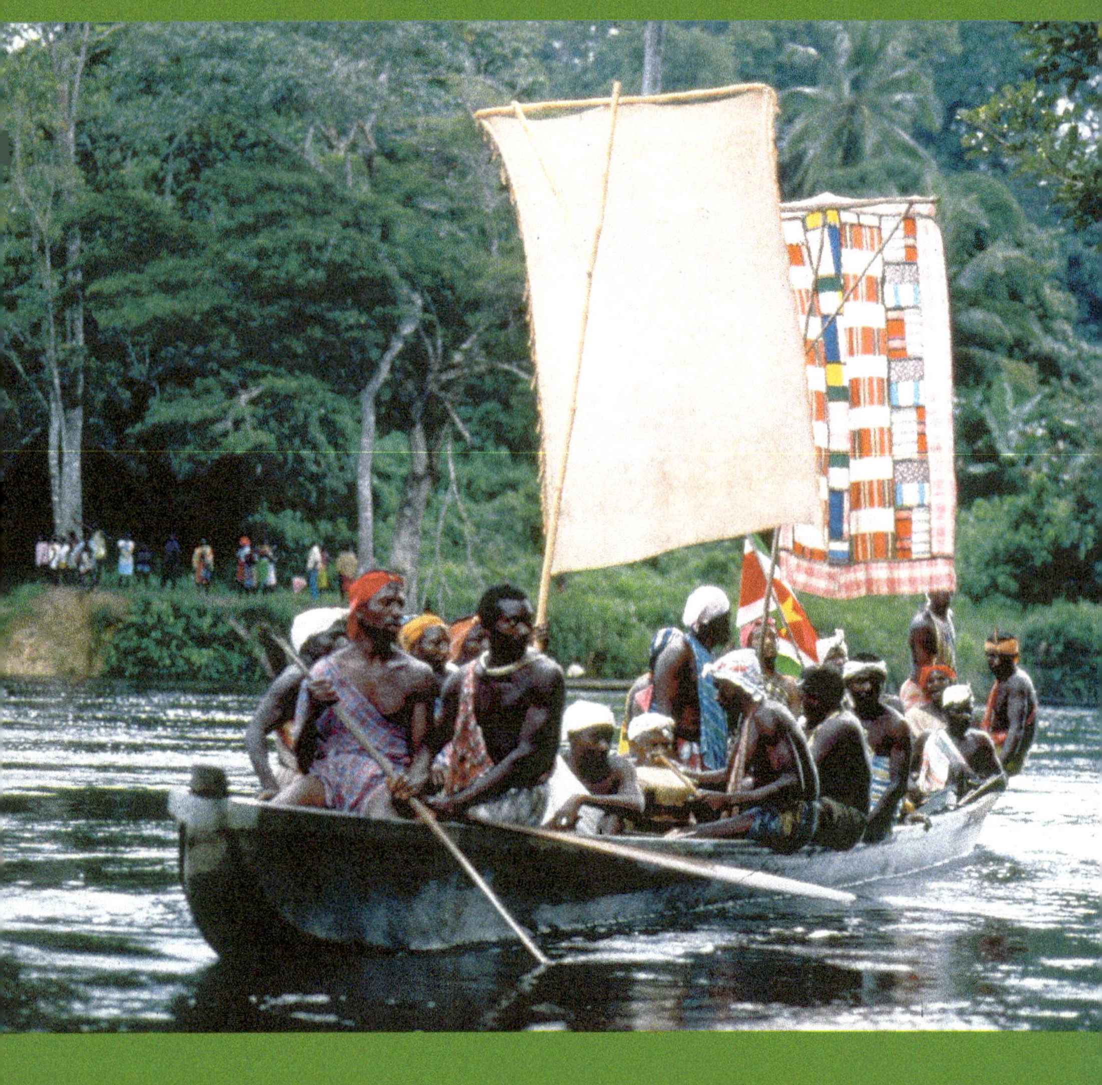

Maroons in Guyane

Past, Present, Future

RICHARD PRICE AND SALLY PRICE

The University of Georgia Press ▸▸▸ *Athens*

A Sarah Mills Hodge Fund Publication

This publication is made possible in part through a grant from the Hodge Foundation in memory of its founder, Sarah Mills Hodge, who devoted her life to the relief and education of African Americans in Savannah, Georgia.

Published by the University of Georgia Press
Athens, Georgia 30602
www.ugapress.org

Designed by Erin Kirk
Set in Warnock Pro
Printed and bound by Sheridan Books
The paper in this book meets the guidelines for permanence and durability of the Committee on Production Guidelines for Book Longevity of the Council on Library Resources.

Most University of Georgia Press titles are available from popular e-book vendors.

Printed in the United States of America
26 25 24 23 22 P 5 4 3 2 1

Library of Congress Cataloging-in-Publication Data
Names: Price, Richard, 1941– author. | Price, Sally, author.
Title: Maroons and Guyane : past, present, future / Richard Price and Sally Price.
Description: Athens : University of Georgia Press, [2022] | Series: Race in the Atlantic world | Includes bibliographical references.
Identifiers: LCCN 2021045241 | ISBN 9780820362458 (hardback) | ISBN 9780820360867 (paperback) | ISBN 9780820361567 (ebook)
Subjects: LSCH: Maroons—French Guiana—History. | Maroons—French Guiana—Social conditions.
Classification: LCC F2471.B55 P755 2022 | DDC 988.2—dc23
LC record available at https://lccn.loc.gov/2021045241

Frontispiece: Gravediggers returning to the village during the funeral rites for the paramount chief of the Saamakas, Agbago Aboikoni, 1989.

Contents

Preface

During our first fifteen years of anthropological research on Maroons in the French overseas *département* of Guyane (French Guiana), our conversations with local people—journalists, politicians, educators, civil servants, and many others—convinced us of the need to replace the pervasive stereotypes circulating about the Maroon populations living in their midst with accurate information. Those encounters inspired us to write a book, in French, to answer that need—*Les Marrons*, which was published in 2003. The book was also intended for young Maroons, many of whom were seriously interested in their own history and able to read French because of having gone to school in Guyane. Our idea was to provide an introduction to the history of the four Maroon peoples in Guyane (Alukus, Okanisis, Pamakas, and Saamakas), clarify the ways in which these groups differ from one another (culturally and linguistically), and trace the main lines of their respective situations at different points in time. This English-language edition provides an update of their fast-evolving presence in Guyane.

▶ ▶ ▶

We begin by calling attention to four key points:

1. **Maroons are not a single people.** They are members of six distinct societies (four of which are represented in the population of Guyane) whose traditional territories are separated by considerable geographical distance and who display significant differences in language, religion, social organization, and myriad other aspects of culture.
2. **Taken together, Maroons now constitute 36 percent of the population of Guyane, which makes them the largest population segment of the *département*.** As of 2020, there were some 100,000 Maroons in Guyane—47,000 Okanisis, 36,000 Saamakas, 10,000 Alukus, and 7,000 Pamakas. With a remarkably high birth rate and strong

ongoing immigration, their proportionate share of the total population continues to rise rapidly.

3. **None of the Maroon peoples in Guyane originated there.** They all came from neighboring Suriname. The groups have distinct histories of arrival in Guyane, having come at different times and in different circumstances, which has much to do with their contrasting political statuses today. These differences have generated rivalries and jealousies that continue to influence the roles that Maroons play in the society of Guyane.
4. **Maroons are known worldwide for the richness of their cultures and their deep historical consciousness.** Their distinctive creole languages are among the most important in the world for linguists. Their arts play a key role in helping us understand historical processes in the African diaspora. Their knowledge of medicinal plants contributes to the pharmacological research of multinational drug companies. And their deep historical knowledge has contributed to a reevaluation of what Claude Lévi-Strauss once called "*la pensée sauvage*."

In contemporary Guyane, the choice of a collective term for these peoples is strongly politicized. Aluku politicians have adopted the term "Buschinengué," rejecting "Noir Marron" and "Marron" as connoting a "European" gaze. Saamakas, who are far more numerous in Guyane but have no political influence (because unlike the Alukus, they are not French citizens), reject "Buschinengué" as a word that appears only in the language of the Alukus and their neighbors.[1]

In this book, we adopt the term "Maroon" both because it is neutral regarding intergroup rivalries and because it has strong connotations of heroism and freedom fighting. (We made a similar choice in the 1960s, when Afro-Surinamese politicians in Paramaribo tried to introduce the term "Boslandcreool" to assimilate Maroons to the Creole political party.) In our view, the heroism of historical Maroons throughout the hemisphere, from Brazil to the United States, and the pride this brings to their descendants today more than justify the use of this term.

Acknowledgments

This book is the fruit of more than a half century of research into the history and culture of Maroons in Suriname and Guyane. It would be impossible to recognize individually the hundreds (perhaps thousands) of people and organizations that have shared their lives and thoughts with us over the years, so we simply thank them collectively here. We would like to express special gratitude to the DAC (Direction des Affaires Culturelles de la Guyane) and the "Canopée des Sciences" association for supporting our research in 2018.

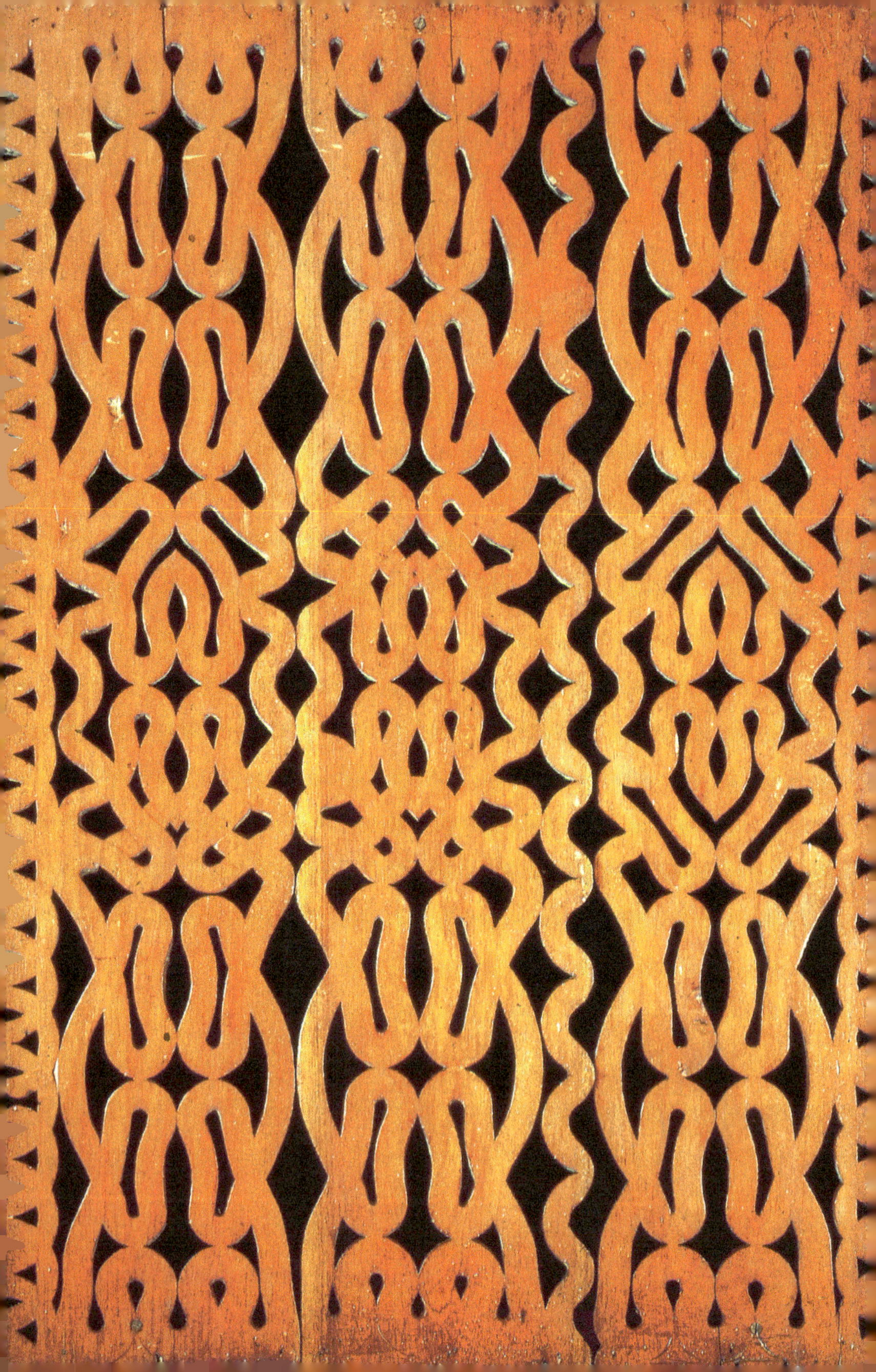

Marronage An Introduction

The English word "maroon" (French *marron*) derives from the Spanish *cimarrón*—itself based on an Arawakan (Taíno) Indian root.[1] *Cimarrón* originally referred to domestic cattle that had taken to the hills in Hispaniola, and soon after it was used to denote enslaved American Indians who had escaped from the Spaniards on that Caribbean island. By the end of the 1530s, the word was being used primarily to refer to Afro-American runaways and already had strong connotations of "fierceness," of being "wild" and "unbroken."[2]

In 1502, the man who would become the first Afro-American maroon arrived on the very first ship carrying enslaved Africans to the New World. In the 1970s, one of the last surviving maroons in the hemisphere was still alive in Cuba. For more than four centuries, the communities formed by maroons dotted the fringes of plantation America from Brazil to Florida, from Texas to Peru. Usually called *palenques* in the Spanish colonies, and *mocambos* or *quilombos* in Brazil, they ranged from tiny bands that survived less than a year to powerful states encompassing thousands of members and lasting for generations or even centuries. Today their descendants still form semi-independent enclaves in several parts of the hemisphere—for example, in Jamaica, Brazil, Colombia, Belize, Suriname, and Guyane—remaining fiercely proud of their maroon origins and, in some cases at least, faithful to unique cultural traditions forged during the earliest days of Afro-American history.

During the past several decades, historical research has done much to dispel the myth of the docile slave. The extent of violent resistance to enslavement has been documented rather fully, including revolts in the slave factories of West Africa, mutinies during the Middle Passage, and the organized rebellions that began to sweep through most colonies within a decade after the arrival of the first slave ships. And there is a growing literature on the pervasiveness

Opposite: Saamaka interior door, carved by Heintje Schmidt, village of Ganzee, ca. 1930.

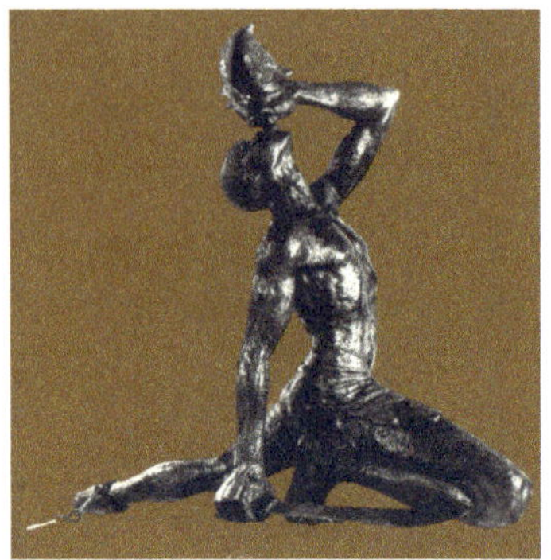

The Unknown Maroon of Saint-Domingue, by Albert Mangonès, ca. 1971, later erected across from the presidential palace, Port-au-Prince, Haiti.

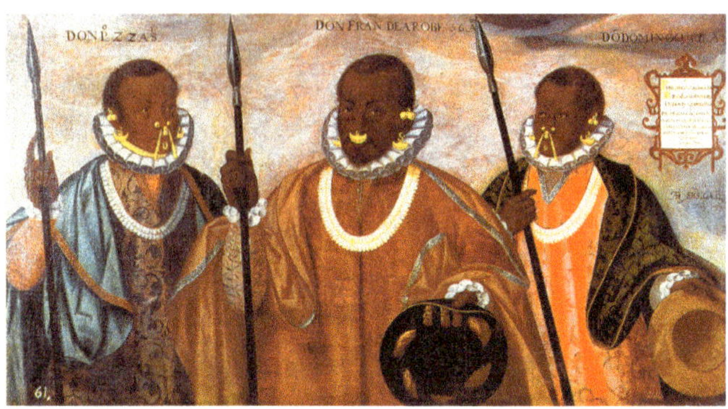

Zambo Chiefs of Esmeraldas, by Andrés Sánchez Gallque, 1599. This painting by an Amerindian master painter shows the Maroon chief Don Francisco de Arobe and his two sons, Don Pedro (*left*) and Don Domingo, in Quito for the signing of a peace treaty. They are wearing the regalia of Spanish lords, but with Amerindian-style ear and nose rings.

of various forms of day-to-day resistance—from simple malingering to subtle but systematic acts of sabotage.

In this context, maroons and their communities hold a special significance for the study of slave societies. For while they were, from one perspective, the antithesis of all that slavery stood for, they were at the same time a widespread and embarrassingly visible part of these systems. Just as the very nature of plantation slavery implied violence and resistance, the wilderness setting of early New World plantations made marronage and the existence of organized maroon communities a ubiquitous reality.

Planters generally tolerated *petit marronage*—repetitive or periodic truancy for such purposes as visiting a friend or lover on a neighboring plantation. But long-term, recidivist maroons received brutal punishments such as the amputation of a leg, castration, suspension from a meat hook through the ribs, or slow roasting to death. And in many cases, these tortures were written into law. *Grand marronage*, in which fugitives banded together to create communities of their own, struck directly at the foundations of the plantation system, presenting military and economic threats that often taxed the colonists to their very limits. Maroon communities, whether hidden near the fringes of the plantations or deep in the forest, periodically raided plantations for firearms, tools, and women, often permitting families that had formed during slavery to be reunited in freedom.

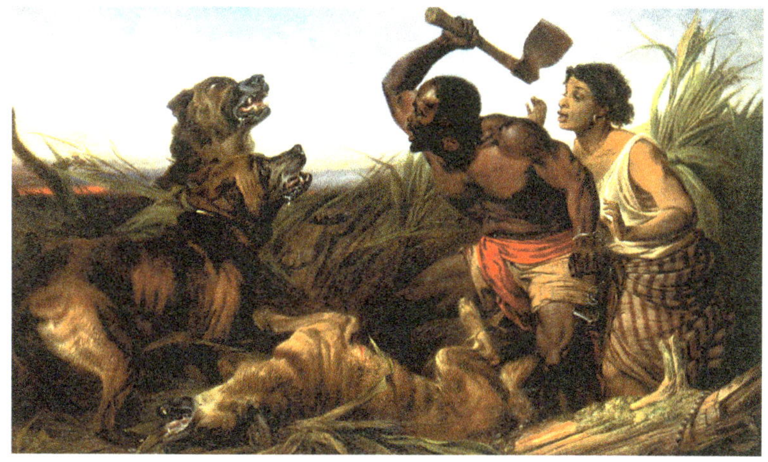

Hunted Slaves, by Richard Ansdell, 1861.

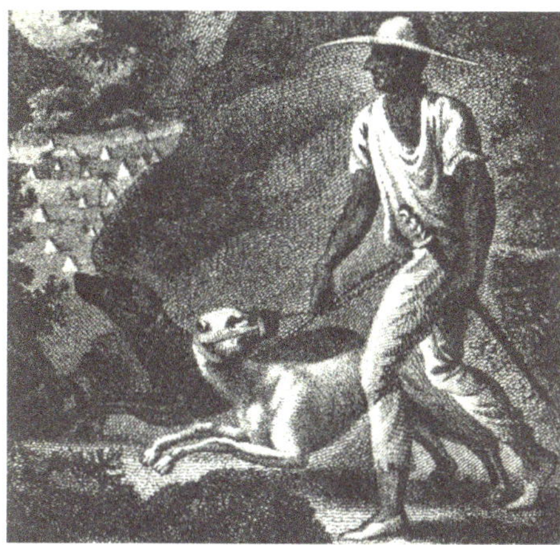

A Cuban hunting maroons with dogs.

In a remarkable number of cases, the beleaguered colonists were eventually forced to sue their former slaves for peace. For example, in Brazil, Colombia, Cuba, Ecuador, Hispaniola, Jamaica, Mexico, and Suriname, whites reluctantly offered treaties granting maroon communities their freedom, recognizing their territorial integrity, and making some provision for meeting their economic needs, in return for an end to hostilities toward the plantations and an agreement to return future runaways. Many maroon societies never reached this stage, having been crushed by a massive force of arms, and even when treaties were proposed, they were sometimes refused or quickly violated. New maroon communities seemed to appear almost as quickly as the old ones were exterminated, and they remained, from a colonial perspective, the "chronic plague" and "gangrene" of many plantation societies right up to final emancipation.

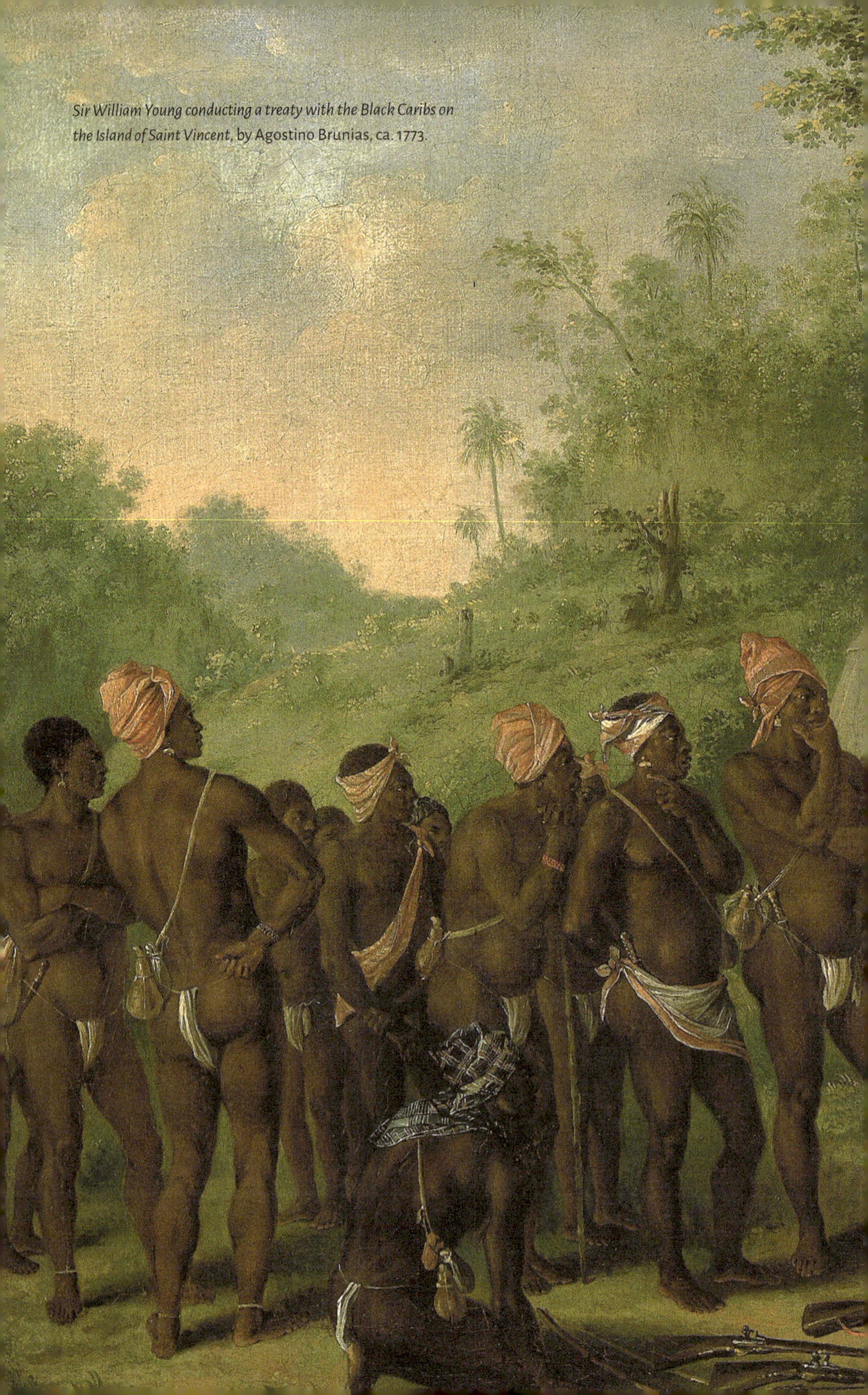

Sir William Young conducting a treaty with the Black Caribs on the Island of Saint Vincent, by Agostino Brunias, ca. 1773.

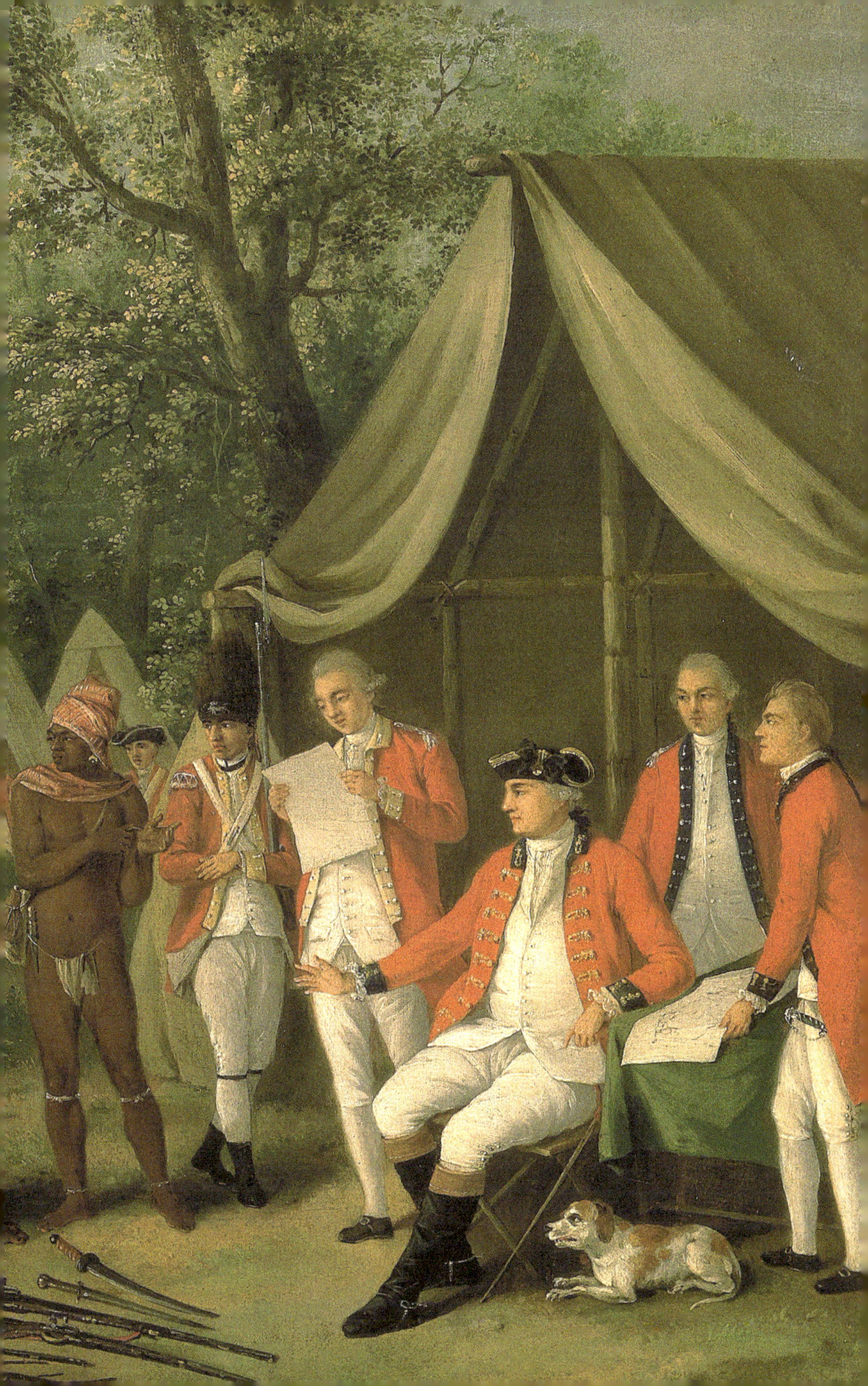

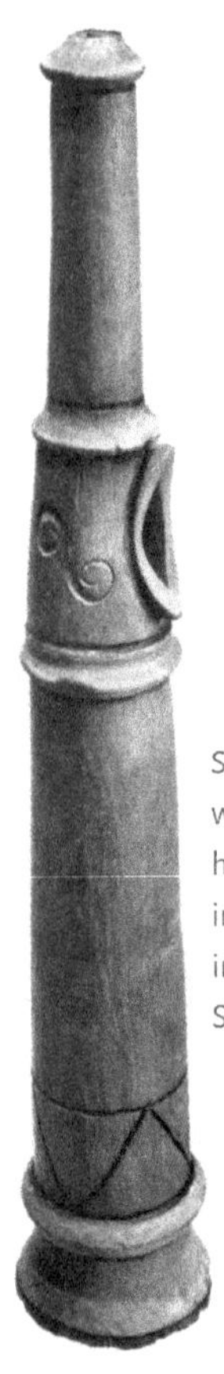

Saamaka wooden signal horn, collected in 1928–1929 in Dangogo, Suriname.

To be viable, maroon communities had to be inaccessible, and villages were typically located in remote, inhospitable areas. In the southern United States, isolated swamps were a favorite setting, and maroons often became part of Native American communities; and in Jamaica, some of the most famous maroon groups lived in the intricately accidented "cockpit country," which was riddled with deep canyons and limestone sinkholes and made inhospitable by a scarcity of water and good soil. In the Guianas, the seemingly impenetrable rain forest provided maroons with a safe haven.

Wherever they established their communities, maroons developed extraordinary skills in guerrilla warfare. To the bewilderment of their colonial enemies, whose rigid and conventional tactics were learned on the open battlefields of Europe, these highly adaptable, mobile warriors took maximum advantage of local environments, striking and withdrawing with great rapidity, making extensive use of ambushes to catch their adversaries in crossfire, fighting only when and where they chose, depending on reliable intelligence networks among non-maroons (both enslaved people and white settlers), and often communicating by drums and horns.

The initial members of each maroon community hailed from a wide range of societies in West and Central Africa. At the outset, they shared neither language nor cultural beliefs and practices. Their collective task, once settled in the forests or mountains or swamplands, was nothing less than to create new communities and institutions, drawing on the various African backgrounds of their members as well as on fragments of the European and Amerindian cultures they had come into contact with in the Americas. In some ways, the cultures of contemporary maroon peoples strike outsiders as being uncannily "African" in feeling, but no maroon social, political, religious, or aesthetic system can be reliably traced to a specific African ethnic provenience. Instead, the cultures of the various maroon peoples exhibit composite heritages, forged in the early meeting of peoples from diverse African, European, and Amerindian cultures in the dynamic setting of the New World.

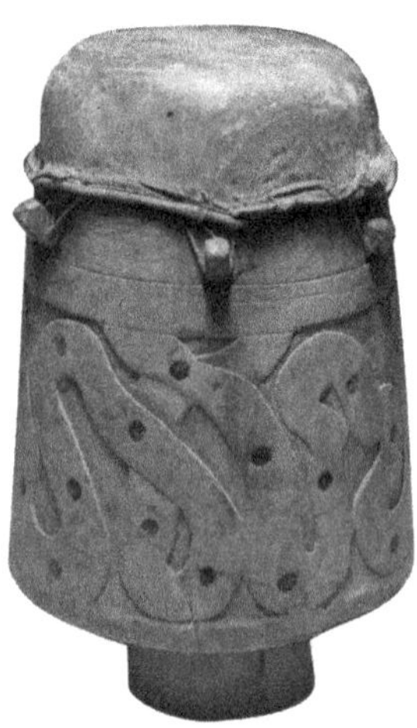

Pamaka *apinti*, collected in the late 1920s on the Guyane side of the Maroni River.

The cultural uniqueness of the maroon societies in Suriname and Guyane rests firmly on their fidelity to deep-level "African" cultural principles—whether aesthetic, political, religious, or domestic—rather than on the frequency of isolated traits that have been rigidly retained through the centuries. As peoples who developed their cultural understandings with relatively little interference from European colonists, Maroons have enjoyed a rare freedom to extrapolate ideas and practices from a whole range of societies in West and Central Africa, adapting them over time in response to changing circumstances and the creative impulses of their members. As a result, their communities have always been in many respects both the most meaningfully African and the most culturally dynamic of all African American societies.[3]

Throughout slavery, maroon communities stood out as a heroic challenge to white authority, as the living reflection of an African American consciousness that refused to be limited by the whites' conception or manipulation of it. It is no accident that today the historical maroon—often mythologized as a larger-than-life figure—has become a touchstone of identity for many writers, artists, and intellectuals, the ultimate symbol of resistance to oppression.

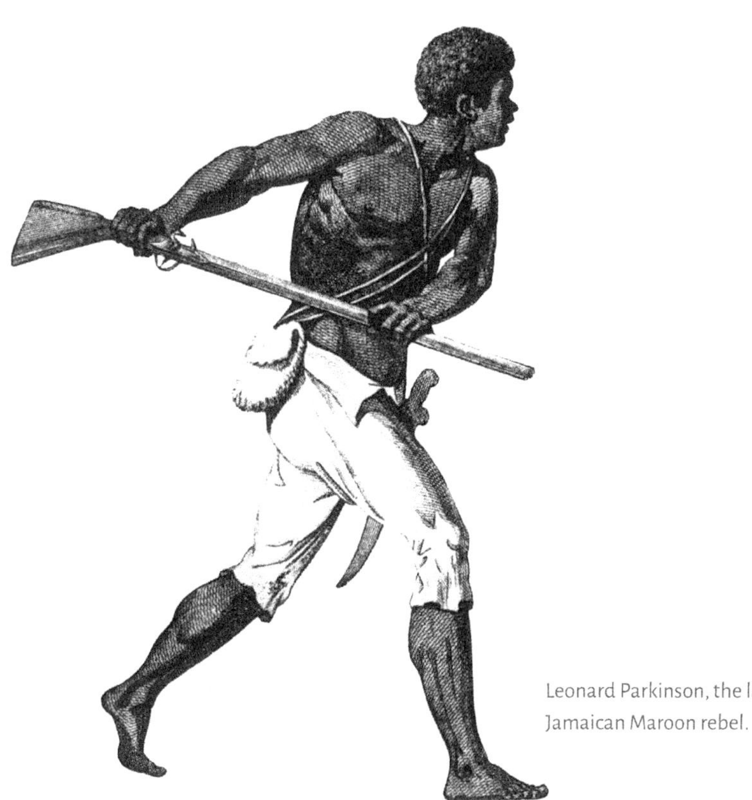

Leonard Parkinson, the last Jamaican Maroon rebel.

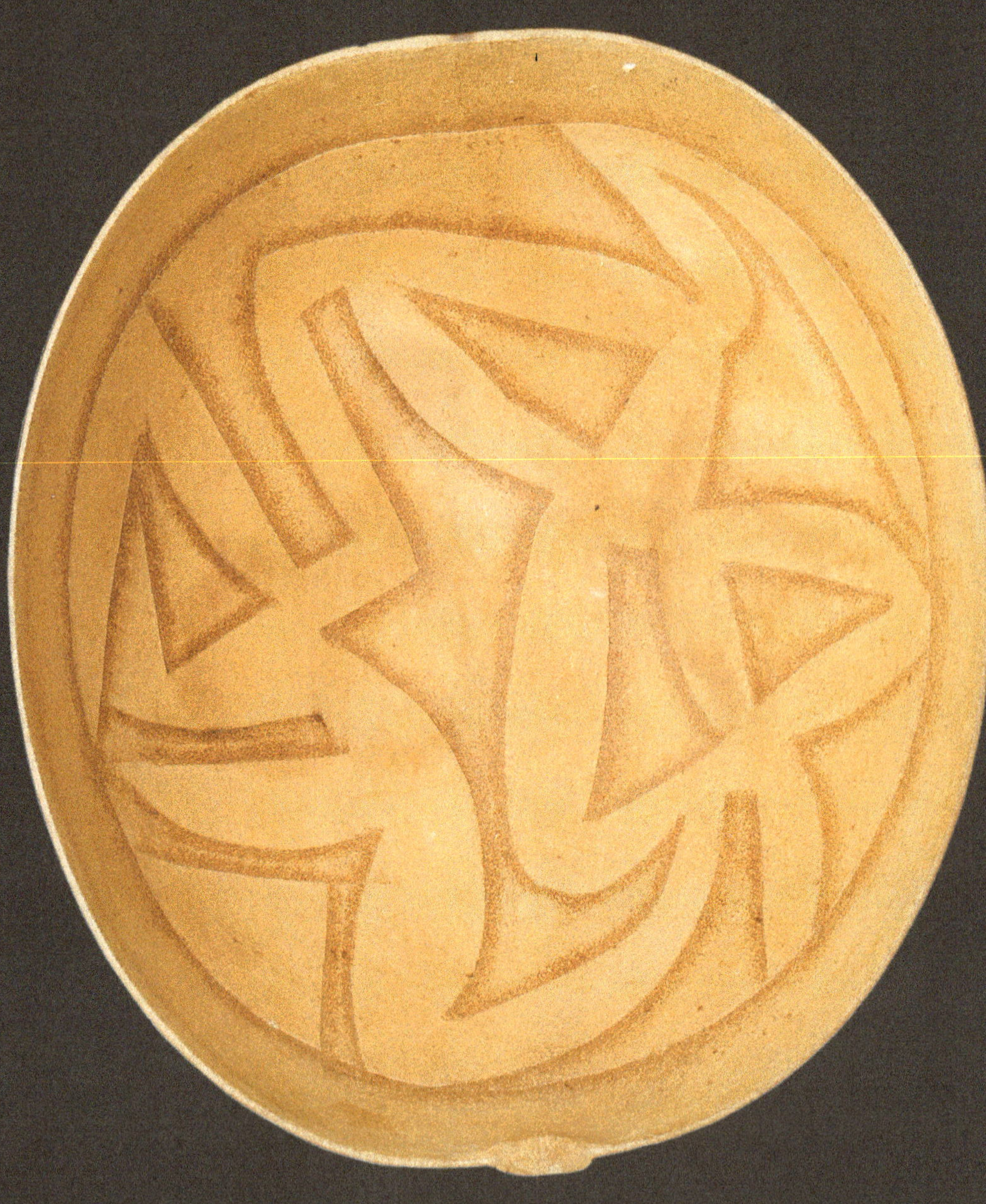

Pamaka calabash bowl, collected in 1991 in the village of Nason.

The Origins of Maroons in Guyane

All four Maroon societies represented in the population of Guyane today—Alukus (Bonis), Okanisis (Ndyukas), Pamakas, and Saamakas—were formed in Suriname (Dutch Guiana) in the seventeenth and eighteenth centuries.[1]

In Guyane, bands of escaped slaves never succeeded in forming long-term communities and rarely numbered more than a few dozen members.[2] Yet there was continual marronage. In 1689, "some thirty slaves accompanied by their wives and children" were spotted not far from Cayenne.[3]

For maroons in Guyane, escape to Brazil offered the best chance for lasting freedom. Throughout the eighteenth century, enslaved people from plantations in Guyane succeeded in crossing the frontier to join already-formed *quilombos* in Amapá.[4] With the abolition of French slavery in 1848, the members of those small Maroon bands that were still extant within Guyane melted back into the population of the newly freed, keeping none of their identity as maroons.

In contrast, marronage in Suriname was continuous and consequent. Between the mid-seventeenth and late eighteenth centuries, large numbers of enslaved people escaped from the coastal

> Toward the middle of the eighteenth century, 150 slaves revolted. One group, on the Montagne de Plomb near Tonnégrande, tried to set up a republic, but the second, near Kourou, was unable to get even that far. Both groups were too small to resist the soldiers sent out by the governor of Cayenne, and were defeated before they could truly organize themselves.
>
> Marie-José Jolivet, *La question créole: Essai de sociologie sur la Guyane française* (Paris: ORSTOM, 1982), 90

plantations, in many cases soon after their arrival from Africa. They fled into the forested interior, where they regrouped into small bands and began forging a viable existence in the new and inhospitable environment. This daunting challenge was made even more difficult by the persistent, massive efforts of the government to eliminate the threat they posed to the colony's thriving plantations.

Each early band of Maroons was composed of Africans who had for the most part been enslaved (for varying periods of time) on the same plantation or on neighboring ones in coastal Suriname, but who came from a number of different ethnic ("tribal") and linguistic backgrounds in Africa. The table illustrates the geographic spread of African ports of shipment to Suriname from the mid-seventeenth century to the late eighteenth.

The colonists in Suriname reserved special punishments for recaptured maroons that were among the most brutal in the hemisphere—hamstringing, the amputation of limbs, and a variety of deaths by torture. The organized pursuit of maroons and expeditions to destroy their settlements date at least from the 1670s, soon after the colony's founding, when a citizen militia was established for this purpose. During the late seventeenth and early eighteenth centuries,

Table 1. African origins of enslaved people in Suriname, 1651–1775 (%)

	1651–1700	1701–1725	1726–1750	1751–1775	Total
Windward Coast ("Mandingos")	2	—	18	38	22
Gold Coast ("Koromantees")	7	16	35	21	21
Slave Coast ("Papas")	30	64	17	2	18
Bight of Biafra ("Calabaris")	16	—	—	—	3
Loango/Angola ("Loangos" or "Kongos")	45	20	30	39	36

In this table, "Windward Coast" corresponds to the coastal regions of modern Guinea-Bissau, Guinea, Sierra Leone, and, especially, Liberia and Ivory Coast; "Gold Coast" is roughly coterminous with modern Ghana; "Slave Coast" corresponds to the coastal regions of present-day Togo and Benin; and Loango/Angola stretches from Cape Lopez south to the Orange River.

The total number of Africans who landed in Suriname was of the same order of magnitude as the number imported into the whole of North America: 295,000 people for Suriname and 388,000 for North America (in both cases about 3 percent of the total transatlantic slave trade). Guyane imported only 31,000 Africans. See "The Trans-Atlantic Slave Trade—Database" (slavevoyages.org/voyage/database), and David Eltis and David Richardson, *Atlas of the Transatlantic Slave Trade* (New Haven, Conn.: Yale University Press, 2010), 205, 241.

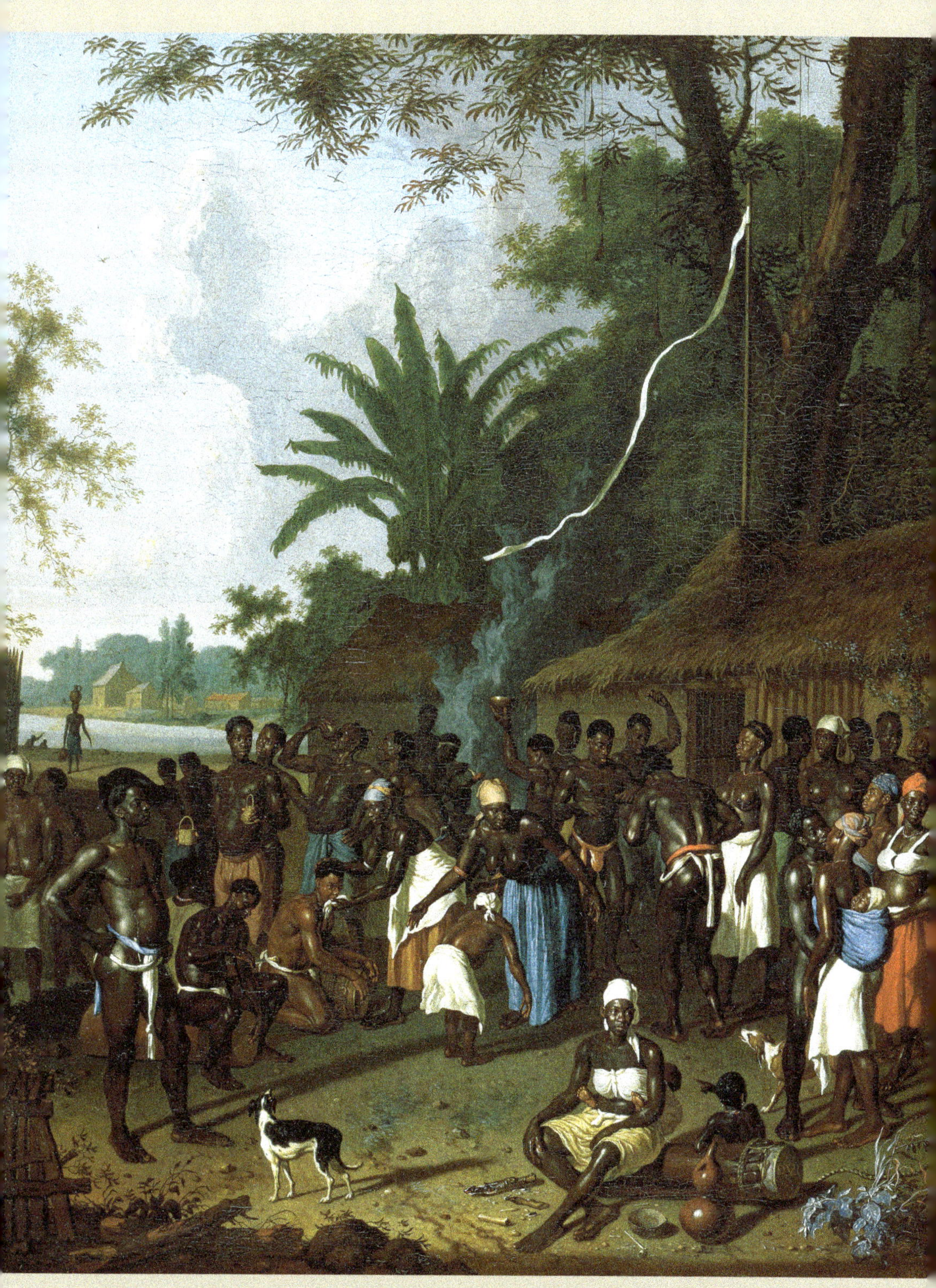

Dirk Valkenburg, 1707, painting of a "play" on the Suriname River plantations of Palmeneribo-Surimombo, from which the ancestors of the Saamaka Dombi clan escaped soon thereafter.

numerous small-scale military expeditions were mounted, sometimes at the personal expense of particular planters. But these rarely met with success, for the maroons had established and protected their settlements with great ingenuity and had become expert at all aspects of guerrilla warfare. It was between the 1730s and 1750s, when "the colony had become the theater of a perpetual war," that such expeditions reached their maximum size and frequency.[5] We know from archival documents, for example, that one was sent out in 1730 that included 50 citizens and 200 enslaved men, and that another one, in 1743, was composed of 27 civilians, 12 soldiers, 15 Indians, 165 enslaved men, and 60 canoes.[6] Although one of the military expeditions of this period returned with "47 prisoners and 6 hands of those whom they had killed," most were fruitless.[7] By the late 1740s, the colonists were finding the expense overwhelming, with typical expeditions costing more than 100,000 guilders and having to traverse (as one document put it) "forty mountains and sixty creeks" before reaching the maroons' hidden villages.[8] It had also become clear to the colonists that the expeditions themselves were contributing to further marronage by making known to the enslaved both the escape routes from the plantations and the locations of maroon villages.

The increasingly costly warfare culminated in a decision by the colonists, during the late 1740s, to sue their former slaves for permanent peace. But peace proved elusive, and in 1754–1755, they decided

In 1730, after two military expeditions captured a number of villagers from the nascent group of Maroons known as Saamakas, the criminal court meted out the following sentences: "The Negro Joosie shall be hanged from the gibbet by an Iron Hook through his ribs, until dead; his head shall then be severed and displayed on a stake by the riverbank, remaining to be picked over by birds of prey. As for the Negroes Wierai and Manbote, they shall be bound to a stake and roasted alive over a slow fire, while being tortured with glowing Tongs. The Negro girls, Lucretia, Ambira, Aga, Gomba, Marie, and Victoria will be tied to a Cross, to be broken alive, and then their heads severed, to be exposed by the riverbank on stakes. The Negro girls Diana and Christina shall be beheaded with an axe, and their heads exposed on poles by the riverbank."

Richard Price, *First-Time: The Historical Vision of an Afro-American People* (Baltimore: Johns Hopkins University Press, 1983), 85

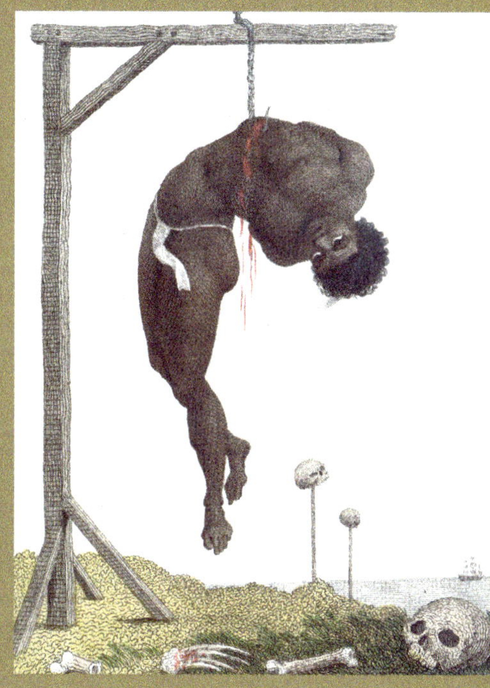

A Negro hung alive by the Ribs to a Gallows, by William Blake, 1792.

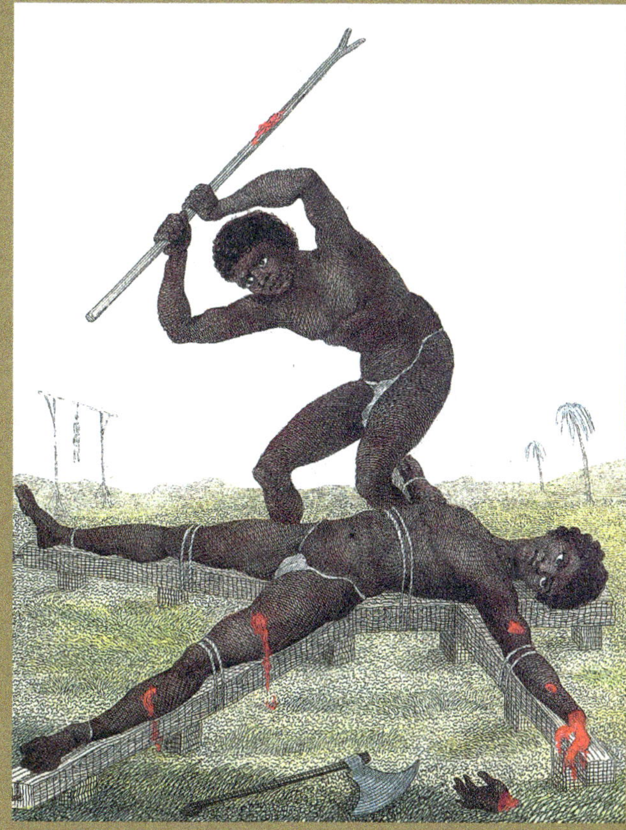

The Execution of Breaking on the Rack, by William Blake, 1793.

to mount yet another massive expedition, consisting of five hundred men, against the Saamakas—"either to make one last attempt at a permanent Peace . . . or else search them out and completely destroy them."[9] In 1760 and 1762, peace treaties were successfully concluded with the two largest Maroon peoples, the Okanisi and the Saamaka, and in 1767 with the much-smaller Matawai. New slave revolts and the large-scale warfare of subsequent decades, for which an army of mercenaries was imported from Europe, eventually led to the formation of the Aluku (Boni) as well as the smaller Pamaka and Kwinti groups. As part of the treaties of the 1760s, the government agreed to recognize the paramount chief, who ruled like a king in each group, as well as a hierarchy of village captains and assistants. The authority of these leaders in political and social matters was from the beginning exercised in a context replete with oracles, spirit possession, and other forms of divination.

In 1710, a recaptured town slave whose punishment was designed "to serve as an example to others" was sentenced "to be quartered alive, and the pieces thrown in the River. He was laid upon the ground, his head on a long beam. The first blow he was given, on the abdomen, burst open his bladder, yet he uttered not the least sound. The second blow with the axe he tried to deflect with his hand, but it gashed his hand and upper belly, again without his uttering a sound. The slave men and women laughed at this, saying to one another, 'That is a man!' Finally, the third blow, to his chest, killed him. His head was cut off and the body cut in four pieces and dumped in the river."

J. D. Herlein, *Beschryvinge van de Volk-plantinge Zuriname* (Leeuwarden: Meindert Injema, 1718), 117

List of objects to be presented to the Saamaka Maroons as tribute, 1763. For each village, this document gives the name of the chief and the quantity of axes, machetes, knives, scissors, chisels, muskets, cloth, thread, cooking oil, salt, pots, razors, needles, and so forth. For details, see Richard Price, *To Slay the Hydra* (Ann Arbor, Mich.: Karoma, 1983), 196–217, 243.

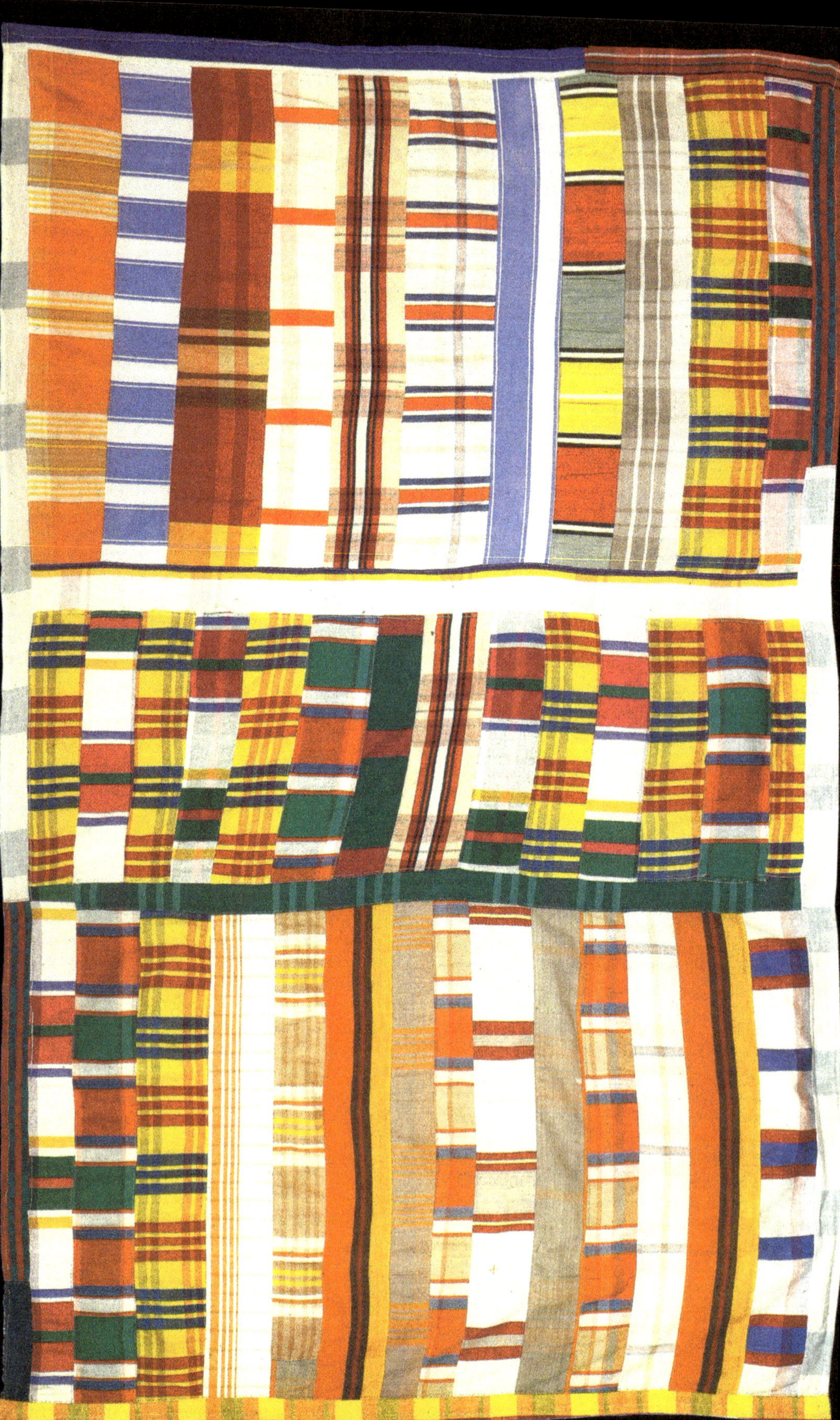

Cultural Similarities and Differences

By the end of the eighteenth century, then, six maroon groups were living in the interior of Suriname. Three of them—the Saamaka, Matawai, and Kwinti—had established their villages along rivers in the center of the colony, and the three others—the Okanisi, Pamaka, and Aluku—had settled in northeastern Suriname and along the border with Guyane. Some movement occurred in these regions during the nineteenth century (see below), and further changes occurred during the twentieth century due to the government's incursions into territory traditionally controlled by Maroons (most notably the construction of a hydroelectric dam that displaced most of the downstream villages of the Saamakas). In 2018, the total population of Maroons from Suriname and Guyane was 263,000—115,500 Saamakas, 115,500 Okanisis, 11,600 Alukus, 11,000 Pamakas, 8,500 Matawais, and 1,200 Kwintis.[1]

These six peoples share many aspects of the life they created in the equatorial forest. Rivers and streams—whether a broad, majestic river like the Maroni, which marks the Suriname-Guyane border, or a small creek like the Sara of central Suriname—are important to all the groups, providing the main means of transportation (in canoes), the daily water supply (for drinking, cooking, bathing, and household chores), a crucial part of the diet (fish), a site of village sociability, and an environment heavily charged with religious signification (housing a wide variety of gods and spirits). Matrilineal kinship is the primary basis for personal identity (though men are close to their children) within the larger society, as well as the foundation for principles of inheritance and succession to political and religious offices. Houses are owned by individuals, not families; couples share a residence for visits of variable length, and if a man has more than one wife (as most men do), each one has her own house (as well, often, as a second one in her garden camp). Details of religious life vary from one group to the next,

Opposite: A hammock sheet sewn in the early twentieth century by Apumba, from the Saamaka village of Pempe, for her sister-in-law Nai, who lived in the village of Dangogo.

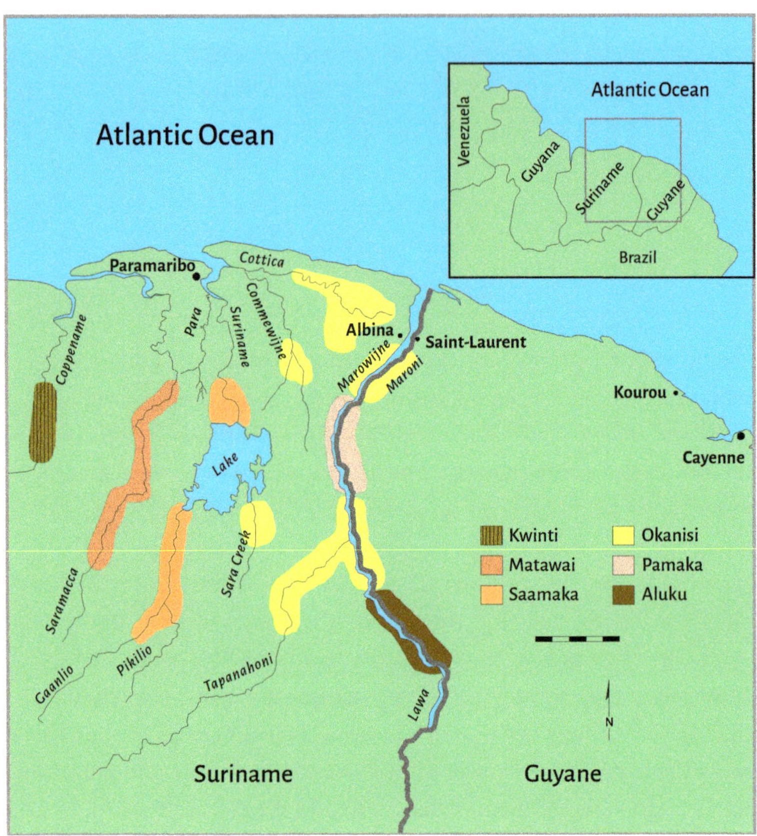

Territories of Maroons, 1960s.

but all pay great attention to the ancestors and to a range of gods and spirits, including (for example) those that inhabit trees or boulders or bodies of water and others embodied in animals such as boa constrictors, caimans, jaguars, and vultures; these powers participate in the life of the community through a wide variety of divinatory processes, from spirit possession to the consultation of oracles.

The adaptation that the early Maroons made to their new environment was rapid and wide-ranging. As early as the 1770s, John Gabriel Stedman, a Scottish mercenary engaged by the planters to fight against the rebels (the ancestors of the Aluku), expressed his admiration for the environmental knowledge possessed by his adversaries. Drawing on their earlier experience in various parts of Africa and the knowledge they had acquired during the years in slavery on the coast of Suriname, they incorporated techniques learned from local Amerindians—all brought together in the context of their own encounters with the plants, animals, and environmental particulars of their new homes.

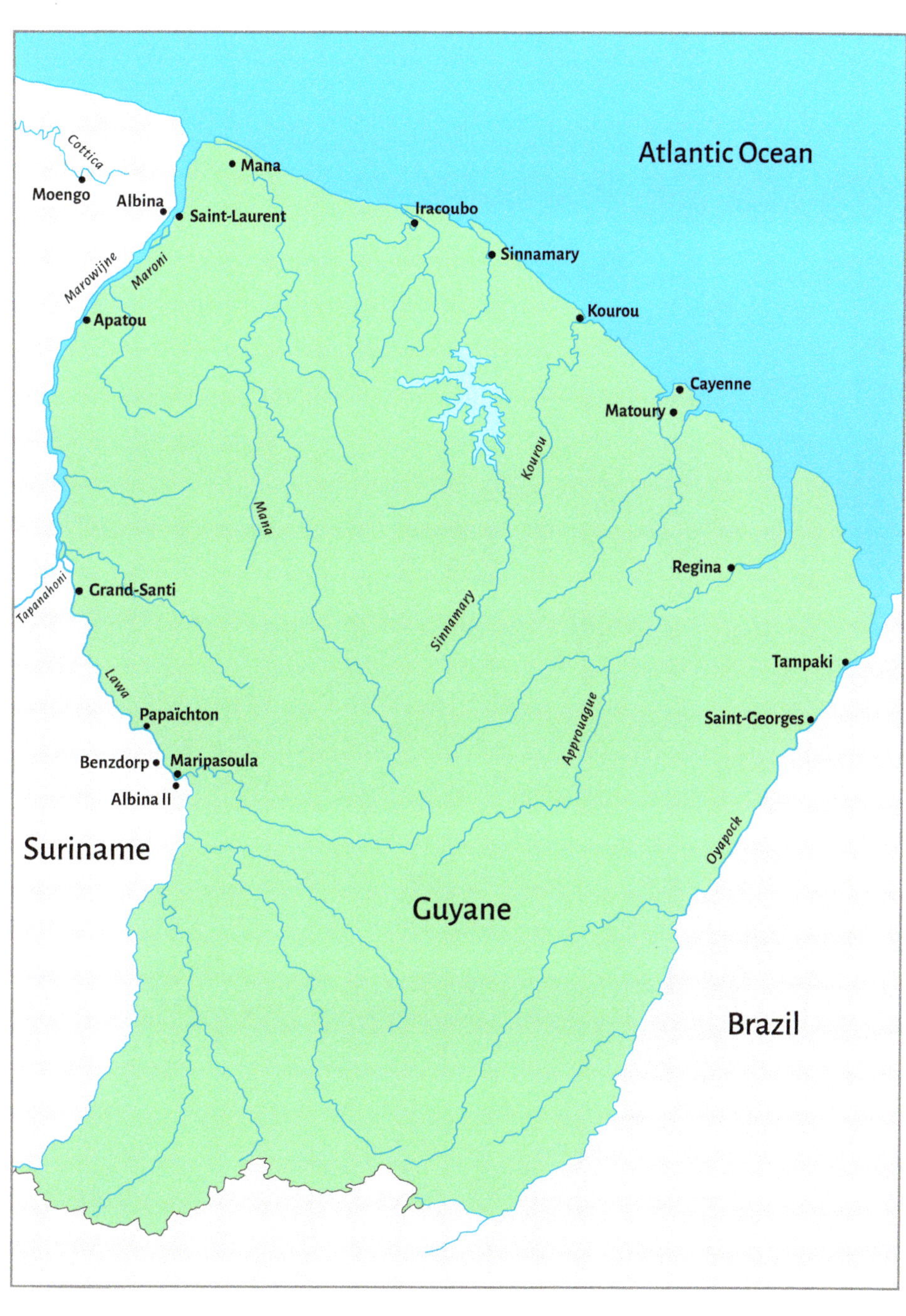
Atlantic Ocean
Cottica
Moengo
Albina
Mana
Saint-Laurent
Iracoubo
Sinnamary
Marowijne
Maroni
Kourou
Apatou
Cayenne
Matoury
Kourou
Mana
Regina
Grand-Santi
Tapanahoni
Sinnamary
Tampaki
Lawa
Approuague
Papaïchton
Saint-Georges
Benzdorp
Maripasoula
Albina II
Oyapock
Suriname
Guyane
Brazil

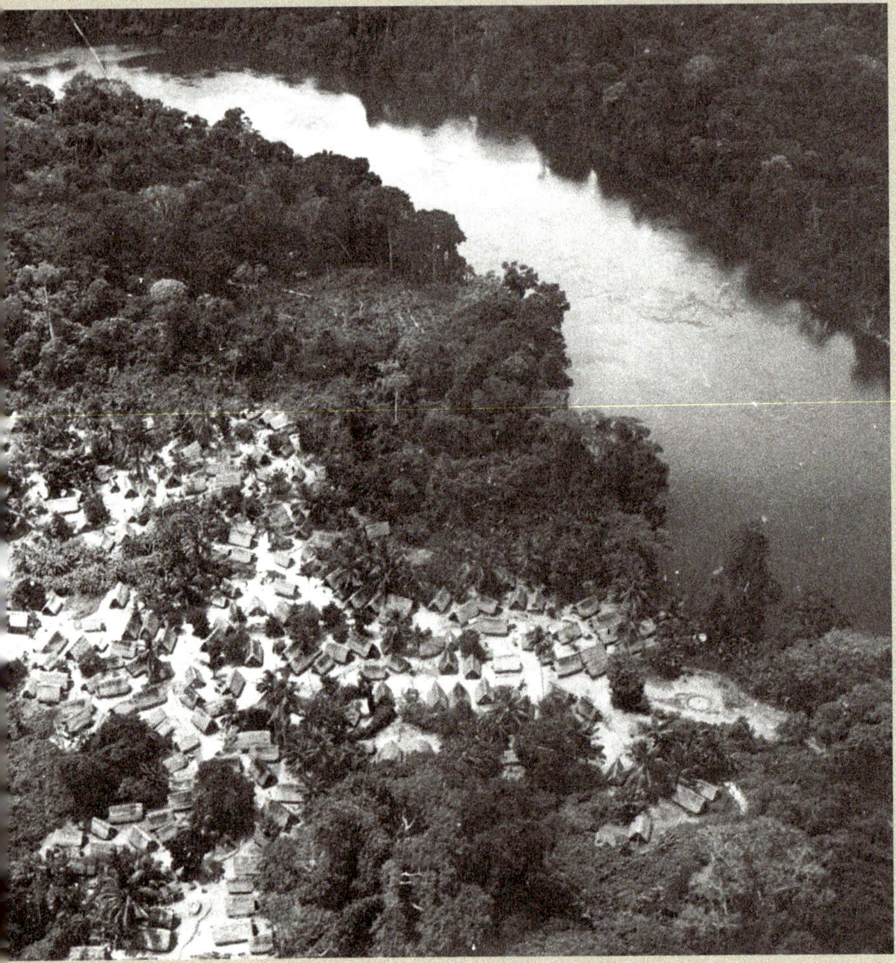

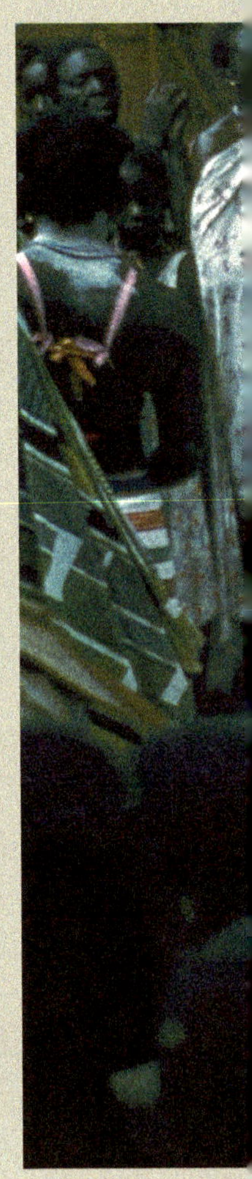

Aerial view of an Okanisi village near the confluence of the Lawa and the Tapanahoni Rivers, 1962.

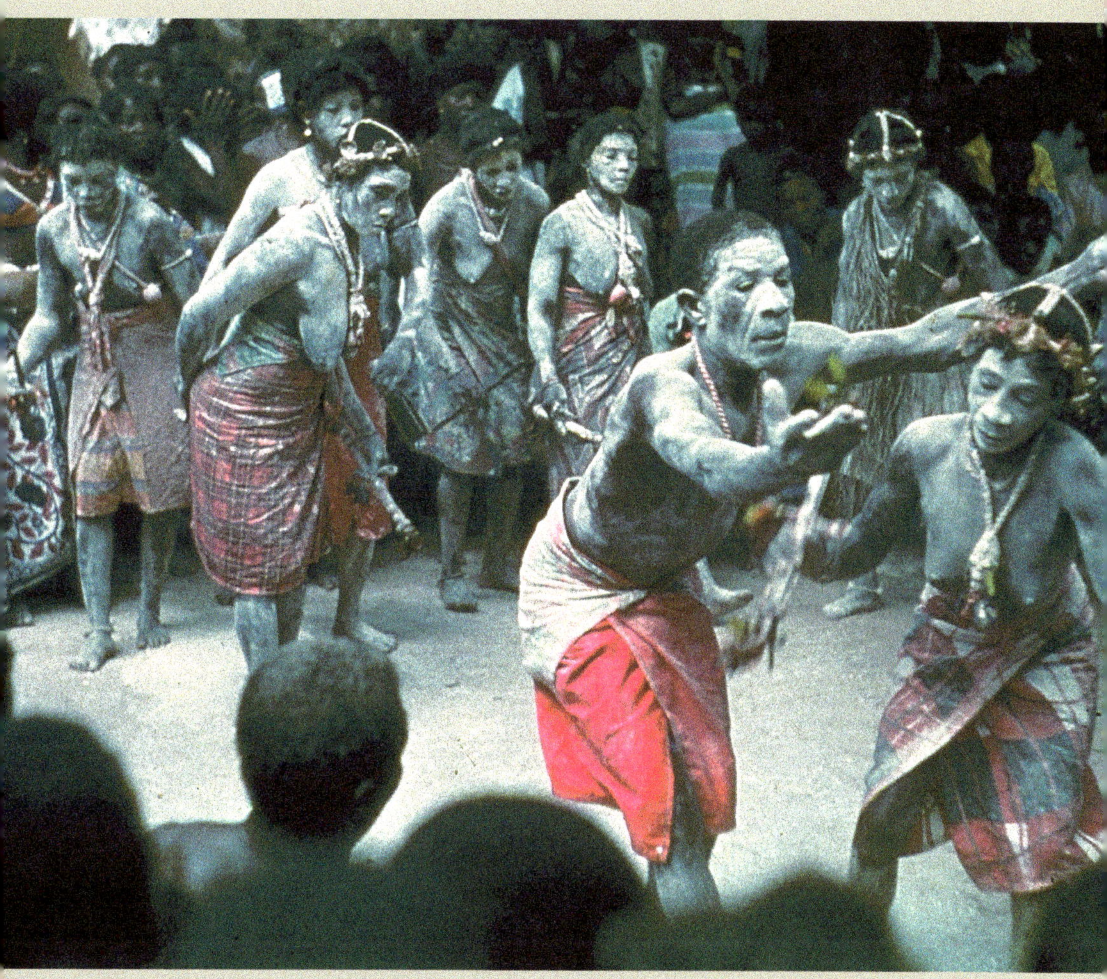

Okanisi ceremony to honor snake gods, 1962.

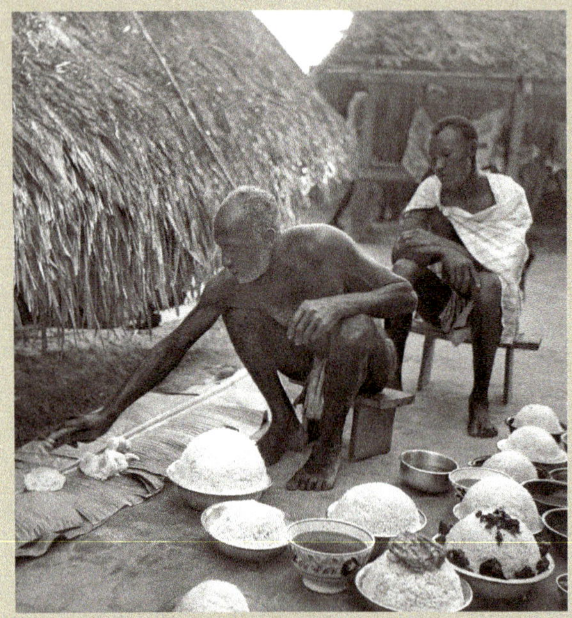

Aluku offering to the ancestors, Papaïchton, 1962.

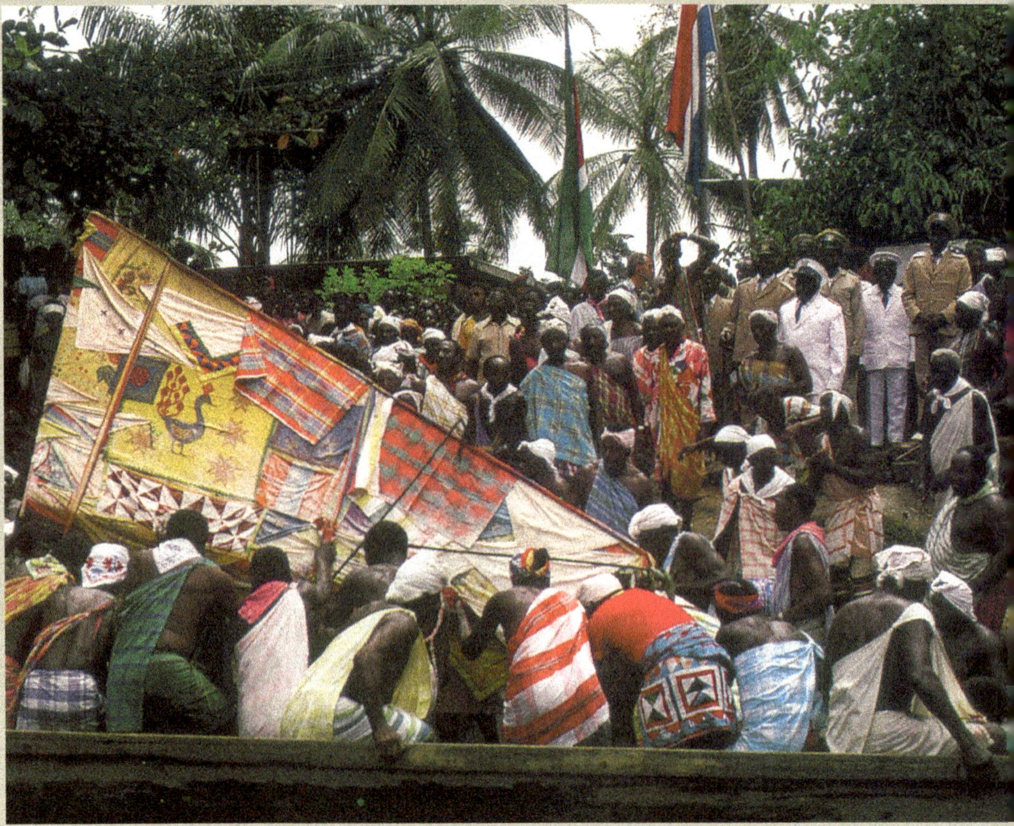

The coffin of Agbago Aboikoni, paramount chief of the Saamaka, being placed in the canoe for its voyage to the cemetery, 1989.

In a State of *Tranquility* they Seemed as they had Said to us Want for Nothing—Being Plump and Fat at Least Such we found those that had been Shot—For instance *Game* and *fish* they Catch in Great Abundance by Artificial Traps and Springs, And Which they Preserve by Barbacuing, While with *Rice, Cassava, Yams, Plantains,* and so on, theyr fields are ever over Stoked—*Salt* they make with the Ashes of the Palm trees like the *Gentoos* in the East indies—Or Use Red Pepper. We even Discovered Concealed near the Trunk of an Old Tree a Case *Bottle* With Excellent *Butter* Which they the Rangers told me they Made by melting and Clarifying the fat of the Palm-tree Worms And Which fully Supplied the Above ingredient While I absolutely found it more Delicious—The *Pistachio* or pinda nuts they Also Convert in Butter, by their Oily Substance & Frequently use them in their Broths—The *Palm tree Wine* they are never in Want of, And which they make by Cutting Deep insitions of a Foot Over Square in the fallen trunk, where the Joice being Gathered it soon ferments by the Heat of the Sun, When it is not only a Cool and Agreeable Beveridge but Strong Sufficient to intoxicate—and Soap they have from the dwarf aloes. To Build their *Houses* the Manicole or Pinda Tree Answers the Purpose, theyr *Pots* they Fabricate with Clay found near their Dwellings While the *Gourd* or Calebas tree gives them Cups &c the Silk Grass Plant and Maureecee tree Provides them in *Hammocks* And even a kind of *Caps* Grow Natural upon the Palm trees as Well as *Brooms*—The Various kinds of Nebees Supply the Want of *Ropes, fuel* for fire they have for the Cutting, While a Wood call'd *Bee Bee* Serves for Tinder to Light it by Rubbing two Pieces on each Other, And Which by its Elasticity Makes *Excellent* Corks—Neyther Do they Want *Candles,* being well Provided with Fat and Oil While the Bees Also Afford them *Wax,* And a Great Deal of Excellent *Honey.*

John Gabriel Stedman, *Narrative of a Five Years Expedition Against the Revolted Negroes of Surinam,* newly transcribed from the original 1790 manuscript, with an introduction and notes by Richard Price and Sally Price (Baltimore: Johns Hopkins University Press, 1988), 409–410

The cylindrical basketry press used for expelling the poisonous juice of the manioc tuber as part of processing it into *kwaka* (a granular grilled staple among the Maroons of the easternmost groups) or *kasaba kuku* (the large round cassava cakes made by all the groups) is an exact copy of the Amerindian model, and much the same can be said of other basketry forms, such as covered containers and fire fans. The ankle bands with vegetable pods that accentuate the rhythm of Maroons performing certain dances are identical to those made by Amerindians, but the dances and the drumming that accompanies them derive from various African cultures. And because Maroons maintained contacts with the coastal society—at the beginning via raids on the plantations, later through the tribute goods provided by the colonial government, and more recently as part of men's wage-labor trips (working, for example, in river transport, logging, or construction, or as artists for the tourist market)—their material culture has always included objects of Western manufacture: salt, cloth, and guns from the beginning, and since the mid-twentieth century, radios and outboard motors. All these influences have come together through a process of creolization in which the Maroons have created new, unique societies and cultures drawing on their varied African pasts as well as their contacts with Amerindian and European models.

In addition to all they have in common, the six Maroon societies display differences that give each its unique character. These differences exist in every domain, from language, art, music, and dance to diet, dress, religion, residence, and patterns of men's wage labor. The most striking differences are between, on the one hand, the three groups that settled in eastern Suriname (Alukus, Okanisis, and Pamakas) and, on the other, those to the west (Saamakas, Matawais, and Kwintis).

For example, while all of them speak "creole languages" (languages formed in a situation of contact between Europeans, Amerindians, and people of diverse African origins), the vocabulary of the central Suriname groups (who speak "Saamaka") includes a strong Portuguese

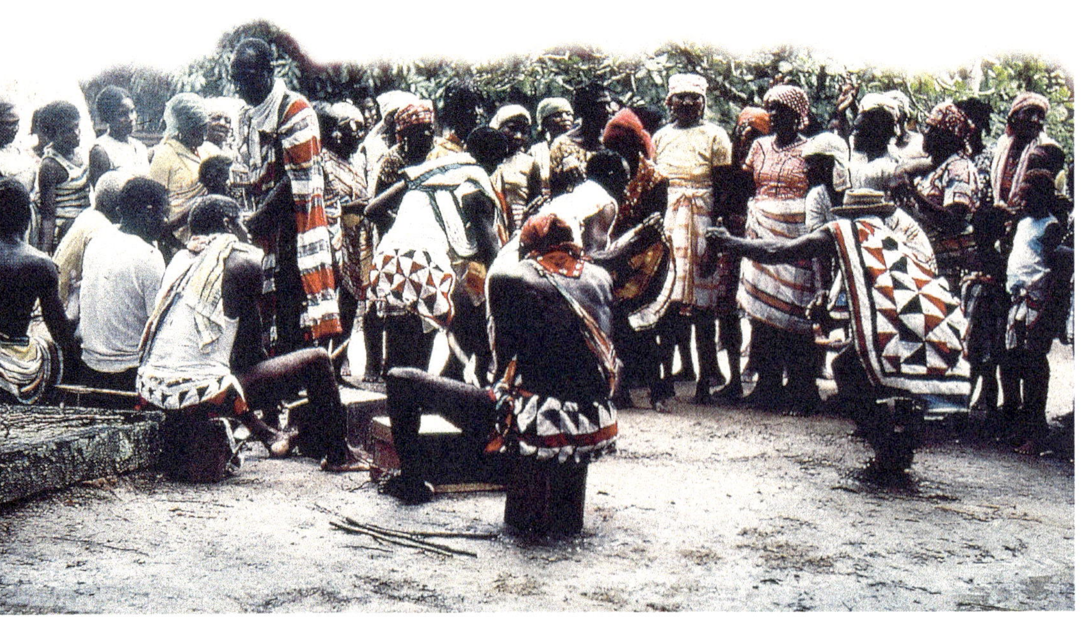

Matawai dancers, 1974.

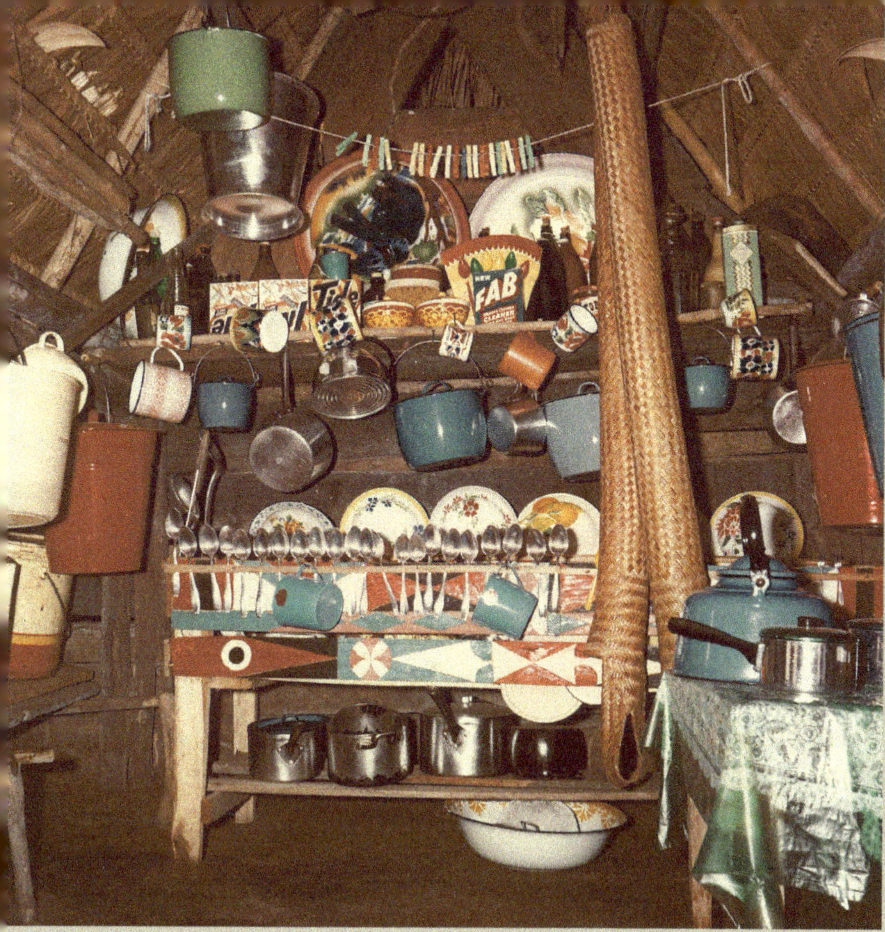

Inside an Okanisi house, Diitabiki (on the Tapanahoni), 1962.

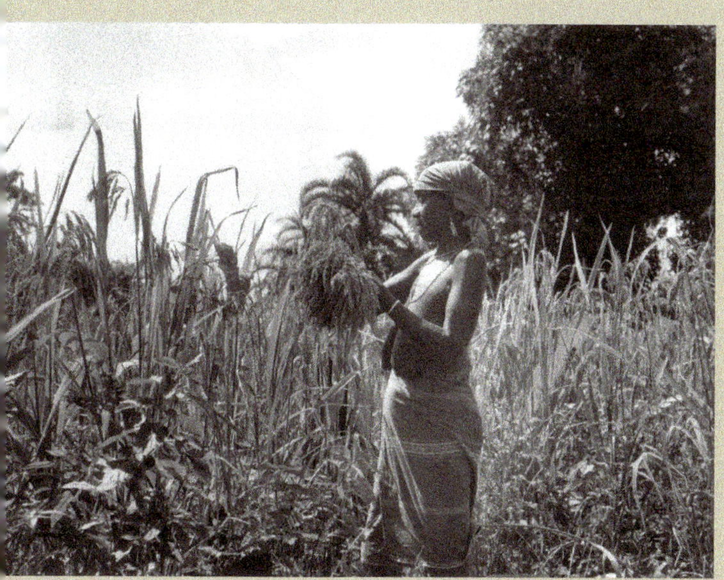

A Saamaka woman harvesting rice, 1968.

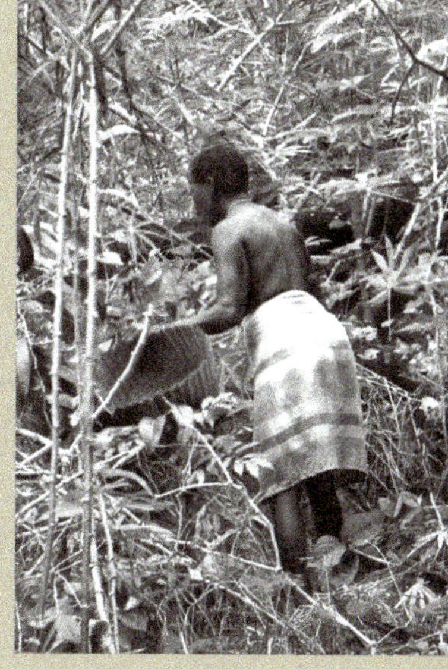

An Aluku woman harvesting manioc, 1952.

Table 2. Origins of some words in the Maroon languages

English	Saamaka		Ndyuka/Okanisi	
		derived from		*derived from*
mouth	buka	Port. boca	mofu	Eng. *mouth*
hand	mau	Port. *mão*	ana	Eng. *hand*
man	womi	Port. *homem*	man	Eng. *man*
woman	muyee	Port. *mulher*	uman	Eng. *woman*
river	lio	Port. *rio*	liba	Eng. *river*
sleep	duumi	Port. *dormir*	siibi	Eng. *sleep*
drink	bebe	Port. *beber*	diingi	Eng. *drink*
spoon	kuyee	Port. *colher*	supun	Eng. *spoon*
ancestral shrine	faaka pau	Eng. *flag* + Port. *pau*	faaka tiki	Eng. *flag* + *stick*
water	wata	Eng. *water*	wata(a)	Eng. *water*
house	osu	Eng. *house*	osu	Eng. *house*
go	go	Eng. *go*	go	Eng. *go*
come	ko	Eng. *come*	kon	Eng. *come*
teeth	tanda	Dutch *tand*	tifi	Eng. *teeth*
pretty	hanse	Eng. *handsome*	moi	Dutch *mooi*
meat	gwamba	African (precise lang. unknown)	switi mofu	Eng. *sweet mouth*
eat	nyan	various African languages.	nyan	various African langs.
talking drum	apintii	Akan [Afr.] *apentemma*	apinti	Akan *apentemma*
covered container	apaki	Twi [Afr.] *apákyi*	pakiba	Twi *apákyi*
hearthstones	makuku	Kikoongo [Afr.] *makukwa*	makuku or doti dii futu	Eng. *dirt three-feet*
calabash	kuya	Tupi [Amerind.] *kuia*	kaabasi	Eng. *calabash*
manioc press	matapi	Kali'na [Amerind.] *matapi*	matapi	Kali'na *matapi*
adolescent apron	koyo	Trio [Amerind.] *kwayu*	kwei	Kali'na *kwai*

component (the language of many of the owners of the plantations from which they escaped) and that of the Eastern Maroons ("Ndyuka/Okanisi") is more influenced by English (introduced to Suriname between 1650 and 1667, the period of British control of the colony).[2] The relationship between Saamaka and Ndyuka/Okanisi is on about the same level as that between Portuguese and Spanish.[3]

In addition to linguistic distinctions, there are intergroup differences in virtually every aspect of life. We cite just a few examples. For Eastern Maroons, the staple of the diet is manioc (especially *kwaka*), but for Saamakas (who rarely make *kwaka*), it's rice. Eastern Maroons spend large amounts of time in their garden camps, which are often as large as the villages; Saamakas build more temporary structures in their garden camps and spend less time in them. For Eastern Maroons, gathering firewood is a man's job, but among Saamakas this is done by women. Traditionally, women in all groups wore a double layer of wrap-skirts, but Eastern Maroon women tied their waist with a cotton sash, topped by a black yarn belt, and Saamakas with a square of cloth doubled over to form a triangle in the back. Eastern Maroon wood-carvers embellish objects with colorful paints, but Saamakas do not.

Eastern Maroon folktales are told as a series of rapid-fire spurts, but

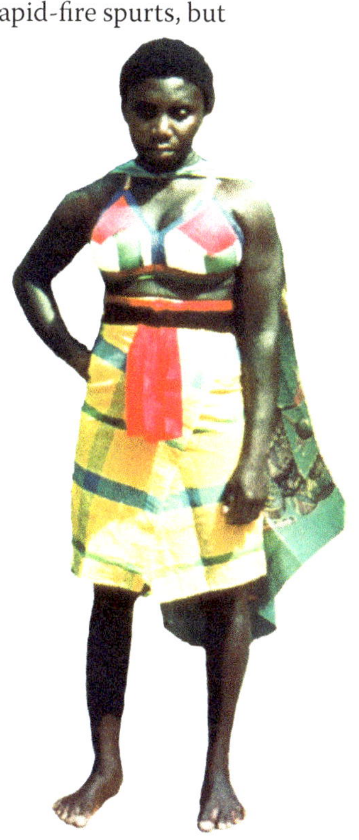

Okanisi women's wear, Diitabiki, 1961.

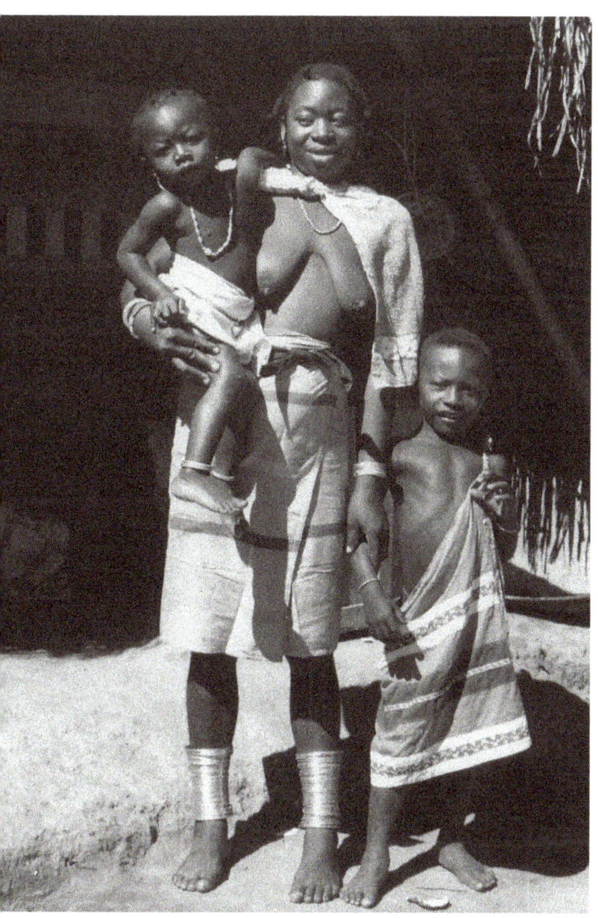

Saamaka women's wear, Dangogo 1968.

those in Saamaka follow a more narrative style. The vocal trill characteristic of much Eastern Maroon singing does not occur in Saamaka songs, and the funerary masks used among the Saamaka have no equivalent among Eastern Maroons. Saamakas traditionally considered houses raised on stilts to be the prerogative of senior men, but Eastern Maroons viewed them as appropriate for women as well.

The degree of cultural difference separating Eastern Maroons from those to their west is roughly equivalent to that which distinguishes the Dutch from the Germans, the Spanish from the Portuguese, or the French from the Italians—that is, in addition to strong similarities, there are enough specificities to make Okanisis, for example, feel offended if they are taken for Saamakas, Saamakas for Alukus, and so forth.

And there are subtler differences even within a single Maroon group—for example, between Saamakas of the upper river and those downstream, or even from one village to another. Maroon men claim that a quick glance at the carving on the prow of a canoe is all it takes for them to tell exactly where in Saamaka the canoe was made. Similarly, regional accents and styles of speech are distinctive, easily signaling an Okanisi's origin as Tapanahoni or Cottica, or whether an Aluku is from a village on the Lawa or the lower Maroni.

The most salient cultural differences separating the various Maroon groups are those between those in the east and those of central Suriname. But there are also lower-level aspects of culture that distinguish the three groups of Eastern Maroons. To cite just a few examples: Alukus and Okanisis are more proficient than Pamakas as canoemen. The Aluku religion gives the oracle-spirit Tata Odun responsibility for major decisions, but this is not the case for Okanisis or Pamakas. The cults responsible for the discovery and punishment of sorcery, which played a decisive role among the twentieth-century Okanisi, have considerably less importance in Aluku and Pamaka societies. And in the domain of language, the differences separating the speech of Alukus, Pamakas, and Okanisis are on about the same level as those that distinguish the English spoken by the people in New York, London, and Melbourne.

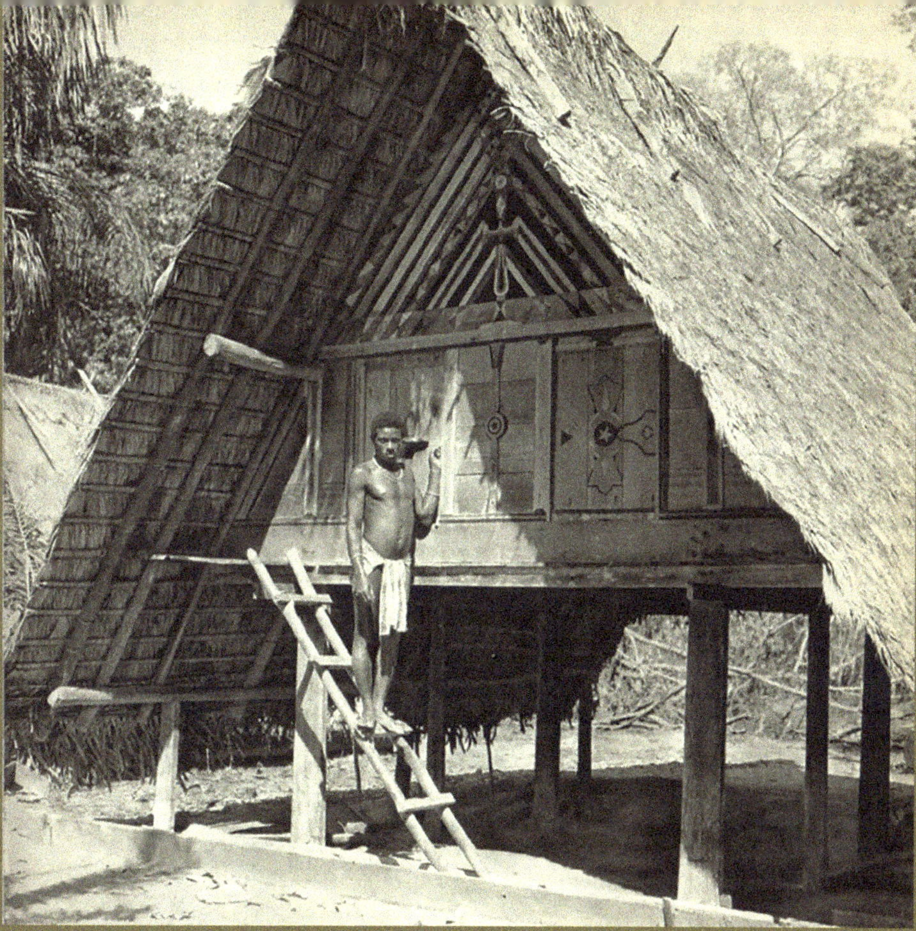

Aluku house, Papaïchton, ca. 1950.

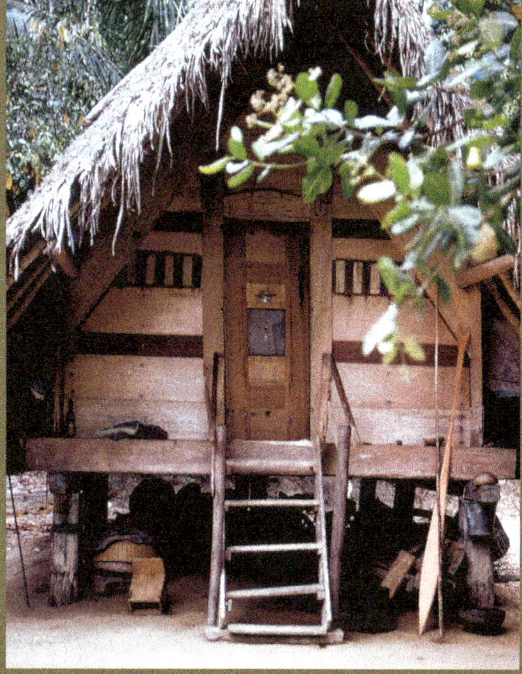

Saamaka house, Dangogo, 1968.

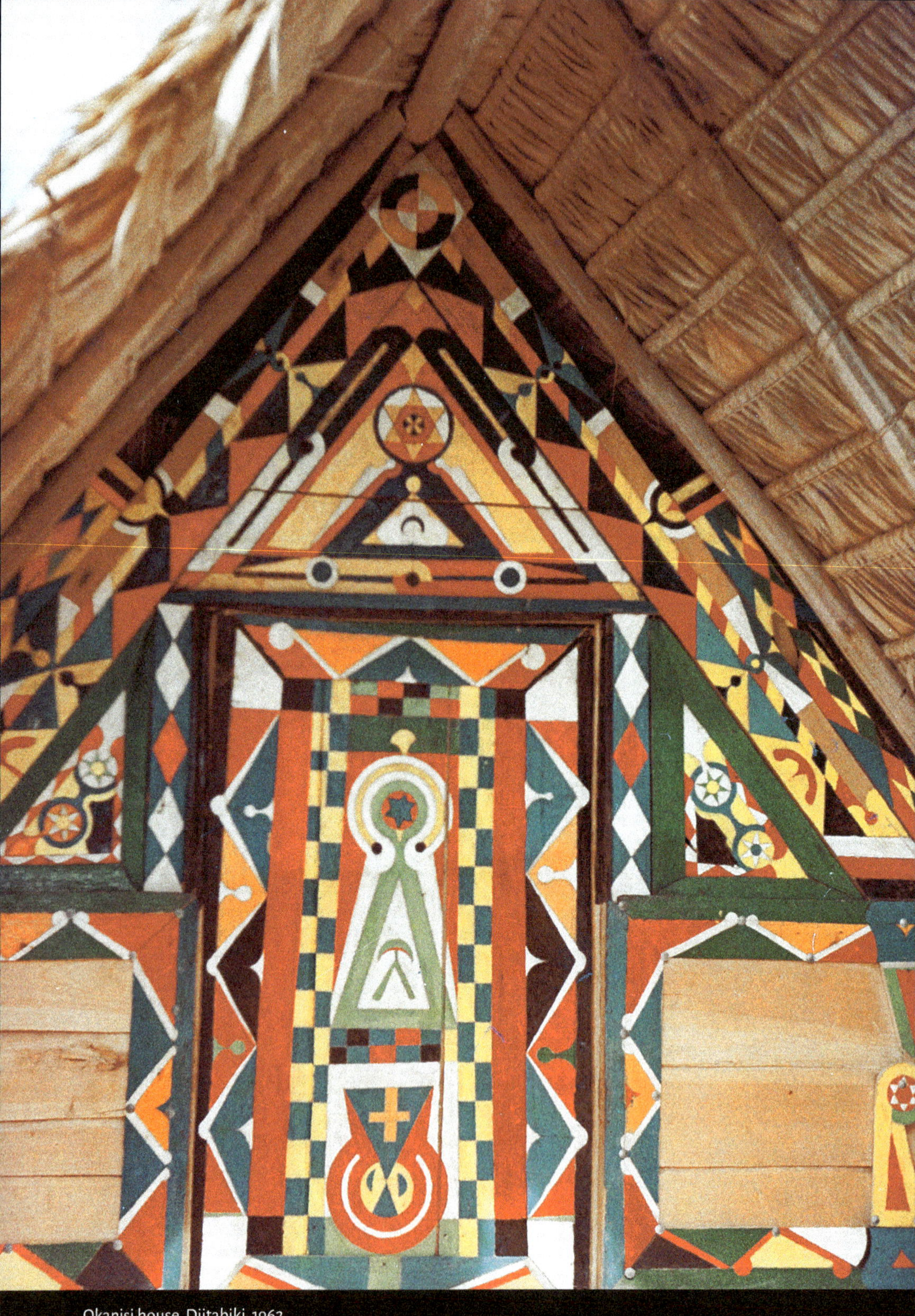

Okanisi house, Diitabiki, 1962.

The Arrival of Maroons in Guyane

The period following the treaties between the Dutch government and the Okanisis and Saamakas in the 1760s witnessed some especially dramatic warfare between new maroon groups and the colonists. Even before the conclusion of those treaties, small independent groups of maroons had formed on the fringes of the plantation areas in the eastern and western parts of the colony. After the treaties, some of these groups continued to hide out in the forest between the Okanisis' territory and the plantation zone. In time, amid numerous cleavages and alliances, three new groups emerged—the Pamaka, the Aluku, and the Kwinti.

Aluku History, 1776–1970

Very little is known about the first days of the Alukus.[1] A few of the initial runaways who were later to form the core of this people are believed to have escaped from Suriname plantations as early as 1712. But the majority fled during the mid- or late eighteenth century. The earliest detailed archival data comes from around 1760. At this time, while the peace treaties with the Okanisi and the Saamaka were being concluded, there were a number of distinct maroon bands dispersed through the eastern part of the Dutch colony. Three of these played a particularly important part in the genesis of the Aluku people. The oldest, the Cottica group, was settled in a swampy region near the Cottica River; this group, headed by a chief named Asikan (or Silvester), numbered about 400 people at its height. It included two especially important historical figures, Boni and Aluku. The second group, the Tesisi maroons, under the leadership of two chiefs named Suku and Sambokwasi, lived in the region to the east of the Commewijne River. The third group, led by a chief named Kormantin Kodjo, had villages in the marshy area between the Commewijne and Suriname Rivers.

The Pamaka and the Kwinti

By the 1780s, the ancestors of the present-day Pamaka, one of the three post-treaty groups, had coalesced into a distinct group living in the Commewijne region. Avoiding contact with both the colonists and the Okanisis, they gradually moved farther south and established a series of new settlements. During the nineteenth century, they founded villages near the Maroni River and came under the control of the Okanisi. Another of the post-treaty fringe groups had earlier migrated to the west, where they eventually settled along the Saramacca and Coppename Rivers; they became the people known today as the Kwinti. Both the Pamaka and the Kwinti kept a low profile and avoided military confrontations with the colonists.

For this period, it is not strictly correct to speak of "Alukus." It seems likely that it was not until the end of the eighteenth century at the earliest that the various bands to which the Aluku ancestors belonged fused into a sociopolitical entity containing most of the sociostructural elements constituting present-day Aluku society. Before this time, the various bands that were later to contribute to the formation of the Aluku people functioned as semiautonomous units under the leadership of their own chiefs, and with their own villages and territories. As late as the 1760s, it would probably be more accurate to speak of the three major bands—the original Cottica group under Asikan and Boni, the Tesisi group led by Suku and Sambokwasi, and the group headed by Kormantin Kodjo—as constituting an alliance or federation of discrete political units rather than a "tribe" or people.

The process by which these diverse elements came together as a single people was similar to that which resulted in the emergence of the other Suriname Maroon societies such as the Okanisi and the Saamaka, although it occurred relatively late in the Alukus' case. At the foundation of this process was the growth of a sense of collective identity among initial core groups or bands of runaways who fled into the forest at the same time or came together soon after taking flight. These bands were called *lo* (a word also meaning "bunch," "flock," "herd," or "group"). Each *lo* eventually became known by the name of a plantation (or the plantation's owner), or sometimes the name of the region from which some of the most prominent original members of the band had escaped. These *lo* names were applied to all the

The Origin of Aluku Clans

Recent archival research has helped establish the local geographic origins of the various *lo*. It appears that the members of the original Cottica group to which Boni and Aluku belonged were the ancestors of the three *lo* that eventually came to be known as Dikan, Yakobi, and Lape. The name "Dikan" is derived from a plantation on the Coermotibo River called Nes en de Camp, owned by a man named De Camp; "Yakobi" is from Jacobie, the name of the owner of a plantation called Groot-Marseille in the Cottica River area; and "Lape" (pronounced "La-pay") is from La Paix, the name of another plantation in the Cottica area. The Tesisi maroons, on the other hand, appear to have been the ancestors of the *lo* known as Kawina; this name is derived from Commewijne, an important plantation district. Finally, the group led by Kormantin Kodjo is now believed to have evolved into the *lo* called Dju; their *lo* name, derived from the English word "Jew," stems from the fact that many of the members of this group escaped from plantations whose owners were Jewish refugees from Brazil or descendants of such refugees.

Kenneth M. Bilby, "The Remaking of the Aluku: Culture, Politics, and Maroon Ethnicity in French South America" (PhD diss., Johns Hopkins University, 1990), 116; see also Wim Hoogbergen, *De Boni-Oorlogen, 1757–1860: Marronage en guerrilla in Oost-Suriname* (Utrecht: Centrum voor Caraïbische Studies, 1985), 413–428.

members of a band even though many members might have originated from plantations other than the one indicated in the *lo* name, and even though new recruits from many different plantations continued to be incorporated over the years. As children were born, a principle of uterine descent was applied, and eventually the *lo* evolved into descent groups. In these groups are to be found the beginnings of the present-day matrilineal clans, still known as *lo*, that are fundamental units of social structure in all the Maroon groups.

At first, it was primarily the Dutch who took the offensive, launching a number of military campaigns against the eastern maroons from the 1740s to the 1760s, most of which were unsuccessful. But shortly after the Saamaka and Okanisi peace treaties of the early 1760s, the Cottica rebels began to display greater aggression. Between 1768 and 1771, they attacked fourteen plantations, with varying degrees of success. Thus began what has come to be known as the First Boni War.

The First Boni War, 1765–1778

During this turbulent period, the Cottica rebels, now headed by Boni, joined forces with the Tesisi group, and together they launched a series of devastating raids on the plantations. The Dutch authorities responded with military patrols that discovered and attacked several rebel villages. The names of some of these have become legendary: Kromotibo, Kormantin-Kodjogron, Nomerimi (meaning "don't provoke me"), and Buku. Buku had special strategic significance because it was protected by palisades and cannons, and surrounded by thick swamps that could be crossed only via secret paths. It was virtually impregnable.

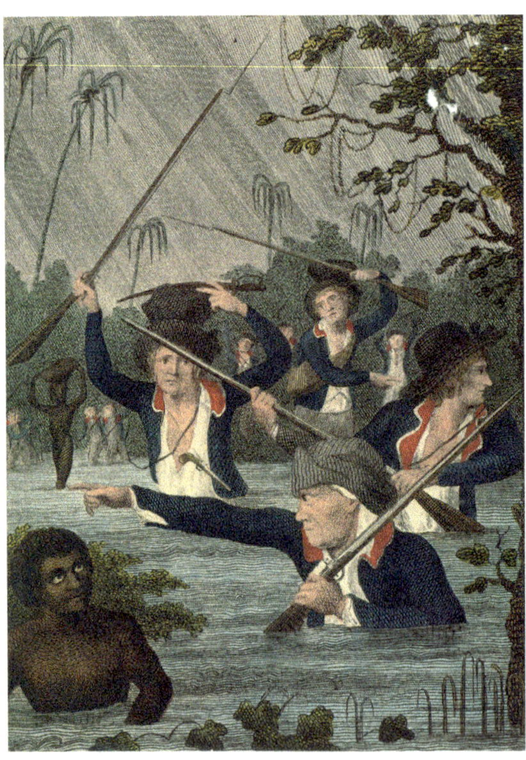

March thro' a swamp or, Marsh in Terra-firma, by William Blake, 1794. Colonial troops and slaves searching for Maroon villages in the Cottica region, 1770s.

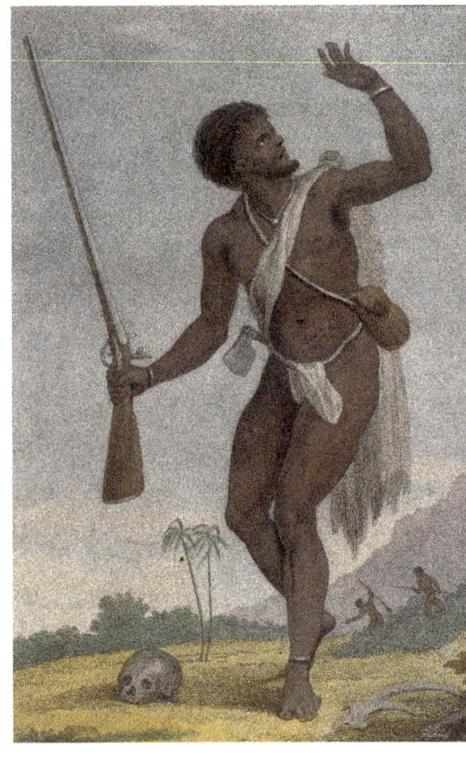

A Rebel Negro armed & on his guard, by Francesco Bartolozzi, 1794. One of the Cottica Maroons in the 1770s.

It was not until a year after their discovery of the village, and only after a continuous five-month-long siege, that the Dutch colonists finally succeeded in capturing and holding it. The taking of Buku in September 1772 dealt a major blow to the Cottica rebels, more than a hundred of whom were captured by colonial troops in the following weeks. The survivors, under the command of Boni, fled farther into the forest. Nearing the point of starvation, they moved to the region between the Commewijne and Suriname Rivers, where they formed an alliance with the band of Kormantin Kodjo, whose provision grounds helped them through the crisis. For the next five years, the Cottica Maroons kept the colony in a state of panic with their surprise attacks on the estates. During this period, some 1,600 soldiers were sent from Holland to root out the remaining rebels. Although the colonial troops discovered and destroyed several villages and managed to keep the Maroons on the run, they never came close to defeating them.

Tiring of the constant harassment by Dutch forces, the rebels decided, after the destruction of their main village, Gado Sabi, to cross the Maroni River and settle in French territory, which they did in August 1776. Their arrival in Guyane happened to coincide with a plan then being devised in Cayenne. The French authorities were at that very moment debating the merits of a proposal to entice those Maroons who had made peace treaties, the Okanisi and the Saamaka, over to the French side by offering them land and material support. These Maroons were thought to number in the tens of thousands, and the advocates of the scheme hoped to use them as a free labor force to farm the coastal plain of western Guyane and to help populate the colony. When word of the Cottica Maroons' flight into French territory reached Cayenne, they too came under consideration for the project. Even after it became apparent that the Okanisi and the Saamaka were unlikely to migrate to Guyane, certain governmental officials in Cayenne continued to harbor hopes that the Cottica Maroons, still bitter enemies of the Dutch, could be coaxed to settle on the coast and contribute to the development of the sparsely populated colony.

The Cottica Maroons, now living in villages along the Sparouine Creek (in French territory), were also interested in treating with the French. Over the next few years, the French authorities sent a number of delegations to the rebel villages to begin negotiations. On several occasions, provisional peace agreements were reached. But growing distrust on both sides hampered negotiations; the French repeatedly failed to deliver promised gifts, while the Maroons vacillated on the question of whether they were willing to resettle in the coastal area between Mana and Iracoubo. Eventually, these Maroons took the decision to withdraw farther upriver along the Maroni, where they founded new villages. During this period, they made peace with both the local Amerindians and the Okanisi, but a full-fledged treaty with the French had failed to materialize.

The Second Boni War, 1789–1793

In 1789, after twelve years of relative calm, a disillusioned faction among the Maroons once again went to war, making a long trek through the interior of Suriname in order to attack several plantations in the central part of the colony. The renewal of hostilities threw Suriname once more into a panic, and the government quickly initiated retaliatory measures, this time with a view to pursuing the Maroons until they could be thoroughly stamped out. Thus began what has come to be known as the Second Boni War. In the fall of that same year, Dutch forces were sent to build a military post on the Maroni River. From this base, Dutch expeditions were sent out against the Maroons. Although the Dutch suffered many casualties, they finally forced the Maroons to abandon their villages and flee yet farther upriver. For a period of a year or so, a temporary standoff was reached. In between minor skirmishes, the Maroons began to send out feelers to see what the conditions might be if they were to surrender. The Dutch, for their part, bided their time, afraid that the Okanisi, who had recently made their own peace with the Cottica rebels, might side with them and go to war once again with the colony of Suriname. Once assured of the loyalty of the Okanisi, however, the Dutch resumed their attacks on the rebels. In 1791, colonial troops succeeded in driving the Maroons even farther upriver, into the Lawa River area. For the next year and a half there were frequent clashes between Dutch soldiers and Maroons, and the colonial forces took possession of a number of Maroon villages. Things looked increasingly bleak for the Cottica Maroons, and they once again began to negotiate the terms for a possible surrender. But the Dutch would accept no less than a total, unconditional surrender, which the Maroons refused.

In 1792, after Okanisi patrols had betrayed a number of the Cottica Maroons and handed them over to the Dutch, the Cottica group decided to break its pact with the Okanisis. In August of that year, they made the fateful decision to attack Animbaw, the village of the Okanisis' paramount chief. During the attack, they took prisoners, plundered the village, and burned down houses. This brazen act of war represented a turning point. Once they were the declared enemies of the Okanisis, there was little hope for them. Not only did they have to contend with the onslaughts of Dutch troops, but now they also had to defend themselves against the much more numerous Okanisis, who, like them, were expert guerrilla fighters, and were amply supplied with arms by the Dutch.

In February 1793, a party of Okanisi warriors under the command of the chief Bambi set off for revenge. Guided by two Cottica Maroon prisoners they had recently captured, they arrived in the vicinity of Boni's village in the middle of the night. Before dawn, they launched a surprise attack, during which Bambi shot and killed Boni in his sleep and then cut off his head and his right hand. By the time the battle was over, eleven Cottica Maroons, including a number of important chiefs, had been killed, and thirty-six taken prisoner. A week later the downriver village of Kormantin Kodjo was attacked, and this important chief was also killed. On the way downriver, however, Bambi's canoe capsized in a rapids, and the canoe, along with Boni's head and the hands of several of his men killed in battle, was lost forever. The story of Boni's death and the disappearance of his head into the seething rapids has become one of the great folk legends of Suriname. For many, it has come to stand for the indomitable spirit of this great warrior who, even in death, refused to submit to defeat.

After the Wars

The deaths of Boni and Kormantin Kodjo signaled the end of the Cottica rebels' power. The survivors of the Okanisi attacks, probably numbering fewer than 150, retreated farther upriver, where they built villages along the Marouini (a tributary of the upper Lawa). Under the leadership of Boni's son, Agosu, they remained in hiding for the next two decades or so. Around 1810, they moved back down to the Lawa River and settled together in one large village just above the area known today as Abattis Cottica. By this time, they had once again made peace with the Okanisis, but for the next several decades, the latter kept them in a state of subjugation. The Okanisis controlled their movements, prohibiting them from leaving the Lawa River area, and restricted their access to material goods from the coast; they also demanded their labor from time to time as a form of tribute. (These relationships were officialized in political contracts between the Dutch and the Okanisi in 1809 and 1837.)[2] Cut off from the coast, the remaining Cottica Maroons were unable to treat with the French. The Dutch, satisfied with this state of affairs, withdrew most of their troops from the area and left the policing of the few surviving Cottica Maroons to their new Okanisi overlords.

As mentioned earlier, during most of the eighteenth century, the various *lo* appear to have functioned as separate political units, each with its own leadership and settlements, although they cooperated at times. But the earliest group to form, the Cottica group originally led by Asikan, seems to have wielded special influence on the loose federation that eventually took shape. Two of the most important early leaders, Boni and Aluku, belonged to this group. It is significant that today the entire group bears the names of both these leaders. (The name "Boni" is most often used as a term of reference by the French, while "Aluku" is the name used by the Alukus and other Maroons.)

Political unification of the various *lo* seems to have occurred only at the end of the eighteenth century, when the separate groups were forced together by adversity. The defeat of the Cottica Maroons by the Dutch and their Okanisi allies and the decimation of the different bands during the war probably made the merging of the fragmented groups of survivors a necessity. Members of the various bands

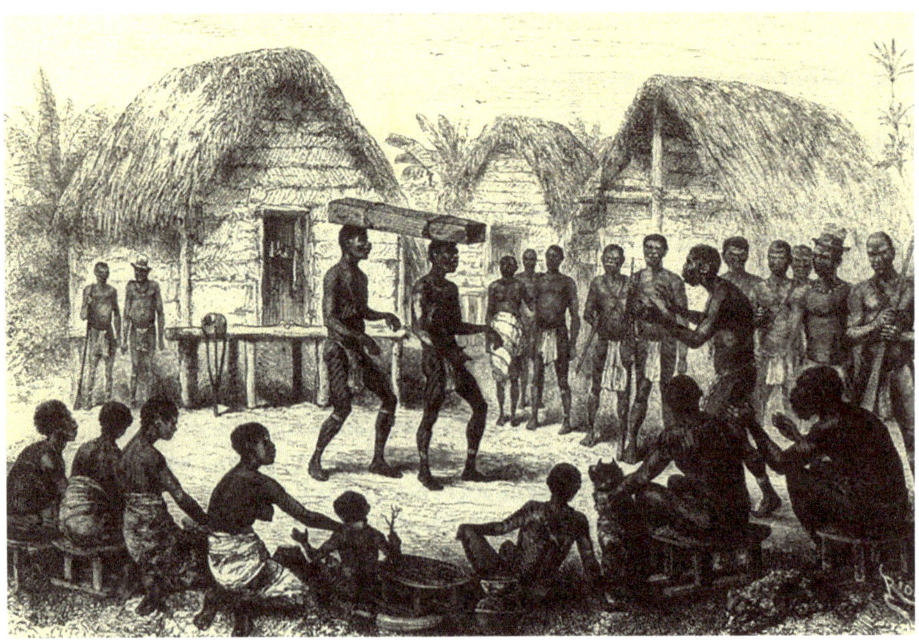

"Among the Boni: Burial of the nails and hair of the grand-man and his wife."

> Corpses are kept unburied for eight days, during which there is much lugubrious dancing and singing. The coffin is carried through the village each morning and evening by men who bend this way and that as if giving salutations. These *politesses* on the part of the deceased as it passes the huts are considered a good sign. The coffin lingers for a while where the council has gathered to receive it. The elders each ask questions to which the coffin answers by moving to the right, to the left, forward or backward. . . . The bodies of the chief and his wife . . . who died on the lower river could not be transported upstream, so instead, just their hair and nails were brought.
>
> Jules Crevaux, "Voyage d'exploration dans l'intérieur des Guyanes, 1876–1877," *Le Tour du monde* 20 (1879): 372

of runaways to some extent already shared a proto-Creole culture learned on the plantations, which itself had drawn on a wide range of African cultural influences. These common elements served as a basis for social and political linkages and coidentification between the groups. Religion played an especially important part in this process.

Archival documents contain numerous descriptions of African-derived ritual oaths used to seal political alliances. In the Alukus' case, the final political unification of the separate bands into a single people seems to have been effected through the subsuming of the different *lo* under the authority of a single set of religious oracles—the oracles controlled by the original Cottica group, led by Asikan, and after him by Boni and Aluku. The divinity originally worshiped by this particular group—a god known as Odun, said by present-day Alukus to have come over from Africa along with the ancestors—thus became the supreme tribal deity, to which all the different *lo* now owed obeisance. At the same time, political unification meant the vesting of ultimate authority in a single paramount chief, who would be recognized by all. It was the chiefs of the oldest band of runaways, most of them members of the Dikan *lo* who controlled the Odun oracles. This may explain why after the unification of the various *lo* into the Aluku people, it was the Dikan *lo* that traditionally supplied the paramount chiefs. From the time of Boni, who died in 1793, until the death of Gaanman Difu in 1967, the Aluku paramount chieftaincy remained, except for a brief hiatus in the nineteenth century, within the Dikan clan.

Alukus and the French in the Nineteenth Century

Once a fragile peace had been reestablished between the Alukus and the Okanisis in the early nineteenth century, the surviving fragments of the different *lo* moved together to the same general area on the Lawa River, where their descendants live today. Here they settled together around 1815 in a single main village, on the Dutch side of the river, with each *lo* occupying its own section. Numbering only a few hundred after the devastating battles of the 1790s, they began to rebuild their lives together. Little is known of this period, but it is certain that the Alukus were eager to escape from Okanisi hegemony. For the next four decades, they sought to treat with the French, in the hope of finding a way out of the onerous condition of vassalage that their former enemies had imposed on them. In 1835 their hopes were raised by a visit from the French botanist and explorer François Leprieur, who assured them that Cayenne was willing to negotiate an agreement with them. But the Okanisis were infuriated when they got wind of the Frenchman's visit and his offer to negotiate with a people they considered to be their vassals. After attempting but failing to intercept Leprieur, the Okanisis protested to the government in Paramaribo, which in turn lodged a formal complaint with the authorities in Cayenne. In 1836, the two colonial governors agreed to an accord that renounced Leprieur's attempts to negotiate, hardened resistance in the French colony to the idea of treating with the Alukus, and kept the latter under the dominance of the Okanisis.

But the Alukus persisted in their attempts to negotiate with the French. Unbearable as their subjugation by the Okanisis must have been, they were unable simply to flee farther into the interior, for they were dependent on coastal society, as they had always been, for certain essential materials—guns, powder, metal tools, pots and pans, and so forth. Even though the Okanisis had set up a blockade to prevent them from traveling to the coast, they kept them supplied with a bare minimum of coastal goods. The French represented the one hope the Alukus had of freeing themselves from the yoke of Okanisi rule. And so they tried to treat with the French again in 1837, sending a delegation to the eastern outpost of Cafesoca to request permission to resettle all the Alukus on the Camopi River, a tributary of the Oyapock. This peaceful overture ended in the tragedy that has came to be known as the Cafesoca Affair. Not only was the Aluku delegation rebuffed, but four of the envoys were summarily executed by a

French firing squad, on the orders of an officer panic stricken at the idea of an impending Aluku "invasion." A few years later, in 1841, the Alukus attempted once again to persuade the French of their peaceful intentions. A new delegation was sent (again via inland routes, without going to the coast) to the Oyapock area, and peaceful contact was made with the French and the local Indians. But this effort, too, ended in disaster. An unfounded rumor began to circulate that the Alukus were behind the murder of two Wayampi Indians, and an armed party was sent out against them. In the ensuing melee, most of the Aluku delegation died, including Paramount Chief Gongo.

In fact, the French authorities were by and large averse to the idea of negotiating with the Alukus. By this time, it was apparent that the Aluku population had dwindled, and with the Okanisis guarding over them, they were no longer seen as a threat. There were fears on the coast that if the Alukus were granted recognition, the coastal slaves might be incited to rebel and demand their own freedom. With the debacle on the Oyapock, which had claimed the life of their paramount chief, the Alukus, for their part, finally came to the realization that there was little hope of an alliance with the French. For the next two decades, except for a brief period of war with the Wayarikule Indians around 1845, they went into a quiet retreat and avoided contact with outsiders.

It was not until 1860 that the Alukus managed to break free of the Okanisis' grip. (At this time their population was several hundred.)[3] More than three-quarters of a century after the first treaty attempt, around 1780, the Alukus finally succeeded in coming to terms with the French. With emancipation of the coastal slaves in 1848, the fears of those who believed that the Alukus might foment rebellion in the colony had begun to subside. France decided that the time had finally come to penetrate the interior of its South American colony, and plans were afoot to begin commercial development along the Maroni estuary. One of the first Europeans to arrive in the area was a Frenchman named Tollinche, who settled on the lower Maroni in the 1850s and launched a series of agricultural projects. Through frequent contact with Okanisis, he learned their language, and by about 1855 he had visited the Lawa River several times and reestablished friendly relations with the Alukus. Through his efforts, the authorities in Cayenne were persuaded that it was in their interest to finally grant the Alukus official recognition. In the fall of 1860, a treaty was signed between the French, the Dutch, and the Okanisi in the Suriname town of Albina, proclaiming the entire Maroni River and its tributaries open to navigation by all parties and recognizing the Alukus as a free people. The treaty was at first vehemently opposed by the Okanisi paramount chief, who agreed to relinquish control over the Alukus only reluctantly and after much wrangling. Ever since this time, the Alukus have been considered French subjects.

By permitting free movement between the interior and coast, the treaty opened the way for the economic development of the previously neglected Maroni region. From the start, the Alukus, as well as the Okanisis and the other Suriname Maroons, were viewed by the French colonial authorities as an important source of labor. But significant economic expansion was never achieved, and little was done during the nineteenth century to encourage large-scale labor migration from the interior into the coastal part of Guyane. In 1857–1858, the community of Saint-Laurent-du-Maroni was founded, about thirty kilometers upriver from where the Maroni meets the Atlantic Ocean. Within a few years, a small number of Alukus were already voyaging to the nearby French prison camp at Saint-Louis to exchange game and handicrafts for the manufactured goods they so desired.[4] But the only economic enterprise that brought substantial numbers of Maroons to the coast at this point was lumbering. To some extent, this involved both the French and Dutch sides of the river.

As early as the late eighteenth century, limited numbers of Okanisis had begun trading lumber, both legally and illegally, with the coastal plantations of Suriname. By the mid-nineteenth century, large groups had migrated to the coast to engage in logging, leading to the founding of new Okanisi/Ndyuka villages in the Cottica River region. In 1856 a law was passed in Suriname to make this sort of economic activity on the coast easier for Maroons, and when emancipation took effect in 1863, Maroons were given further encouragement to participate in trade with coastal society.[5] In the following decades, many Alukus as well as Okanisis became loggers. After cutting and hauling timber, they would tie it together in rafts and float it downstream to depots on both the French and Dutch sides of the Maroni. The timber included both lumber used for local construction and precious woods exported to Europe for their oils and scents or for use in furniture making. The production of lumber enabled Alukus and other Maroons to enter the cash economy of the coast and gain access to the desired material goods they could not produce themselves without losing their cherished independence. The bulk of labor was carried out without external supervision and was organized on their own terms; and migration to coastal towns or settlements was temporary and usually limited to brief visits. During this period, Alukus had only limited and rather superficial contact with coastal society.[6]

The Gold Rush

A major change came in the late nineteenth century with the discovery of gold in the interior of Guyane. According to one account, "As early as 1877 Crevaux signaled a placer in Boni territory that counted one thousand miners."[7] In 1883, deposits were found on the Tampok River (a tributary of the Lawa), in 1887 on the Lawa itself—in the heart of Aluku territory—and in 1900 on the Inini. It has been estimated that 5,000–6,000 people suddenly poured into the area between the Lawa and the Tapanahoni Rivers once word of the discoveries reached other parts of the colony.[8] Settlements of *orpailleurs* (gold miners) sprang up overnight along the Lawa and its tributaries. A brisk trade was set up between these villages and the coastal towns of Albina and Saint-Laurent. None of this would have been possible without the cooperation of the Alukus and other Maroons, since they alone possessed the skills needed to navigate the many difficult rapids between the coast and the interior. The miners, who produced only a small portion of

Aluku canoemen on the Maroni, 1955.

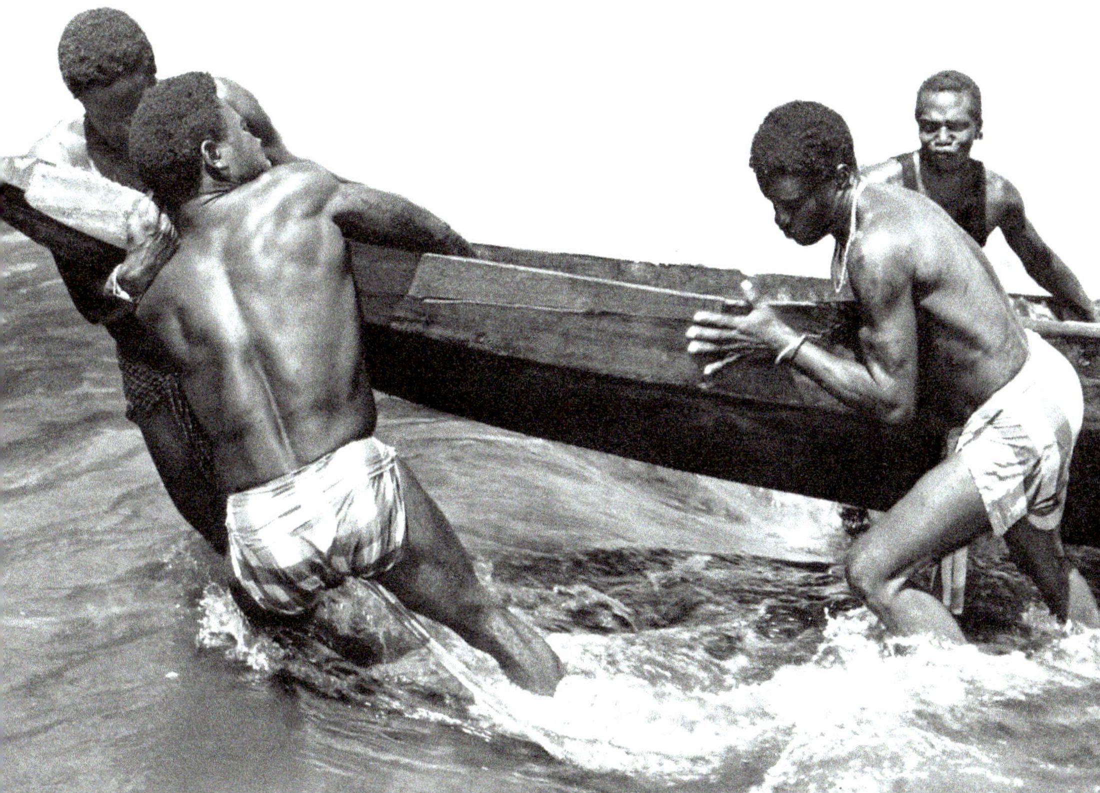

their own food, were almost completely dependent on the Maroons for provisions as well as for general transportation between the mining camps and the coastal towns. Jean Hurault estimated that at the height of the gold rush, the annual traffic on the Maroni amounted to no less than three thousand voyages to the coast and back, with cargoes averaging one ton per canoe.[9]

The Maroons were quick to take advantage of their position, charging steep fees for their services and regulating the passage of gold through their territory. During the early years, Gaanman Anato, the paramount chief of the Alukus, levied taxes at will, laying claim to 15–20 percent of all gold exiting his territory. One observer estimated that by 1888, Anato had acquired the equivalent of more than one hundred thousand francs in this manner.[10] According to another estimate, between 1900 and 1910 the Maroon boat crews plying the Lawa

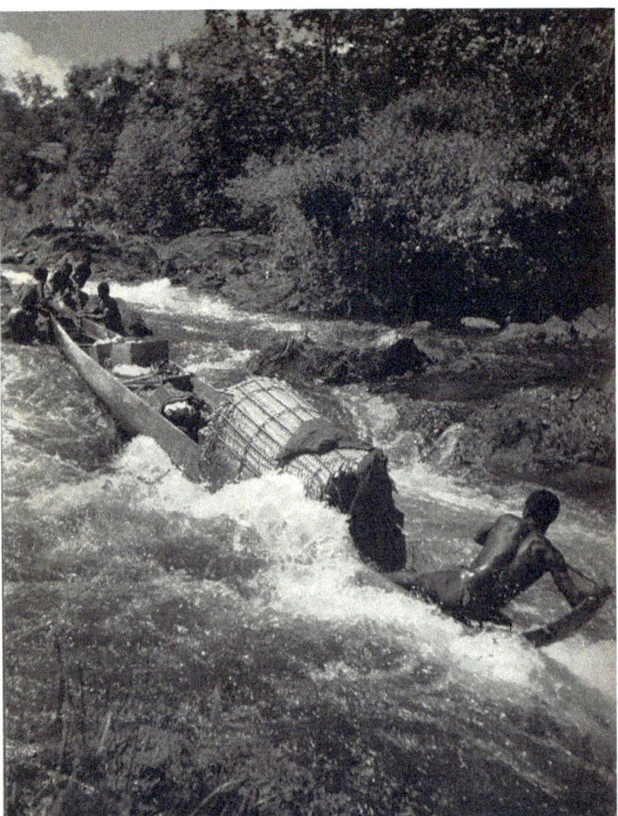

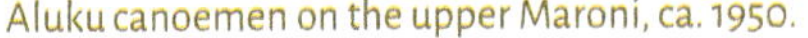

Aluku canoemen on the upper Maroni, ca. 1950.

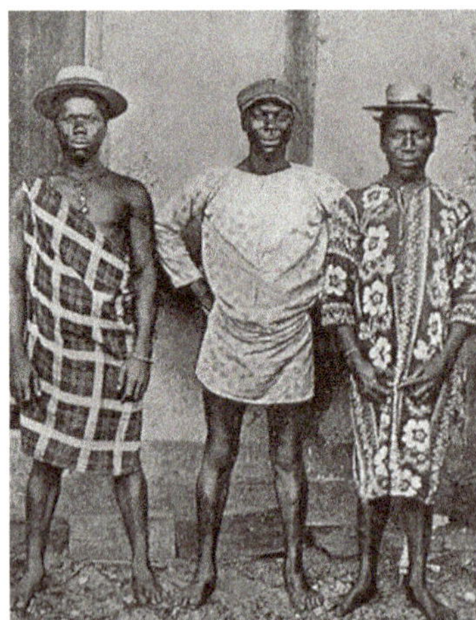

"Boni canoemen, suppliers for the gold miners, ca. 1910."

and its tributaries (which included Aluku boatmen) boasted an annual collective income of about six hundred thousand florins (some U.S.$6 million in today's money); individual canoemen averaged something like U.S.$40,000 annually in today's money.[11] The gold rush thus allowed the Maroons to achieve an unprecedented degree of affluence. Western goods flowed from the coast into their communities as never before; and differential accumulation of wealth created internal social pressures. Among the Okanisis, these powerful economic changes led to major religious upheavals and transformations during the nineteenth and early twentieth centuries.[12] Among the Alukus, however, for reasons that are not yet fully clear, the impact on religious life was much less marked.

What the gold rush did do for the Alukus, other than enriching a number of boatmen, was to provide them with their first prolonged, intensive contact with those they call *bakaa*—coastal people, or Westerners in general. The foreigners who came flocking to their territory, building temporary villages alongside theirs, hiring their services, and trading with them, were primarily immigrants from the French and British Antilles.[13] Through continual and often intimate contact with these Creole adventurers, the Alukus got their first taste of a foreign way of life that they equated with white society. They learned to speak French Creole, borrowed certain cultigens and house-building techniques from their Creole neighbors, and became increasingly sophisticated in their economic dealings with those from beyond their borders. This experience helped prepare them for the large-scale migration to the coast that was to take place in later years. But for the moment, in spite of the presence of this large Creole population in their midst, neither their basic social and political institutions nor the fundamentals of their culture were greatly affected. Although Aluku and Creole individuals mingled a good deal, the distance between the two societies was clearly maintained.

The discovery of gold brought to a head the territorial dispute between France and Holland over the mineral-rich area between the Lawa and Tapanahoni Rivers. The matter was submitted to Tsar Alexander III for arbitration, and a decision was handed down in 1891: thenceforth, the Lawa River was to be considered the boundary between Guyane and Suriname. This posed something of a problem for the Alukus, who had villages and camps on both sides of the river. By the middle of the nineteenth century, some of the *lo* had already split off from the main Aluku village (then called Pobiansi) on the western

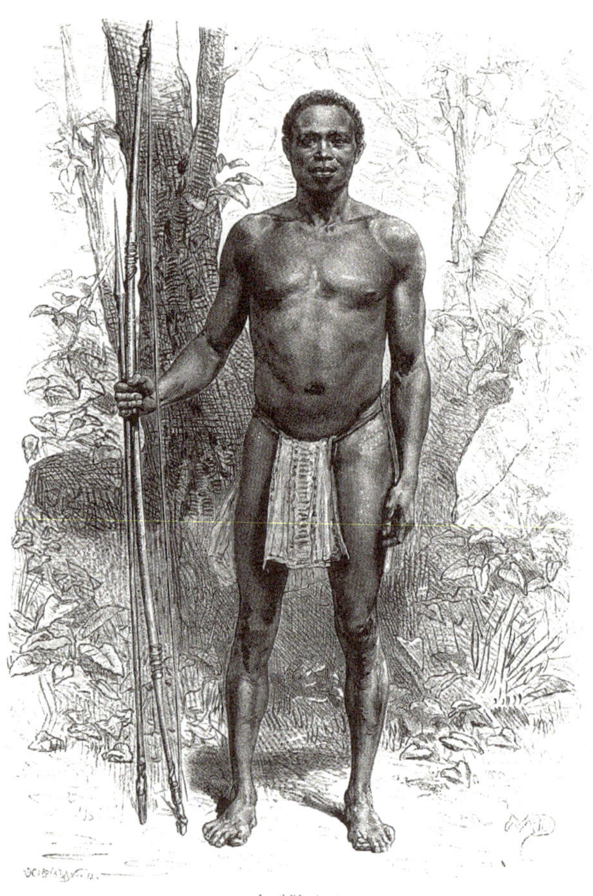

"Le fidèle Apatou" (The Faithful Apatou).

(Dutch) side of the river, where all of the Alukus had once lived, to establish new villages on the eastern (French) side. The process continued over the years, one *lo* after another crossing the river to start new settlements, until only a single village, Kotika, remained on the western side. As the oldest continuously inhabited settlement and the then residence of the paramount chief, Kotika was one of the most important Aluku villages. When the land on which it sat definitively became Dutch territory in 1891, the residents insisted on staying. For a number of years they tried to have it both ways, claiming to be French subjects living on Dutch soil, but they ended up declaring allegiance to the Dutch. The resulting split between the Dutch-affiliated Alukus of Kotika and the French-affiliated Alukus of all the other villages holds

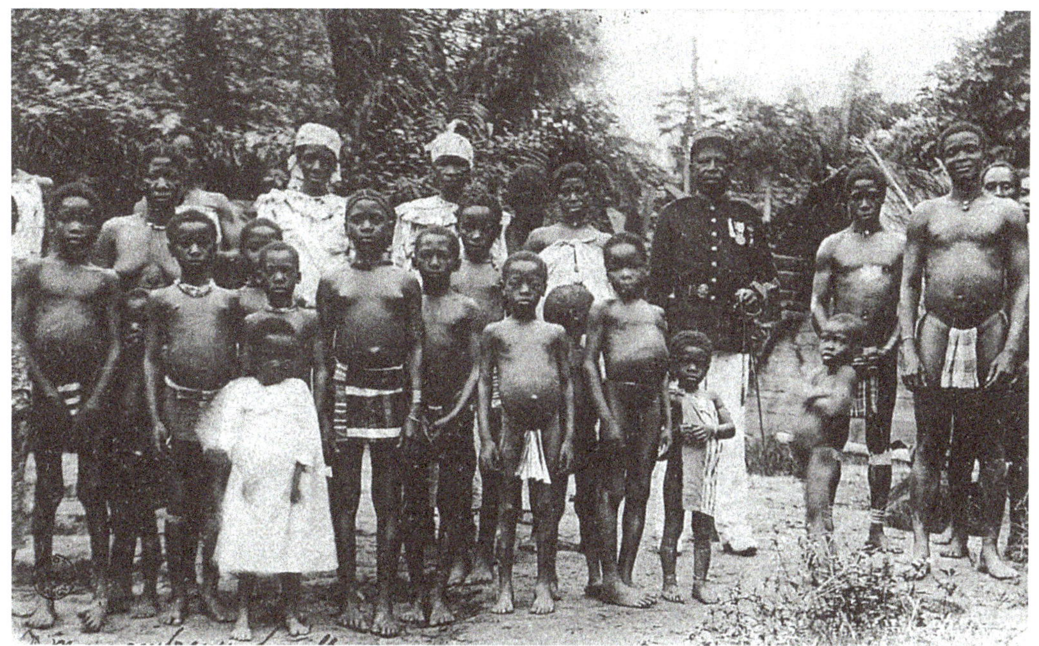

"Boni Captain Apatou and His Family" (postcard). Apatou served as a faithful guide for the explorer Jules Crevaux in the 1870s and was rewarded with a trip to Paris. In 1882, he founded the downstream village of Motende, which is today the center of the commune of Apatou. He was named captain in 1887. See Kenneth Bilby, "The Explorer as Hero: *Le Fidèle Apatou* in the French Wilderness," *New West Indian Guide* 78 (2004): 197–227.

to this day. But in spite of this political division, for the great majority of the Alukus—those living on the French side—the boundary dispute had the effect of reaffirming long-standing French sympathies.

The Twentieth Century

After the gold rush declined in the early twentieth century, the interior of Guyane was never again to become the focus of such intense economic activity. To keep themselves supplied with coastal goods on the scale to which they had become accustomed, the Alukus needed to find other sources of revenue. This led to a certain economic diversification. By the 1950s, wage-earning opportunities for adult males included several standard options. Substantial numbers were employed in forestry projects on the coast or as guides and laborers with French geological or geographic expeditions into the interior. Others continued to work as boatmen, transporting freight between the coast and the interior for the remaining miners and the few shopkeepers who

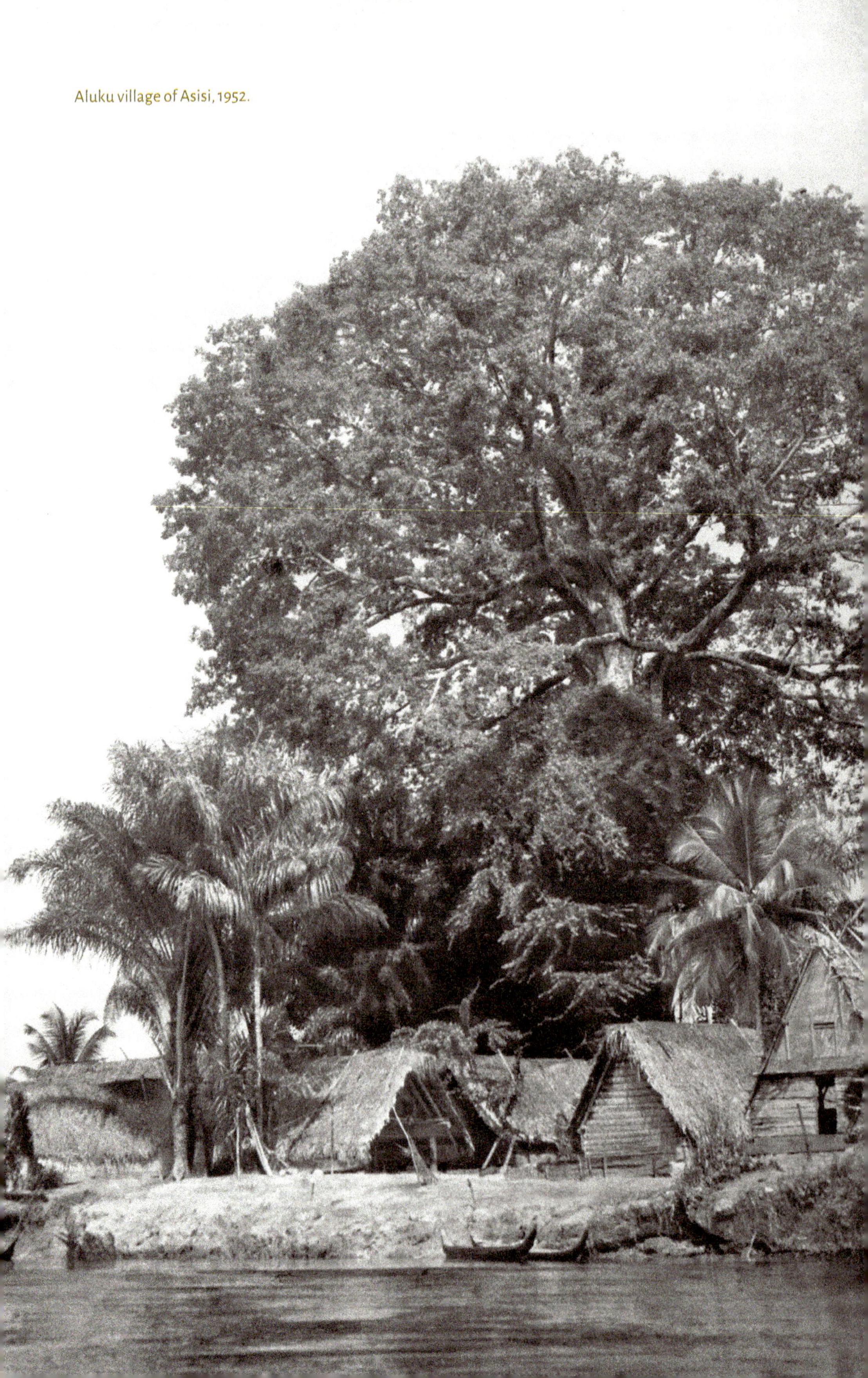

Aluku village of Asisi, 1952.

supplied them. Still others were able to earn a substantial income by becoming professional fishermen, selling their catches to Creoles and to French or Dutch officials stationed in the villages of Maripasoula or Benzdorp. Certain men also worked seasonally in the forest as independent gold miners or balata bleeders. An able-bodied man working as a boatman or a fisherman at this time might expect to earn 200,000 francs (ca. U.S.$500) per year.[14]

Clearly, the Alukus were no longer an isolated society, remote from Western influence. For more than half a century they had been surrounded by Creole gold prospectors. They had ongoing relations with the Okanisis and with the Wayanas. And during the first half of the twentieth century, significant numbers of migrant Saamaka men from Suriname had settled for a time in Aluku villages, taking wives, fathering children, and influencing Aluku woodcarving styles. The growing dependence of the Alukus on wage labor tied their own fortunes to those of a number of distant economies. For instance, at several points during the twentieth century, changing demand caused by fluctuations in the U.S. market strongly affected the opportunities available to Aluku balata bleeders.[15] With the introduction of substantial numbers of outboard motors in the 1950s, the arduous journey from Saint-Laurent to the Aluku territory upriver was reduced from a week (under ideal conditions) to only two or three days.

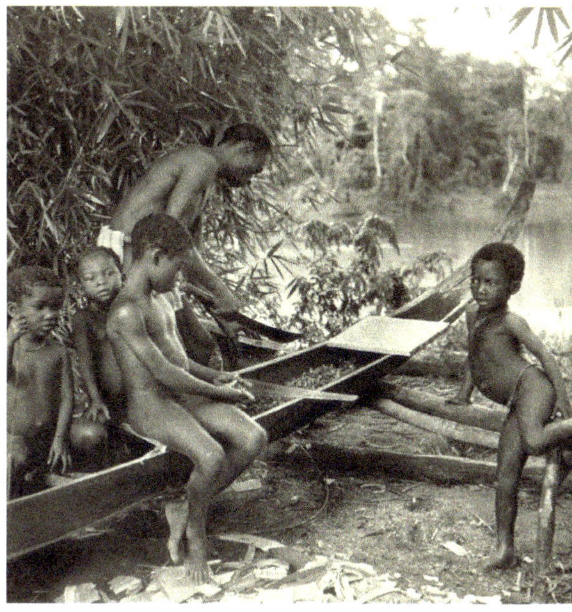

Construction of an Aluku canoe, Boniville, 1952.

Nevertheless, these changes were less far-reaching than might be supposed. Up until the 1960s, traditional Aluku villages looked much as they had during the previous century; nor did their social and political structure show evidence of any major departure from past models. Ever since 1930, the area where the Alukus lived had belonged to the separately administered Inini territory (administered directly by the governor of the colony), and the French seldom intervened directly in the internal affairs of the Alukus. The principle of local autonomy was respected, and most of the dealings between the government and the Alukus were conducted by the paramount chief or his specially appointed representatives living downriver in Saint-Laurent, who served as intermediaries. The French presence in the territory was

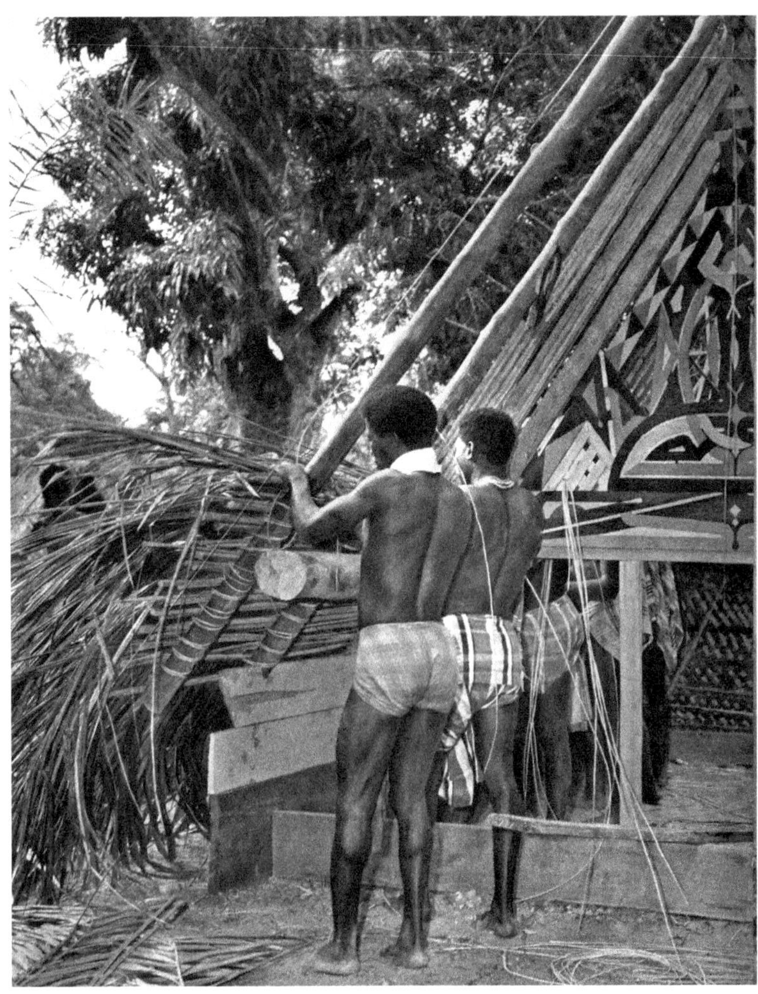

Aluku house building, Loka, 1957.

limited to a small circle of gendarmes, Catholic clerics, medical personnel, and other officials who had been based in the Creole village of Maripasoula since 1949. The Creoles who had stayed on after the gold rush continued to interact frequently with the Alukus, but the two groups remained socially and politically separate. And the handful of Dutch officials posted at the mining company village of Benzdorp on the Suriname side of the river had only superficial contact with the Alukus.

It should be added that during the period before 1970, permanent emigration from Aluku villages to the coast was of only minor significance. The majority of the Alukus still made a living in the interior. In 1958, about a quarter of the adult male population found employment with forestry projects or with governmental missions in the coastal area, but this migratory movement formed part of an established pattern of temporary wage labor.[16] The engagements of Aluku laborers on the coast generally lasted no longer than four to six months, and most of their time was spent in the traditional territory. There was a clear reluctance to migrate for longer periods, and permanent emigration at this time was almost unheard of. In short, by the 1960s, Alukus had been able to adapt to the larger economy, with which they were gradually becoming integrated, without forfeiting their cultural and political autonomy or otherwise upsetting the fundamental integrity of their traditional way of life.

Saamakas in Guyane, 1860–1970

Saamaka historians recount in detail the personal exploits of their early ancestors, creating a patchwork of stories that keep alive a heroic account of rebellion, wars of liberation, and the formation of a new society and culture in the forest.

The fragment of Saamaka oral history in the following sidebar begins a saga of rebellion, escape, and the formation of a new people. The full story is beyond the scope of this book, but it is worth noting that the ancestors of today's Saamakas escaped at the end of the seventeenth century and the beginning of the eighteenth from plantations on the Suriname River, whose proprietors were for the most part Portuguese Jews who had come from Brazil.[17] By the middle of the eighteenth century, they had established numerous villages between the Gaanlio and the Saramacca River, far enough from the coast to protect themselves from the colonists' military expeditions, yet close

Ayako had a sister who lived on the same plantation. One day she was at work, with her baby tied to her back. The child began crying but the white man didn't want her to sit down to nurse. It kept crying. She kept working. The child still cried. Then the white man called her, "Bring the child and I'll hold it for you." So she took the baby off her back and handed it over and returned to work. He grasped the child by the legs, held it upside down, and lowered its head into a bucket of water until it was dead. Then he called the woman and said, "Take the child and tie it on your back." She tied it on and returned to work until nightfall when they released the slaves from work. The child was dead, stiff as a board.

Well, Ayako saw this and said, "What sadness! My family is finished. My sister has but one child left and when she goes to work tomorrow, if the child cries, the white man will do the same thing. I'll be witness to the annihilation of my family. Now, when I was in Africa, I wasn't a nobody. I will make a special effort and see if I still have my powers intact." Then he got himself ready. And he escaped! He ran off with his sister and her baby daughter. It wasn't considered humanly possible to escape from that plantation, but he did it!

At the edge of the forest, he called out his praise name: "I'm the one. *Okundu bi okundo.* The largest of all the animals. I may not have tools but I can still take care of my family!" Then they entered the forest and continued on till nightfall. All he carried was the great Lamba gourd. Whenever they were hungry, they simply ate from that gourd. That was our food in those days.

Captain Kala of Dangogo, teaching R.P. in 1978, adapted from Richard Price, *First-Time: The Historical Vision of an Afro-American People* (Baltimore: Johns Hopkins University Press, 1983), 47–48

enough to the plantations to be able to raid them for manufactured goods and to liberate further recruits. After nearly a century of continual warfare, the Saamakas forced the Dutch colonists to propose a peace treaty; after an initial attempt failed, a treaty was concluded in 1762. By this time, they had created a strong and vibrant culture, language, and polity (a strong state within a state). The treaty required the government to furnish periodic tribute that included axes, guns, pots, cloth, and a host of other goods. By 1850, in the waning days of coastal slavery, tribute had ended, and the Saamakas had shifted to logging and trading agricultural items on the coast. With general

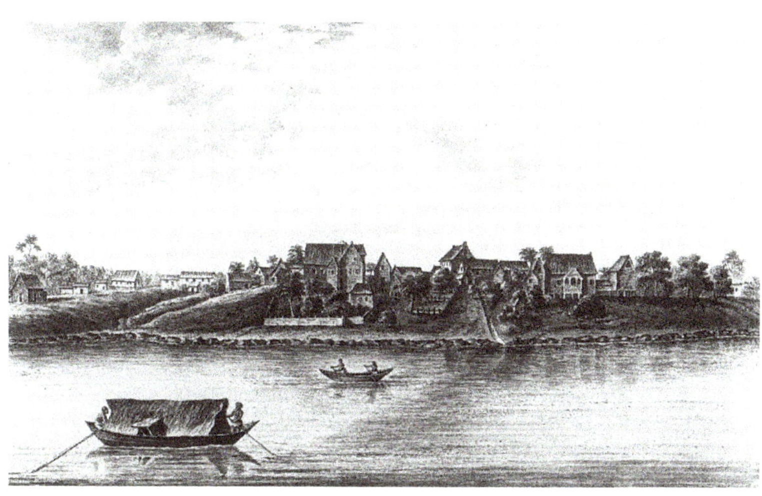

"View of the Jews Savannah" ca. 1800. This was the heart of the plantation region from which the ancestors of the Saamakas escaped.

emancipation in 1863, Saamakas felt freer (and somewhat more comfortable) going to coastal Suriname.

Two major labor opportunities opened up for Saamaka men at this time, and most men eventually combined the two—logging along the Suriname and Saramacca Rivers (a seasonal pursuit that took men from their home villages for only several months at a time) and river transport in Guyane (which caused men to be absent for several years at a stretch). Between the 1860s and the Second World War, men combined these two kinds of jobs outside Saamaka territory, with the balance depending on the ups and downs of particular labor markets.

During the Second World War, when Guyane suffered under the Vichy regime, American army engineers in the Dutch colony of Suriname built the large air base that later became the country's international airport, and Saamakas found many jobs there. Likewise, during the war, Suralco, an Alcoa subsidiary, expanded its aluminum activities in Paranam, creating additional jobs for Saamakas in coastal Suriname. And in the early 1960s, large numbers of Saamakas were employed in building the hydroelectric dam at Afobaka on the Suriname River, designed to power Suralco's aluminum smelter. Unlike logging and river transport, in which Saamakas operated independently, these jobs put them in the position of wage earners working under supervision.

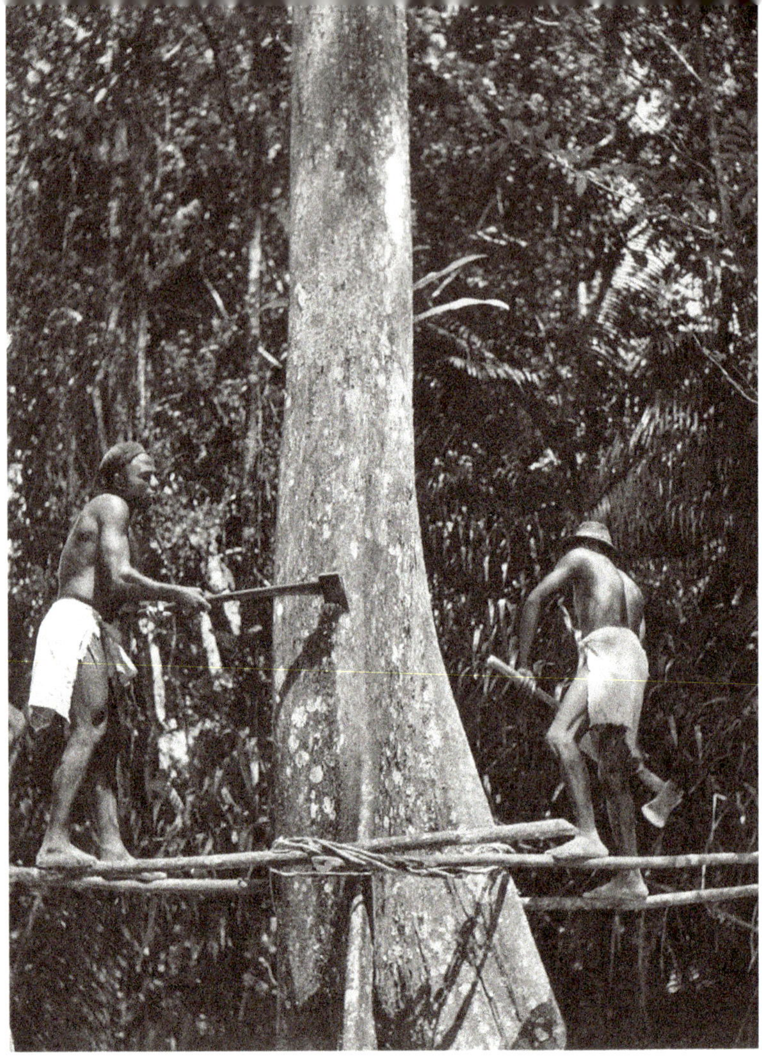

Tree felling, ca. 1950.

Beginnings

Since the 1860s–1870s, Guyane has been the preferred destination for Saamaka men. They saw it as a comfortable place to earn money and even to settle down. In contrast, when doing wage labor or conducting logging or trading trips to the coast of Suriname, they felt embedded in a rigid colonial system, and they were keenly aware that other ethnic groups saw them as low men on the totem pole. While coastal Suriname continued to represent the very world from which the Saamakas' early ancestors had extricated themselves by force of arms, Guyane was perceived as having a looser system, a "homier" atmosphere, and a more relaxed environment, and as a place where they could earn good money far more freely, in occupations that left them considerable independence. Older Saamaka men liked to say that while Suriname was their "*mamakonde*" (their matrilineal [home] village), Guyane was their "*tatakonde*" (their "father's village," their sentimentally favored place to be).

Arriving in Guyane during the early days of the gold rush, Saamakas quickly monopolized major supply routes to the interior and became the colony's rivermen par excellence, taking their pay from Antillean prospectors in bags of gold dust and living high off the hog with what their descendants still remember as gorgeous Creole women who were always available, they say, for men with gold in their pockets. The relative welcome felt by Saamakas in Guyane, as opposed to the coldness they always sensed in coastal Suriname, was clearly expressed during the late 1970s, when the situation of Maroons in newly independent Suriname was already beginning to deteriorate, by the aged Gaama Agbago (Aboikoni): "If only I were a few years younger," he said, "I would simply pull up stakes and lead my whole [Saamaka] people across the Marowijne."

When river transport slowed with the waning of the gold rush, Saamakas switched to other forest endeavors—logging, rosewood extraction—but they continued to earn their money in occupations that left them largely free to set their own schedules and pace of work. Depending on the place and time, many worked in the balata-bleeding industry and even more in cutting rosewood (*bois de rose*), especially during the first three decades of the twentieth century (though a small rosewood mill was still operating in Tampaki on the Oyapock in the 1950s). A Saamaka resident told us that when he first arrived, in 1939, there were still at least three hundred people living in Tampaki, and a rosewood mill was working around the clock. During the 1920s and 1930s—until the trees were depleted and the industry moved to the Brazilian Amazon—Guyane was the world's largest producer of rosewood oil, the essential ingredient in Chanel No. 5 perfume. From the nineteenth century to the present, a number of Saamaka men have also worked mining gold.

From the beginning, men took their preadolescent sons and sisters' sons to Guyane for several years to be socialized into this "other half" of the world in which they would someday have to function as men. And until recently, men continued these trips well past middle age, until ill health finally forced some of them into the undesirable position of economic dependence. Economic necessity put practical limits on variations in the rhythm of coastal trips. No married man could afford an unbroken stay of more than three years in Saamaka unless, because of chronic illness or other personal misfortune, special arrangements had been made. After two years, his supplies of such items as cloth, kerosene, ammunition, and rum would be seriously depleted, and his wives would have passed the halfway point in expending their salt, soap, cloth, and so forth. In spite of fluctuations in wages and consumption patterns over the past half century, there was a fairly stable ideal that a man, having gone to work on the coast (except on logging trips), should bring back supplies to last his wives four to five years, until his next return. During the twentieth century, most Saamaka men spent nearly half of their life in Guyane.

Some Saamaka men never came home from Guyane, instead founding large families with Creole women. Many of their daughters and their daughters' daughters later married Saamaka immigrants. But the very great majority of Saamakas in Guyane returned to Suriname, often going back and forth at several-year intervals during their entire adult lives until they came home to die.

In the mid-1960s, labor opportunities in Guyane took a new turn for Saamakas with the establishment of the European Space Center (now the Centre Spatial Guyanais) in Kourou. As large swatches of forest needed at first to be cleared, and later as carpentry became important during the construction of the vast new town of Kourou, Saamakas flocked to the region, leaving home villages during the late 1960s with few young men. As with other post–Second World War jobs in Suriname and Guyane, the building of Kourou brought with it a new way of life for Saamaka men. They now lived in company towns, wore Western clothes, cut their traditional braids, and were making genuine attempts to speak the creole language of Guyane. Nevertheless, labor trips remained, as much as ever, a thoroughly institutionalized aspect of Saamaka life. While on the coast, men remained conceptually and physically close to other Saamakas, maintaining frequent communication with their home villages, primarily via tape-recorded messages carried by men going and coming.

The departure for the French missile base (or other sites in Guyane), which we witnessed many times in Saamaka, has always been preceded by a complicated series of rituals performed over many days (and often in several different villages) to protect the man from the various kinds of supernatural dangers and pollution still associated with the world outside. A man departing from the village of Dangogo, for example, would be escorted by Dangogo's village oracle-deity and its two bearers, a "priest" (*basi*), and attendants as he prepared to board the waiting outboard-powered canoe. At the missile base, in off-duty hours he would stay largely with other Saamakas, follow Saamaka gossip, and use imported Saamaka oracles and other forms of divination whenever he had a personal problem. And on his triumphant return, soon after the other villagers had finished trekking back and forth to the loaded canoe, carrying supplies intended to last several years, he would begin rituals to be purified from the various kinds of contamination to which he had been exposed on the coast.

Between the final decades of the nineteenth century and the end of the twentieth, the number of Saamakas in Guyane at any one time was greater than the number of Maroons from any other group—even more than the entire population of the Alukus. These men contributed a large number of children (some recognized, some not) to the population of Guyane and played a key role in the economy of the colony. Until the 1970s, the Saamaka presence was almost exclusively male and largely in the form of temporary (several-year-long) visits. Today, as we shall see, many Saamaka men live in Guyane with their Saamaka wives and children.

Special Arrangements: French Authorities and the Saamakas

The first Saamakas arrived in Guyane in the 1860s, in the early years of the colony's gold rush, on the Sinnamary, Mana, and Approuague Rivers.[18] (In 1887, one group of one hundred Saamaka men was reported to be returning home from a nine-year stay at Mana.)[19] On both the Approuague and the Mana, the upriver placers were as far as 350 kilometers upstream, through innumerable treacherous rapids, and took some sixty days to reach.[20] By the early twentieth century, there were usually about twelve thousand gold miners in the interior—including Creoles from both Guyane and the Antilles—though some estimates put the figure at twenty-five thousand.[21] During the early years of the rush, "there were so many accidents on the river that a decision was taken to summon to the Mana, the Approuague, and the Oyapock really expert canoemen, the Saamaka Maroons of Suriname. Toward this end, the governor of Guyane signed an official agreement in 1883 with the paramount chief of the Saamakas."[22]

These Accords of 1883 set up an administrative system for the French colonial government in Cayenne to handle Saamaka immigration and residence, and they gave the Saamaka canoemen considerable autonomy and privilege.

Saamaka canoes, wider than those of the Okanisis or Alukus, were better suited to carry large loads upriver, where the rapids were practically impassable to a Creole canoe. A sixteen-meter-long Saamaka canoe could bring as much as 45 *barils* (4,500 kilos) of merchandise to the gold miners upstream.

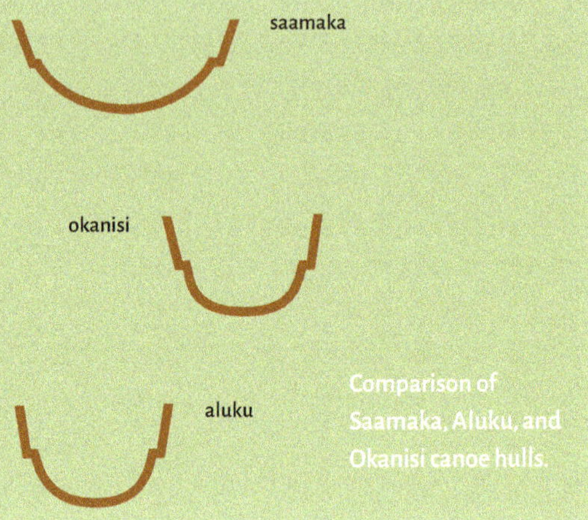

Comparison of Saamaka, Aluku, and Okanisi canoe hulls.

Beginning in 1883, then, Saamakas enjoyed a special status in Guyane, remaining throughout their stays under the legal authority of the Saamaka paramount chief in Suriname. No other group of people in Guyane had this legal independence from the laws of Guyane or France—only Saamakas. Indeed, to our knowledge, these accords have never been officially rescinded or renegotiated. In 1892, an additional contract was signed in Cayenne between A. Bally, the owner of

In effect, the immigrants were placed under the authority of a chief designated by the Granman and recognized by the governor of Cayenne with the title "commandant." This chief went to live on the lower Oyapock, at the place that was later to become Tampaki, the base for canoemen on that river. But the Oyapock was hardly the only river with navigational challenges—in addition to the Maroni, which was the domain of the Boni (and Okanisi), there were the Approuague and the Mana, and two other groups of Saamakas took over there. At the head of each of these groups was a "captain" named by the governor with the approval of the Saamaka commandant. Assisted by a "lieutenant," whom he chose and who was also recognized by the governor, the captain was charged with maintaining discipline within the group. To accomplish this, he stayed in close touch with the mayor and the gendarmes, but these latter never intervened directly in the affairs of the group. When there was a dispute between two Saamakas, it was solely the captain who had authority to find a solution. If the dispute involved a Saamaka and a Guyanais—which in fact very rarely occurred—the gendarme would always go first to the captain and then, with his help, resolve the problem.

Marie-José Jolivet, *La question créole: Essai de sociologie sur la Guyane française* (Paris: ORSTOM, 1982), 154–155

various placers and a member of the colony's *commission d'immigration*, and Gaama Akoosu, paramount chief of the Saamaka, who was on a visit to Guyane.

Bally added a personal note at the bottom of his agreement with Akoosu: "In order to persuade the Saamaka Granman to agree to this treaty I had to give him numerous presents—among others, a very fine little cannon with powder."

In the 1940s, the colonial governor made reference to the Bally-Akoosu treaty, writing in a circular on the subject of the Saamakas that "the origin of their coming to Guyane and the special advantages

In the name of all my captains, village chiefs, and all my subjects, I, Akrosoe Abraham, Granman of the tribe of Saamakas established in Dutch Guiana, wishing to recognize the services rendered to my tribe by M. Adolphe Bally, citizen of France and ex-president of the *conseil général*, have concluded a peace treaty that includes the following clauses:

Granman Abraham agrees to furnish all canoe transport requested by M. Bally, either for himself or for his friends. He further agrees to furnish all necessary personnel for this task.

He also agrees to send M. Bally families of Saamakas both for logging and the extraction of balata and for making gardens which will furnish various crops in whatever regions of the country M. Bally designates.

For his part, M. Bally agrees to provide every aid and assistance to the Saamaka men. He assures Granman Abraham that French laws, which protect the freedom of labor and the equality of men, will cause no interference with the free execution of the present treaty made with the good faith of both contractual parties.

A. Bally

Akrosoe Abraham

Cayenne, 1 April 1892

This document is in a folder labeled "Saramacca" in the Archives Départementales. The document cited here, which is dated "1882," is a typescript copy of an 1892 manuscript (now apparently lost). All the other documents in the folder specify the date of the original as 1892. Thus, the "1882" on the typescript is a typo. Indeed, Akrosoe did not even become *gaama* until 1888. In addition, another copy of the document, which is in the archives of the Musée des Beaux-arts de Chartres, fonds Bougé, is labeled "copie d'un traité d'amitié passé avec les Saramacas et M. Bally de Cayenne en avril 1892 pour le transport par canotage sur le territoire de la Guyane française."

they enjoy date from 1892, when a treaty was made with the Saamaka *Gaama* (paramount chief). Every special privilege they enjoy (entry without official papers, entry without a deposit against repatriation, residence without registration, exemption from all levies and taxes) was designed to facilitate, under the best possible conditions, transport on the rivers."[23]

At the very least, these agreements would seem to give Saamakas reason to expect special consideration in immigration matters from the French authorities today.

Favored Places

In the 1860s, the coastal town of Mana became the first main target of Saamaka settlement, and there was a strong Saamaka presence for one hundred years, with several hundred men in residence at any one

Today, Saamakas have precious memories of their pioneer ancestors who "opened up" Guyane for them: the first men who went to Mana. They tell, for example, about Asimadyo from the village of Dangogo, who left Saamaka in haste in the wake of the scandal caused by his having slept with a mother's brother's wife, walked for days through the forest to the east until he arrived at the Okanisi villages along the Tapanahoni River, and was welcomed there by his Okanisi friend Hansibai. He and his friend each made a canoe and, accompanied by the sons and sister's sons of Hansibai, paddled down the Maroni to its mouth and entered the Mana. In the town of Mana, Asimadyo learned to speak Creole and saw how Creoles from Guyane, along with a handful of Okanisi and Aluku Maroons, controlled the river transport trade. He saw that Creole canoes were far smaller than Saamaka ones, holding but 6 *barils* (600 kilos) compared to Saamaka ones, which held up to 45 *barils*, and that the Creoles maneuvered exclusively with paddles rather than with the poles that Saamakas always used at the prow of the canoe to get through the rapids. "The Creoles were dying in the water and the goods weren't getting to their destination . . . and neither Alukus nor Okanisis were up to the task either," an old Saamaka told R.P. Hansibai and Asimadyo succeeded in the transport trade, working the lower river for some time. And when Asimadyo made his triumphal return to Saamaka, bringing back a case of fancy French soap and a magnificent French sword, large numbers of men were ready to follow in his footsteps.

►►►

The work was tough, very tough, remember Saamakas. They tell about Akoni, another pioneer in Mana and the first to try to bring a load all the way up to the mines at St.

time. As early as 1883, a shopkeeper in Mana wrote about the advantages offered by Saamaka canoemen: "It was common to see a flotilla of twenty-five canoes leaving for the upper Mana, transporting a full fifty tonnes of merchandise"—and at half the price charged by Creole canoemen.[24] Once they had brought the merchandise to the upriver camps, Saamaka canoemen were paid in gold: "Tremendous precautions were taken with the payments in gold. They would be coated with lead and placed in a sealed case attached to a float. That way, if the boat sank the case containing the precious metal could be recovered."[25]

Soon, Saamakas had an absolute monopoly of river transport on the Mana. Around 1900, the colonial administration decided for the first time to recognize a Saamaka captain in Guyane. Agaduhansu, selected for the post, deferred in favor of Samuel, who became the captain of

Léon, on the upper river. Unable to get through the rapids at Saut Continent, he and his crew built a platform in the forest, stored the merchandise there, and went downstream to seek help. His father-in-law, who lived in Mana, went upriver, found the load, and was able to bring it some distance farther, but when he got to the rapids called Saut Par Hasard, he too was stymied, so he and his crew built a platform for the goods and went back downstream. Tata Agaduhansu, who was at the place called Délices with his sister's sons Asantifutu and Akaaso and with Tata Koga, said they'd do it. And they did! They found the goods and, using their poling technique, brought them far upstream. At the mouth of Crique St. Leon, a tremendous fallen tree blocked their entry. They cut at it with their axes for a whole week but couldn't get through, so they unloaded the canoes, made a camp, and called their gods for consultation. Tata Koga had a god called Ma Kambo, Agaduhansu one called Miisi. The gods said, "If you give up and go back now, you will die. Cut the tree." They worked at it for three more days and called the gods again. This time the gods said they would work with them the following day. As the men were cutting at the tree, they saw two ducks and shot them. (It was the gods who'd brought the ducks.) The Creole gold miners upriver at St. Leon heard the gunshots and figured the Saamakas didn't know where to find them and were signaling with their guns. So they answered with their own guns and went down to meet them—a moment of joy still remembered by Saamakas with emotion. As Saamakas say, "Honors for opening up the upper Mana go to Tata Agaduhansu and Tata Koga, and those for the lower Mana go to Asimadyo, but not to him alone, for it was his Okanisi friend Hansibai who first told him there was a river over there with work to be had."

Mana. In the period 1910–1920, there were so many Saamaka men in Mana that there was active discussion between France and the Netherlands of establishing a Dutch subconsulate in that tiny town.[26] In 1947, from twenty to twenty-five Saamaka canoes were still working between the town of Mana and the upstream goldfields.[27] In the 1960s, when job opportunities had shifted to Kourou, there were still some forty Saamaka men, most of them elderly, working in logging and river transport in the area around Mana. By the end of the twentieth century, the Saamaka presence in the town had shrunk to three aging men and several of the (Saamaka-speaking) daughters whom they had fathered with Creole women. The last Saamaka captain of Mana died about 1989. On the other hand, a number of young Saamaka men have since arrived from Suriname with their families and settled along the road between Mana and Saint-Laurent, earning their living by offering woodcarvings for sale at roadside stands.

The second major site for the pioneer generation of Saamakas in Guyane was the Approuague River—first in the coastal town of Guisambourg and later, beginning in the 1920s, in the town of Régina. By the late nineteenth century, several thousand gold miners of varied origins were working on the upper river, and the area had more than twenty factories for processing *bois de rose*. As Sophie François notes, “Saamaka canoemen quickly gained a monopoly on river transport

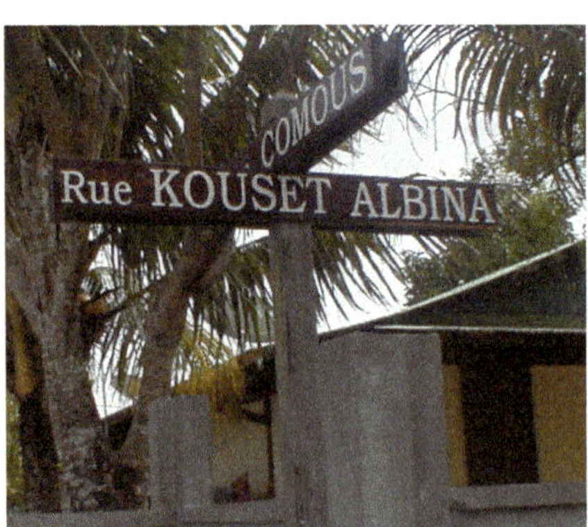

Street sign in the public housing tract of Sables Blancs, Saint-Laurent-du-Maroni, where many Saamakas live.

Saamakas in Guyane recount with pride the story of “Kouset, Albina” (also known as “Nyamisi”), who worked in Mana and in 1939 enlisted in the army, joining the French forces fighting in Europe in the Second World War. After returning to Guyane aboard the *Saint-Domingue* in 1945, he fathered twenty-one children in Saint-Laurent and returned to his village in the interior of Suriname just before his death in 1974.

The story of Kouset, who was a POW in a stalag in eastern Germany, is recounted in detail, on the basis of oral and archival sources, in Richard Price, *Travels with Tooy* (Chicago: University of Chicago Press, 2008), 66–78.

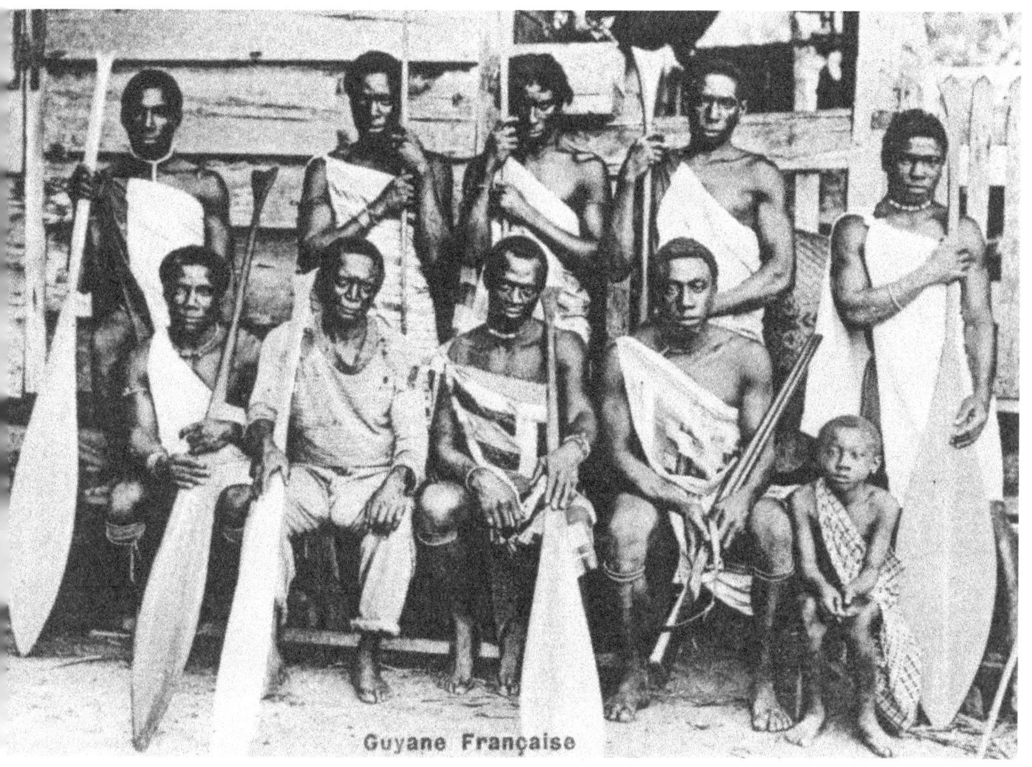

Saamaka canoemen in Guyane at the dawn of the twentieth century (postcard).

along the Approuague."[28] Saamakas still remember their pioneer ancestors in the region by name: Tata Tamenu and his sons Konima and Tomasie. Another, Tata Abaasa, is remembered as having brought an important carry-oracle from Saamaka and taken it with him to the Carsewene goldfields, where large numbers of Saamakas worked in the 1890s before returning to the Approuague around 1900, when Carsewene officially became part of Brazil.

From a Saamaka perspective, the glory days of the Approuague stretched from the 1880s to the mid-twentieth century, when river transport and cutting *bois de rose* offered steady work. At its height, the Saamaka presence "is said to have numbered 400 men."[29] Between 1920 and 1940, there was always a Saamaka community of 200–300 men in Régina, as well as the numerous children they had with Creole women.[30] According to Saamakas, unlike the women of Saint-Georges (see below), many of those in Régina refused to recognize the Saamaka fathers of their children, preferring to take a Creole husband as soon as they realized they were pregnant. (Indeed, an old song from the

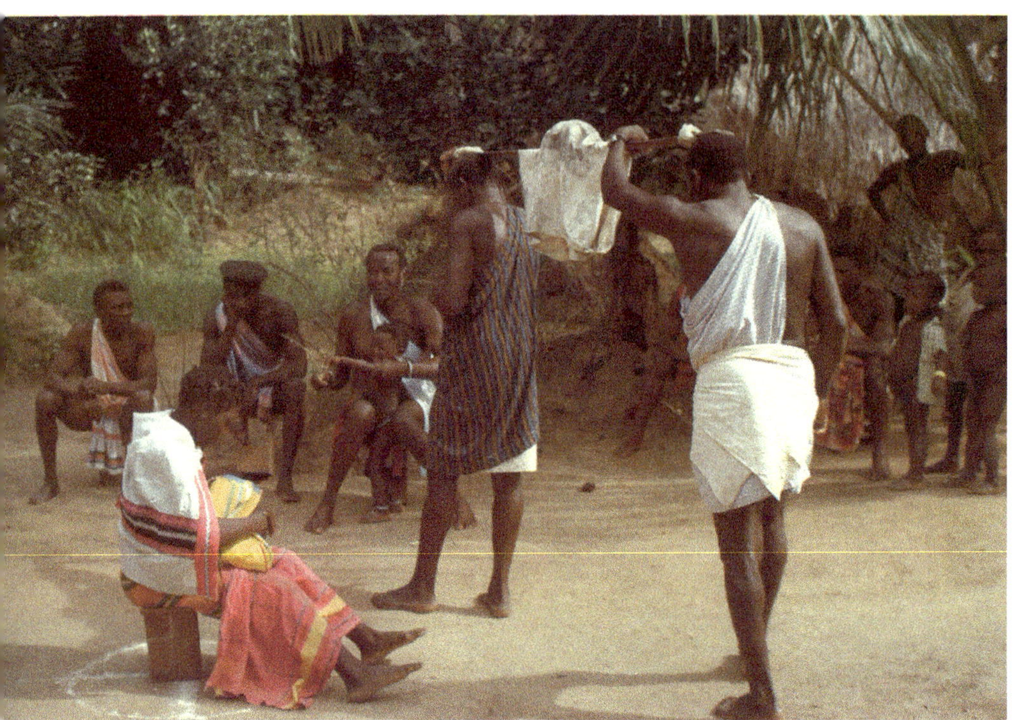

A Saamaka newborn is formally introduced to her village, Dangogo, 1968. A local head-carried oracle that was consulted frequently during the mother's pregnancy supervises the ceremony, pushing its two bearers forward, backward, or sideways to respond to the questions posed by its priest (*seated at left*).

Régina carnival makes reference to these shenanigans.)[31] In the late 1960s, there were still some 30 Saamakas working as loggers and canoe makers in and around Régina.[32] When we visited in 1991, we were shown the "Village Saramaka," which consisted of the overgrown ruins of more than one hundred houses; there were only three old men still alive, all three of whom were still there in 2001. In 2018, two of these men were still there, but Brazilians had built a new village on the site of the old Village Saramaka.

At the very end of the nineteenth century, Saint-Georges-de-l'Oyapock became the third—and most important—center for Saamakas in Guyane. Founded as a penal center in 1853, with a prisoner and guard population of some two hundred, it became the jumping-off place for gold miners in the Oyapock basin, which had a gold rush after 1855. The population was unusually mixed: by 1874, eighty-one East Indians, fourteen Africans, and five Chinese had been imported as immigrant laborers to the region, and there were a number of immigrants from the French Antilles, metropolitan French people working in government services, and Brazilians from across the river.[33] Saamakas, with their special status, monopolized river transport on the Oyapock, but it was only after 1900, when a large migration of French and Antilleans, with their Saamaka canoemen, came back to the Oyapock from the now-Brazilian Carsewene goldfields, that the region really took off economically and demographically.

It was in the wake of this reflux from the Carsewene that Saamakas built their village of Tampaki, a few kilometers downstream from Saint-Georges. Of all the towns in Guyane, Saint-Georges developed the reputation among Saamakas as the place where Creole women were most available to them as wives, and soon Tampaki was a thriving village of some three hundred residents—Saamaka men, their Creole wives, and their children. By 1910, Tampaki was said to have

Saamakas remember Tualu, who had been working in Mana, as their pioneer on the Oyapock, and also as the first Saamaka to take a Creole wife. When he arrived in Cayenne from Mana at the end of the nineteenth century, there were already many Saamakas working in the area. Margarite, his wife, suggested they go to the Oyapock, where she and her husband formed a river transport team, Tualu at the prow of the canoe with a pole and Margarite steering at the rear, bringing goods up as far as Camopi and from there to the placers of Bienvenue. Before long, Tualu returned to Cayenne and told other Saamakas about the opportunities on the Oyapock, and he was soon followed there by Abeliti, Kodyobii, and Tata Kodyi (a famous curer who had just arrived from Haarlem, on the Saramacca River in Suriname), as well as a group of men from the Pikilio in Suriname: Gasiton, Kositan, Agbago, Wenwenkaka, Gide, and Kodyo.

Saamakas tell how a "French captain" in Saint-Georges who was about to be sent to Cayenne to have his leg amputated was instead cured by Kodyobii, at which point the French authorities in Cayenne encouraged Saamakas to settle in the area. They had offered Kodyobii the first captain's position on the Oyapock but he declined in favor of his elder, the already-respected Kodyi, who then served for two decades until his death in 1923. (After Kodyi's death, his son—today remembered as "Commandant Kodyi"—took the position, and he was in fact named by the French colonial government, in 1942, to be the first commandant of all the Saamakas in Guyane.[1]

1. According to a document in the Archives départementales, "André Coggie" was named "Commandant des Saramacas de la Guyane Française et du Territoire de l'Inini" in January 1942, having served as "Chef des Saramacas de l'Oyapok" since August 4, 1923.

the largest ancestor shrine of any Saamaka village anywhere. In 2001, one Saamaka resident told us that when he first arrived in 1939, there were still some three hundred people living in Tampaki.

With the opening of the European Space Center in Kourou in the 1960s, work opportunities shifted and the Saamaka population of Tampaki never recovered. In 2001, only seven elderly men remained (plus three in Saint-Georges along with two younger, more recent arrivals), including the Saamaka captain Lalani, who was the successor to Commandant Kodyi (see sidebar). The village was increasingly populated by Amerindians from Brazil. Nonetheless, the Saamaka imprint on the region of Saint-Georges remains important. A significant portion of the Creole population has at least one Saamaka grandparent or great-grandparent (for example, the mayor of Saint-Georges, Georges

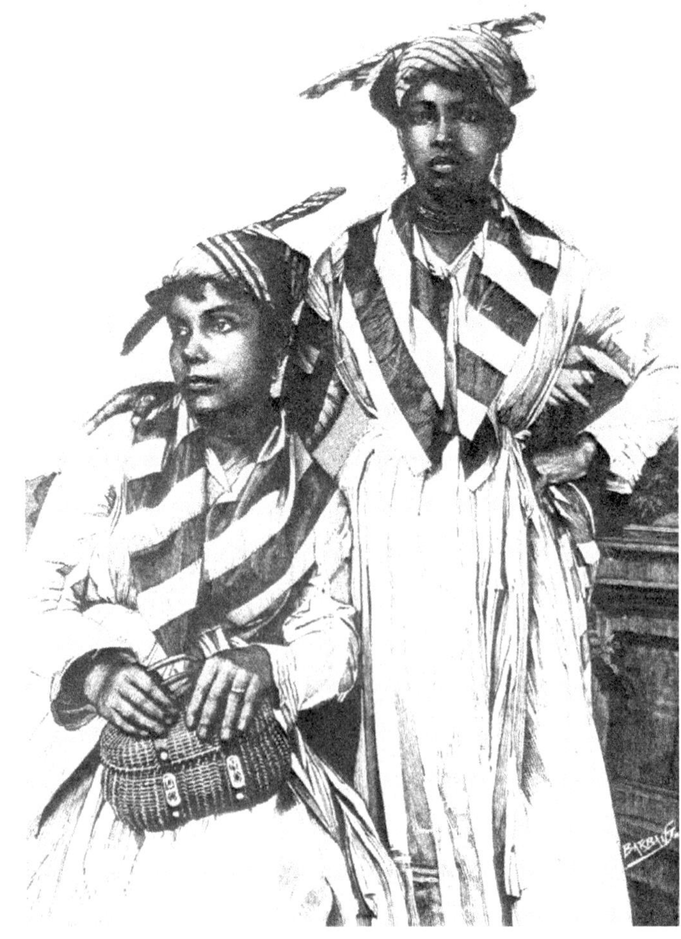

"Women of the Placers," ca. 1890.

Elfort, who is proud of his Saamaka grandfather),[34] and a number of Creole women with Saamaka fathers still speak Saamaka.

Today, the Oyapock is the spiritual center of Saamakas in Guyane. The river is speckled with sites sacred to Saamakas—including places where annual rites to the sea gods are still performed. In early 2001, for example, rites at sacred sites both downriver and upriver from Saint-Georges attracted more than a hundred people: some fifteen Saamakas, seventy of their Creole descendants, and fifteen or so Amerindians who live in Tampaki. And at numerous other sacred sites, all the way up to Camopi and Bienvenue, the deeds of Saamaka pioneers in the region, such as Kodyi, are periodically commemorated.

Since the end of the nineteenth century, Saamakas have also exercised a river-transport monopoly on the Sinnamary, where they had an official captain (as on the Mana, Approuague, and Oyapock), but their village there never achieved the size of those in Mana, Régina, or Tampaki.

Saamakas and the Penal Colony

Some Saamakas served the French penal colony as bounty hunters. In one celebrated case, a Saamaka named Voisin—probably the man brought up by Kodyi (the father), who inherited many of his powers—brought in a recidivist escapee in 1939.[35] And Saamakas—some thirty of them, according to old men today—often lost their lives in this activity, as did innocent Saamakas who were attacked by escaped prisoners in the forest. Escapees in the forest were often starving, and Saamakas preserve numerous stories of their attempts, sometimes successful, to ambush, rob, or kill Saamakas who happened to cross their paths.

Something of the excitement of this period was expressed to us when we lived in Suriname, where older Saamaka men used to tell us about their tremendous fear of escapees from the penal colony. Well into the 1970s, Saamaka mothers still disciplined disobedient children by repeating the adage, "Little children cooked up with dasheen, that's the convicts' favorite dish!" Books on the *bagne* (penal colony) recount how four particularly fierce North Africans, who had been sowing mayhem throughout Guyane for several months since their escape in early 1934, fell upon a Saamaka garden camp along the Oyapock and killed a woman. Before they could cross the border to Brazil, they were captured by Saamakas and, in return for a reward, turned over to the authorities on the other side of the colony in Saint-Laurent-du-Maroni. (Another account suggests that the Saamakas lynched them

Saamakas who killed escaped prisoners from the penal colony? That's not something we like to talk about—it risks invoking avenging spirits. But sure, they killed them! Men like Tata Maayani, who met up with a group of them just below the Saut Tamanoa rapids, on the Mana. He had his camp there. All, of them—I think there were six—snuck into his camp to steal his canoe and his gun. But that man had a *komanti* [warrior] god in his head! He heard them saying they wanted to get away to Brazil. His *komanti* was really something else! That's why the prisoners didn't manage to kill him. He told them he knew the way to Brazil and that he'd take them as far as Roche Bardo, just above Kakioko Creek. When they got out of the canoe there, Old Man Maayani killed them all and left their bodies in the forest! Then he took his gun, got back in his canoe, and came home. He'd killed all six. By himself. I myself saw Maayani at the end of his life at Mana.

Captain Adaïsso, Kourou, 2002

with machetes and clubs.) Saamakas still say that "*alabi poite*" [Arab convicts] were "the worst of the lot."[36]

Saamakas in Tampaki also had to deal with escapees from the Brazilian penal colony of Clevelândia do Norte, just across the Oyapock, where large numbers of rebels and anarchists from the 1924 revolution in the south of Brazil had been sent. Elderly Saamakas still remember bloody encounters with these escapees during the late 1920s. One man described to us how his father and three others were attacked on the Brazilian bank by men who tied their hands, put them up against a tree, pressed long guns to their bellies, and threatened their private parts with razors before the Saamakas succeeded in escaping back to Tampaki.

The Effects of the Saamaka Diaspora on Saamakas in Suriname

From the beginning of the Saamaka presence in Guyane, Saamaka authorities (as well as Dutch colonial officials in Paramaribo) expressed concern about the effects of a male labor shortage for the clearing and cutting of women's gardens, as well as for other political and religious functions, back home in Saamaka.[37] And food shortages in Saamaka, because of the lack of male labor, were signaled throughout the first half of the twentieth century.[38] In 1935, the recently installed Gaama Atudendu expressed grave concerns about the number of Saamakas then in Mana and Sinnemary who were living with Creole wives and neglecting their families in Saamaka.[39] Various measures—from fines to incentives—were tried by both the Saamaka and Suriname governments to bring men in Guyane back to their home villages, nearly always without success. Formal admonitions not to remain longer than necessary are a central part of the normal leave-taking ceremonies. The kin of any man absent more than three or four years exert considerable pressures on him to return; both council meetings and oracles frequently instruct an outgoing villager to bring back a lingering relative, and occasionally special delegations are sent for this express purpose. Absent men are often designated to assume a political office; we know one captain and two assistant captains of one upriver village who were coerced to return to accept their new offices, abruptly terminating trips of twenty, twenty-two, and eleven years. Any man who succeeds in bringing back a *fikama* ("a man who has stayed a long time") enjoys very special honors, and the returning *fikama* is greeted with a large celebration, offered wives, and fully encouraged to fit himself back into village life as quickly as possible. Advanced age and a lengthy stay away pose no special problems; in the 1960s, we witnessed the return of an eighty-year-old man who had been in Guyane for a half century, and who, after several months in the village, was married, serving as the medium of an important god and holding an honored role in local council meetings.

The demographic imbalance between men and women created by men's absences in Guyane had a profound effect on life in Saamaka villages. Earlier, the practice of polygyny had meant a perceived shortage of women in the marriage pool, and several customs reflected the resulting pressure on the system. During the nineteenth century, for example, girls were often promised in marriage well before puberty, and both betrothal in the womb (aimed at marriage if the baby was a girl, at formal friendship if a boy) and "widow inheritance" (in which a man would be given his deceased brother's wife in marriage) were common. Men were required to show marked deference to their in-laws, with a variety of gifts and services, and were in a poor position to insist that the woman leave her village to come to live with them. And it was not unknown for women to initiate divorce, since the chances of finding another husband were relatively good. But in the late nineteenth century, once men began leaving the villages and spending years at a stretch in Guyane, the situation was altered. Polygyny became much more common; betrothal in the womb and widow inheritance became a memory from the past; residence in the man's village increased as women felt more pressure to compete for their husband's

Overall, at any time during the first half of the twentieth century, 1,500–2,500 Saamaka men (depending on the date) resided in Guyane, making enormous contributions to the economy and fathering large numbers of children, both recognized and unrecognized. In 1920, there were 2000 Saamakas in Guyane.[1] In 1936, the figure was independently put at 2,000—approximately 60 percent of all Saamaka men.[2] Even in 1941, when the war had made Guyane much less hospitable, there were still some 1,000 Saamaka men living there, according to the Suriname government.[3] And in 1966, when France began to build the European Space Center, Saamakas provided the largest component of the workforce; by 1968, they officially numbered more than 700 on the local payroll, but because of subcontracting and other, more informal methods of hiring, the figure was probably more than 1,500.[4] In 1968, approximately half the men in the Saamaka village of Dangogo (the southernmost village on the Pikilio and the most distant from Paramaribo) were away in Kourou. And other Saamakas continued to live and work in other sites throughout Guyane.

1. L. Junker, "Herinneringen aan het oerwoud: Uit mijn dagboek van 1921," *Nieuwe West-Indische Gids* 26 (1944–1945), 120.

2. E. Wong, "Hoofdenverkiezing, stamverdeeling em stamverspreiding der Boschnegers van Suriname in de 18e en 19e eeuw," *Bijdragen tot de Taal- Land- en Volkenkunde* 97 (1938): 323.

3. Ben Scholtens, *Bosnegers en overheid in Suriname: De ontwikkeling van de politieke verhouding 1651–1992* (Paramaribo: Afdeling Cultuurstudies/Minov, 1994), 84.

4. Marie-José Jolivet, *La question créole: Essai de sociologie sur la Guyane française* (Paris: ORSTOM, 1982), 445.

favor; and gender-based behavior came to reflect, in a variety of small ways, the shift toward male dominance in domestic power. Men's participation in the gathering of firewood, for example, was discontinued, and girls were taught, as a mark of deference, to avoid addressing their husband by his first name.

Okanisis and Pamakas in Guyane up to the 1970s

Until fifty years ago, Okanisis and Pamakas were mainly visitors in Guyane. The home villages of both groups were exclusively in Suriname, though some of their gardens were on the French side of the Lawa or Maroni Rivers, and many Okanisis spent a good deal of their time in these *kampu* (garden-settlements), returning to their villages mainly for rituals, including funerals. Okanisis had long lived along the Tapanahoni in Suriname, using the Maroni as their highway to the coast. Pamakas had descended the Paramacca Creek in

Suriname and established their villages on islands in the Maroni only at the beginning of the twentieth century, and during those early years on the river, they were subjected to frequent harassment by Okanisis, who claimed the river as their own and raided Pamaka gardens with impunity.[40]

Unlike Alukus, who had long lived on French soil, and Saamakas, who had a long tradition of labor migration to many parts of Guyane, both Okanisis and Pamakas restricted themselves largely to the Maroni, which was their route to Albina and thence to Paramaribo. As we have seen, Okanisis, but not Pamakas, worked the Maroni as boatmen, and men from both groups also visited Saint-Laurent occasionally to buy supplies—in general, goods were cheaper and more abundant in Paramaribo—or to provide manual labor.

In the early years of the twentieth century, the transport industry on the Maroni was controlled by Okanisis, Alukus, and, to a lesser extent, Saamakas. (Pamakas did not participate in transport work.) Indeed, from the beginning of the gold rush, there was active competition among these three groups for transport privileges on the Maroni. During the 1880s, the Aluku *gaama* was attempting, unsuccessfully, to keep Okanisi canoemen out of the Lawa;[41] similarly, the Okanisi *gaama* was threatening the Alukus with an interdiction on the use of the Maroni (cutting them off from the coast), though this dispute was eventually settled peacefully.[42] And not long after, the Okanisi *gaama* was trying to keep Saamakas off the Maroni, again without success. Meanwhile, all three Maroon groups were playing the French authorities off against the Dutch, bringing their trade (and the state taxes that went with it) either to Albina (Dutch) or Saint-Laurent (French), depending on the conditions of the moment. There was nationalistic talk by each of the colonial governments as well; a French report of 1893, for example, recommended the exclusive use of Aluku canoemen rather than Okanisis.[43] And over the years, the governments had many discussions with mining and rubber-tapping companies about which group should be used on the Maroni as various companies made exclusive contracts with Okanisis, Saamakas, or Alukus.[44]

Throughout the period, French officials stressed that the population of Alukus was much smaller than that of Okanisis and Saamakas. For example, in 1893 the French governor wrote that the Aluku population totaled "several hundred," but that the Okanisis numbered some 4,000, and that immigrant Saamakas had already established "a colony" on the Maroni.[45] (Our best estimates for total Maroon populations around 1900 are 4,000 Okanisi, 4,000 Saamaka, 600 Matawai, 400 Aluku, 400 Pamaka, and 200 Kwinti.)[46]

The Great Strike of 1921

For three months in 1921, the Maroni was the scene of "the greatest strike in the history of the colony" of Suriname—or of Guyane.[47] There had been an overcapacity of transport available since the end of the First World War, when both gold and balata activity decreased. Prices of imported goods had risen considerably during the war. And by the end of the war, the French franc—the main currency in the trade—had been devalued by 60 percent against the Dutch guilder. So Maroon canoemen were finding less work and lower wages, yet faced higher prices for their purchases. In early 1921, the Okanisi *gaama*, Amaketi, managed (temporarily) to chase Saamaka canoemen from the river. (Saamakas, he claimed during a 1919 meeting, were taking away the Okanisi boatmen's business, undermining the price structure, working in Okanisi territory, and stealing Okanisi men's wives.)[48] Shortly thereafter, Amaketi made an agreement with Aluku Gaama Awensai for Okanisi and Aluku canoemen to halt all traffic between the coast and the Lawa placers, and from February 21 to May 30, 1921, nothing at all moved on the river. Both the Dutch and the French were taken by surprise. "In terms of the strikers' organization, it was amazingly solidary," wrote a journalist in Guyane as all river traffic stopped and the economy of the region fell into disarray.[49] There was an attempt by the Dutch government to bring in Saamakas as strikebreakers, but they refused to interfere with what they saw as a legitimate Okanisi strike.[50] Dutch troops were also brought in. The issues involved were complex and varied: Gaama Awensai hadn't received his government salary in three years, the Okanisis were demanding schools for their children, and various internal Okanisi and Aluku political affairs also played into the strike. By its end, when the canoemen received partial satisfaction for their demands, the so-called Albina Commissie, set up to investigate the causes of the conflict, concluded that the demands of the Maroon canoemen regarding prices, devaluation, and reduced incomes were largely justified.

Details aside, the story of the 1921 strike shows the power that Maroons, in this case Okanisis and Alukus, already exercised over the economy of Guyane, with both the Paramaribo and Cayenne governments frantically involved in trying to bring it to an end. (Maroon canoemen conducted briefer strikes, mostly successful, in 1904, 1906, and 1925.)[51] At various other times, the Dutch and the French tried to force particular contractual conditions on Maroon canoemen, to place taxes on the goods that Maroons carried upriver, and to impose other restrictions—but never with much success, as the Maroons remained kings of the river.[52] During periods of relative Maroon prosperity, such as the gold-rush years at the turn of the century, outside observers expressed wonderment at Okanisis buying "tea sets, clocks, and boxes," taking them up the Maroni, and dragging pieces of fancy European furniture over the rapids back to their villages.[53]

Until about 1990, however, both Okanisis and Pamakas remained resident in their villages on the Suriname side of the river, except when they were in their garden camps, and it is only more recently that some of them have moved their residences into Guyane.

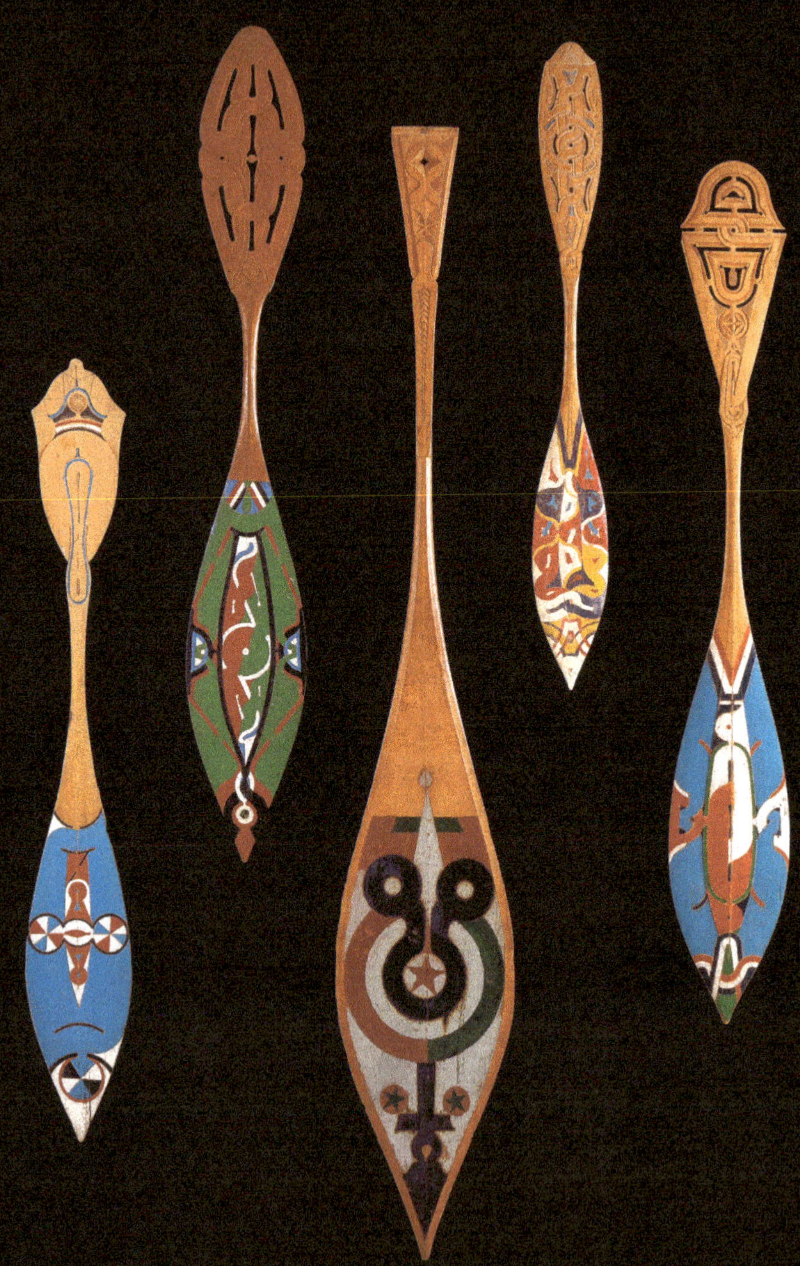

Eastern Maroon paddles. *Left to right*: Okanisi, pre-1971; unknown provenience; Okanisi 1920s; Paamaka child's paddle; Okanisi pre-1971.

Maroons in Guyane 1970 to the Present

In 1970, there were only about 7,500 Maroons in Guyane—3,000 Saamakas (men who were working there for periods of several years) and 2,000 Alukus (essentially, the entire Aluku population, all of whom were now citizens of France), as well as 2,000 Okanisis and 500 Pamakas who had their garden camps on the French side of the Maroni or had moved into the Saint-Laurent area. The great majority of these Maroons were living on the Maroni and its tributary, the Lawa, or in the new town of Kourou.

Over the past five decades, the world of the Maroons has undergone dramatic transformations. A very high birth rate—almost twice that of Guyane in general, which is already "one of the highest in South America and the Caribbean"[1]—has caused a veritable demographic explosion among Maroons. Though there is vague awareness of a recent increase in the Maroon presence, few Guyanais have any idea of its scale. In 2000, Christiane Taubira-Delannon, the *députée* from Guyane to the French National Assembly, expressed the official consensus: "The Maroon communities in Guyane, divided among Bonis (Alukus), Okanisis, Pamakas, and Saamakas, now number 7,000 people," and a 1999 article in the newspaper *Libération* estimated the number of Maroons in Guyane at 4,000.[2] But in fact, today there are about 100,000 Maroons living in Guyane (some 47,000 Okanisis, 36,000 Saamakas, 10,000 Alukus, and 7,000 Pamakas), with a rough parity of males and females. This means that Maroons, taken together, now constitute about 36 percent of the population of the *département* and that, taken together, they form the largest single population segment. They live in a large number of towns in Guyane.[3]

A glance at the past may help contextualize the migratory movements of Maroons to Guyane during the last fifty years.

In the 1960s, when we began our fieldwork, the lives and concerns of the Maroons of Suriname and Guyane were securely anchored in the rain forest. The six Maroon groups were still being referred to by

Table 3. Distribution of Maroons in Guyane, by commune, 2018

Saint-Georges	3
Regina	6
Roura	300
Remire-Montjoly	700
Cayenne + Matoury	9,000
Macouria	3,000
Kourou	12,225
Sinnemary	350
Iracoubo	180
Mana	4,000
Saint-Laurent	46,000
Apatou	6,660
Grand-Santi	7,500
Papaïchton	4,500
Maripasoula	5,450
Total	**99,874**

anthropologists as "tribes" that functioned as "states within a state." Running their own political and judicial affairs, they were known to outsiders for such exotic practices as polygyny, oracular divination, spirit possession, body scarification, and ancestor worship, as well as distinctive styles of music, dance, and plastic arts, and countless other aspects of daily life that reflected their uncompromised heritage of independence and their radical difference from the other populations of Suriname and Guyane. Maroons' dealings with the outside world were largely limited to the men's wage-labor trips, which provided the cash needed to buy soap, salt, tools, cloth, kerosene, kitchenware, and other necessities for life back in the villages of the rain forest. Maroons felt tremendous pride in the accomplishments of their heroic ancestors and, on the whole, remained masters of their forest realm.[4]

The period of the 1950s–1970 witnessed relatively gradual modernization, such as the introduction of outboard motors, which facilitated mobility within and beyond the interior, and radios and tape recorders, which allowed closer communication with the coast. In Suriname, gasoline-powered generators in some villages brought electric lights and the occasional refrigerator, and there was an increase in the number of missionary schools that prepared boys, and sometimes girls, for contact with Creoles and other non-Maroons. All these changes were monitored by public consensus through community meetings and the consultation of gods, ancestors, and local divinatory instruments such as oracle bundles.

The first major change came in Suriname in the 1960s when the colonial government, in collaboration with Alcoa, summarily dispossessed (without consultation or compensation) some six thousand Saamakas of lands that had been guaranteed under the 1762 treaty, in order to construct the hydroelectric dam at Afobaka. Deprived of their villages, their gardens, their hunting grounds, and their most important religious sites and shrines, these people were forced to relocate, often to government-built towns far from the river. But with the important exception of this dam-building project, Maroons in both Suriname and Guyane remained largely in control of their destinies.

The 1970s brought more dramatic changes that affected all Maroons. Suriname moved away from its ties to Europe, becoming an independent republic in 1975, and Guyane moved closer to Europe as Paris targeted it for rapid development in connection with the establishment of the European Space Center in Kourou. Each of these

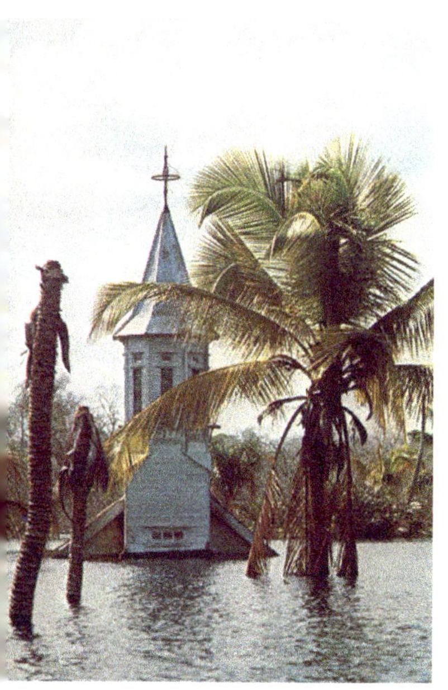

The church in Ganzee, the largest of the forty-three Saamaka villages flooded in the mid-1960s by the Afobaka hydroelectric project.

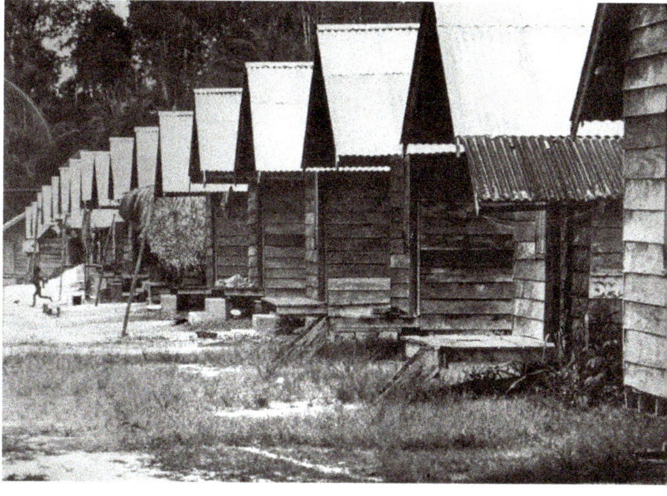

Brownsweg, Suriname: a row of houses constructed for some of the six thousand Saamakas whose villages had been flooded by the hydroelectric dam and lake.

shifts eventually had profound consequences for Maroons in terms of territorial sovereignty, political independence, cultural integrity, and economic opportunities, not to mention basic issues of health and personal dignity.

In Suriname: The State versus Maroons

Recent events in Suriname have had a profound effect on Guyane, especially as they affect the migration of Maroons. Since independence in 1975, successive governments in Suriname have been pursuing an increasingly militant policy against Maroons, stripping them of their land and its potential riches, and endangering their right to exist as distinctive peoples. In 1980, the Suriname Army seized power in a coup d'état, and the young republic began a downward spiral from which it has never recovered—a plummeting economy, a massive brain drain, and a notable increase in poverty, drugs, and crime.

In 1986, civil war broke out between Maroons and the national Creole-run military, sending thousands of Maroons fleeing across the border into Guyane—some ten thousand Okanisis as refugees, confined to camps enclosed by barbed wire, and countless others (mainly

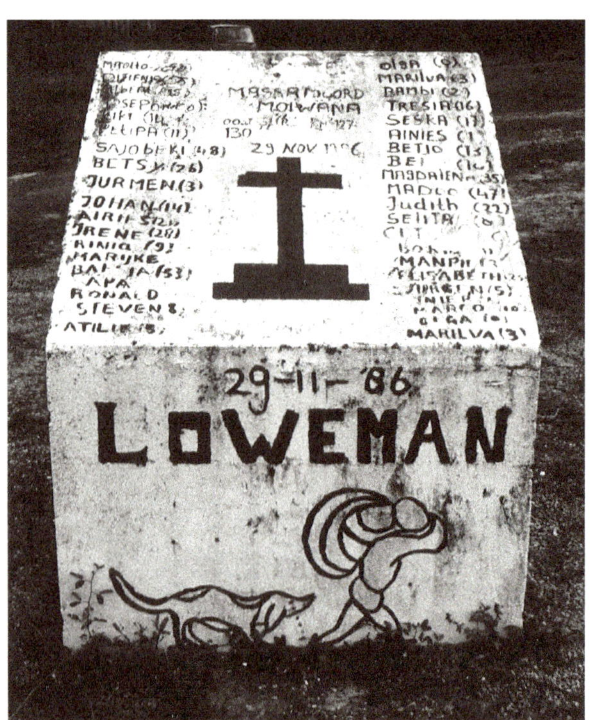

Monument to the victims of the Moiwana massacre, erected by the Okanisi community of Charvein, commune of Mana, Guyane.

The turning point . . . came in November and December 1986, when a military campaign in eastern Suriname resulted in more than 150 civilian deaths. In a number of Cottica River Ndjuka villages, unarmed Maroons—including pregnant women and children—were rounded up and massacred. . . . Within a few weeks, more than 10,000 of these Maroon refugees had arrived in French Guiana. Witnesses narrated horrific accounts of defenseless villagers being lined up and mowed down with automatic weapons while they pleaded for their lives. I was there when the refugees began to pour into Saint-Laurent, and I spoke to several of these eyewitnesses, only days after the massacres took place. Of the many atrocities related, one in particular seemed to stand out for its brutality. In the settlement of Moiwana, not far from Albina, a soldier had torn an infant from its mother's arms, placed the barrel of his gun in its mouth, and pulled the trigger.

Kenneth M. Bilby, "The Remaking of the Aluku: Culture, Politics, and Maroon Ethnicity in French South America" (PhD diss., Johns Hopkins University, 1990), 505–506

Saamakas) as *clandestins* attempting to build a new life while remaining invisible to French authorities charged with the expulsion of illegals. The fighting, which raged from 1986 to 1992, pitted Maroons against the national army of Suriname, bringing back to life many of the horrors of their ancestors' struggles for freedom. African medicine bundles that had lain buried for two hundred years were unearthed and carried into battle. Okanisi and Saamaka men and boys, often armed with shotguns, confronted the army's automatic weapons, tanks, and helicopter gunships dropping napalm. Whole villages, particularly in the Cottica Ndyuka (Okanisi) region, were razed, and soldiers killed hundreds of women and children with machetes and guns.[5]

In 2005, the Inter-American Court of Human Rights rendered its judgment in the case of *Moiwana Village v. Suriname*, ordering Suriname to identify and punish the perpetrators of the massacre, to change the country's laws in order to recognize the rights of Maroons and Amerindians to the collective ownership of their territories, and to make other major changes, all of which, as of this writing, remain unimplemented.[6]

In Suriname, post-civil-war Maroon life has been transformed, perhaps irreparably, by rampant poverty and malnutrition, severe degradation of educational and medical resources, and the arrival in force of

AIDS and prostitution. The official restoration of peace in 1992 came at a price, as the Maroons were pushed into signing a treaty largely focused on rights to land, minerals, and other natural resources—all of which are now claimed unambiguously by the Suriname state. The government has clearly undertaken a unilateral program to abrogate the Maroons' eighteenth-century treaties and to erase their historic accomplishments. In the case of Suriname, scrapping Maroons' history—their heroic struggle for freedom and their hard-won treaties—in the alleged interest of national unity is tantamount to ethnocide.

The government insists that under Suriname law, neither Maroons nor Indigenous peoples hold any special rights and that priority must be given to "the interests of the total development of the country"—which increasingly means the private interests of governmental officials and their cronies.[7]

During the 1990s, Saamakas suddenly found their territory invaded by Chinese, Canadian, and other multinational logging and mining companies which were extracting resources, with the explicit permission of the state. The constitution of Suriname specifies that all non-titled land and resources belong to the state, rendering Maroon peoples such as the Saamaka, as well as Suriname's numerous Indigenous peoples, little more than guests on government lands. The constitution also denies the possibility that an Indigenous or Maroon people could have a juridical personality and therefore collective rights to property (or to anything else). After Chinese loggers began to devastate their territory, Saamakas managed to organize their more than sixty villages strung out along the Suriname River for the coming legal battle. In 2000, they petitioned the Inter-American Commission on Human Rights, eventually winning a signal victory in 2007 before the

The State has long held the position that "Indigenous peoples and Maroons are permissive occupiers of privately held State lands and that whatever rights they may have will always be superseded by the larger interests of the State. Further, these rights are simply temporary protections conceded by the State during a transitional period in which Indigenous peoples and Maroons are to be assimilated into the larger, and inherently superior, Surinamese society and economy."

Ellen-Rose Kambel and Fergus MacKay, *The Rights of Indigenous Peoples and Maroons in Suriname* (Moreton-in-Marsh, UK: Forest Peoples Programme, 1999), 178

Inter-American Court of Human Rights in Costa Rica. The court's judgment in the case of *Saramaka People v. Suriname* required Suriname to change its laws (and if necessary its constitution) in order to grant the Saamaka People collective title to their traditional territory and considerable sovereignty over it—a legal precedent that henceforth applies to all Indigenous peoples and Maroons in the Americas. It is sad to report that in 2020, as we write this book, the government has refused to honor that decision. The rights of the Saamaka People, like those of other Maroons and Indigenous peoples in Suriname, remain

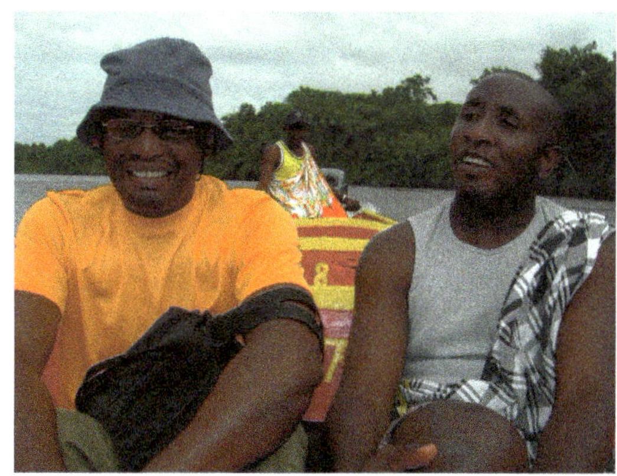

Two Saamaka leaders, Head Captain Wazen Eduards and law student Hugo Jabini, on their way to a village meeting.

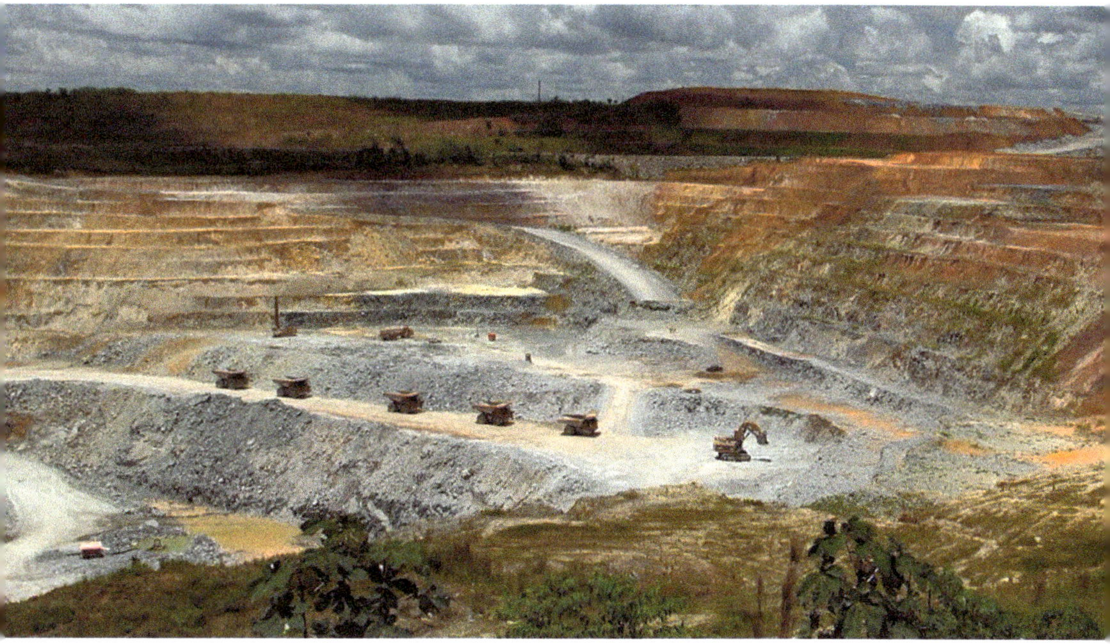

A Canadian open-pit gold mine, Rosebel, owned by Iamgold, in Saamaka territory.

profoundly threatened despite continuing efforts—by the Saamakas, their lawyers, the Inter-American Commission, and ourselves—to persuade the government to adhere to the orders of the court.[8]

Today, much of the forest for which the ancestors of the Maroons spilled their blood is still being auctioned off by the government to American, Canadian, Chinese, Indonesian, Malaysian, Australian, and Brazilian timber and mining corporations. We must hope that international cooperation and pressure will goad the government of Suriname into finding ways to safeguard the rights of the Maroons, to preserve their irreplaceable forest resources, and to encourage Maroon economic development (particularly in terms of much-needed hospitals and schools) while still respecting the Maroons' autonomy and their right to a separate identity.

Suriname is routinely described by foreign journalists as a "narcocracy" where shady business interests in collusion with the army fly light planes across the forest to exchange arms for drugs with Colombian guerrilla groups and then transship the drugs to Europe. A Dutch court's 1999 conviction in absentia of Desi Bouterse, Suriname's former president and commander in chief who led the 1980 coup d'état, for international arms and drug trafficking, and his sentence to sixteen years in prison and a fine of U.S.$2.3 million, had little effect on the country's general malaise. In 2015, his favorite son, Dino Bouterse, was sentenced in New York to more than sixteen years in prison for drug trafficking and terrorism; he remains in a federal prison in Yazoo City, Mississippi. In July 2010, Desi Bouterse—ex-dictator, convicted drug dealer, and convicted murderer (in 2019) of fifteen political opponents in the infamous "December Murders" of 1982—was chosen by Parliament to be president of Suriname. In 2015, he was reelected.

The overall decline in the prosperity of Suriname during the past forty years has had strong trickle-down effects on Maroons. State services in Maroon territories—clinics, hospitals, schools—function poorly. Medical facilities and other essential services are consistently far below even the deteriorating standards on the coast. Moreover, the basic rights of Suriname Maroons—to be free from discrimination, to own and enjoy their lands and resources, to participate in decision making, to practice their cultures, and so forth—are routinely violated in policy and practice, through, among other actions, the enactment of assimilationist policies and laws, the issuing of logging and mining concessions without any consultation, environmental degradation, dispossession, and the disregard of legal agreements such as Maroon treaties.[9]

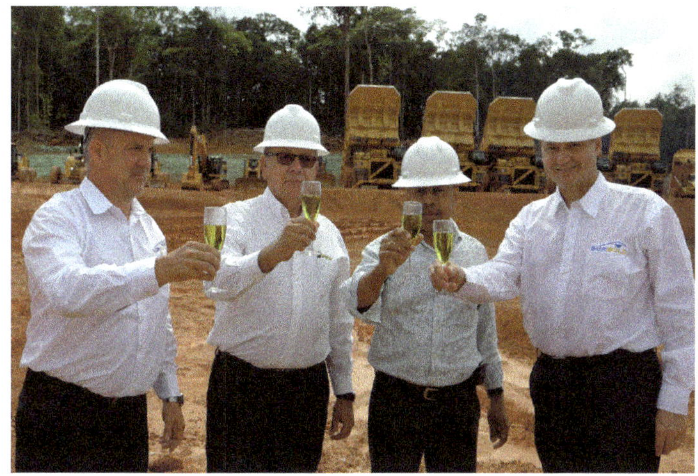

Inauguration of the Newmont mine in Pamaka territory, 2014.

In 2016, the U.S. multinational Newmont Mining (the biggest gold producer in the world) began operating in eastern Suriname. Despite the opposition of Maroon and Amerindian leaders, the company opened several mines in Pamaka territory, at a reported cost of some U.S.$1 billion. (By 2020, this was the second-largest gold mine in all of South America.)[10] The Pamaka capital, Langatabiki, has become a ghost town, and the rest of Pamaka territory has been largely abandoned.[11] At the same time, a company based in Dubai has opened a refinery in Suriname designed to produced sixty tonnes of gold each year.[12] Meanwhile, Suriname's rate of inflation reached 40 percent in August 2020.

There are no signs that the national government has any plans for its Maroon and Indigenous peoples other than their assimilation (the sooner the better) into the urban underclass, leaving the country's forested interior free for extractive industries. Suriname now has the shameful distinction of being "the only state in the western hemisphere in which indigenous peoples and Maroons live that does not in some way legally recognize their rights to own their ancestral territories."[13]

In Guyane's Interior

The Saamaka presence that was so vibrant in the interior of Guyane during most of the twentieth century has faded to mere traces today. For the interior of Guyane, the Maroon story has shifted almost exclusively to the regions of the Lawa and Maroni Rivers, where recent changes have been dramatic.

Since the 1970s, those Maroons who are officially French citizens by virtue of having been born east of the Maroni and Lawa have been adapting to an aggressive program of *francisation*. This program disseminates the language and culture of the French state, provides generous welfare benefits, redefines the nature of Maroon political leadership, attempts to convert collective land ownership to a regime of private property, encourages consumerism (both in the stores of Guyane and through European mail-order catalogues), and recasts Maroon visual and performative arts as part of the cultural patrimony of Overseas France.[14] It has brought about a situation in which fewer than one in ten Alukus lives in one of the traditional villages that existed before *francisation*, in which some 40 percent of the population lives in one of the two new towns developed by the French, and in which social problems (in part due to gold-mining activities) have reached devastating proportions. (The other Alukus live either on the coast or, in smaller numbers, in Europe.)

Francisation

The massive change in the lives of Maroons in Guyane began on March 17, 1969, when the Territoire de l'Inini—essentially, the entire interior of Guyane—was dissolved by decree. Traditional Aluku territory was divided between the two new communes of Maripasoula and Grand-Santi–Papaïchton.

The momentous changes that ensued were unlike anything the Aluku had ever experienced. With drastic suddenness, an alien administrative system was superimposed on the traditional sociopolitical structure. The Aluku villages, with their clans and chiefs, became part of a commune modeled on its metropolitan equivalents; it was to be governed by a mayor, his deputies, and a municipal council. Governmental schools, clinics, and gendarmeries were quickly built in the heart of Aluku territory. Since few Alukus spoke French or had any idea of what a commune was, certain concessions had to be made. Local elections were postponed, and in the meantime, the Aluku paramount chief—who had already been recruited into the RPR party—was appointed mayor. In this capacity, he presided over the distribution of an unprecedented influx of public funds. A host of paid administrative positions were instituted, and virtually the entire Aluku population suddenly became eligible for a variety of social subsidies: family welfare, social security, retirement money, and more. Adding to the sense of upheaval during this period was the rapidly growing incidence of semipermanent migration to the larger coastal towns, spurred in part by the construction of the new town of Kourou.

In 1976, the commune of Apatou, with a largely Aluku population, split off from Grand-Santi–Papaïchton, and in 1993, Grand-Santi–Papaïchton was divided into two new communes, Grand-Santi (largely Okanisi) and Papaïchton (which remained the Aluku capital). A 1982 census along the Maroni, above Saint-Laurent, showed a population of 2,558, but by 2020, that figure had exploded to 39,000—almost certainly an undercount.[15]

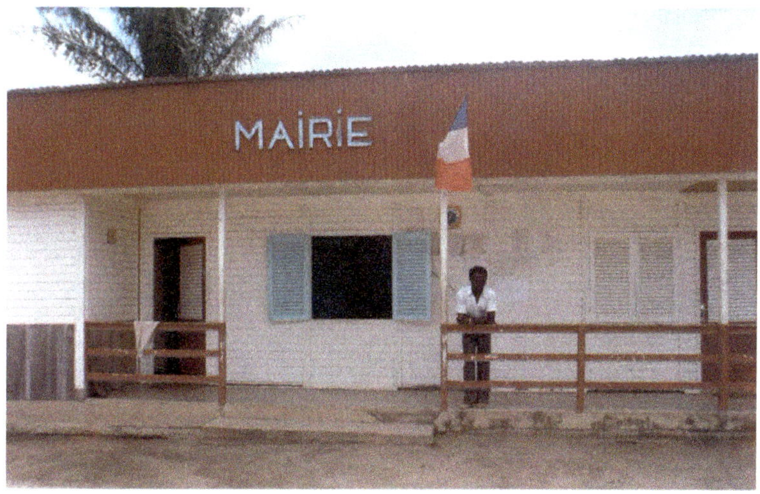

The mayor, Fossé Omissi, in front of the *mairie* of Papaïchton, 1986.

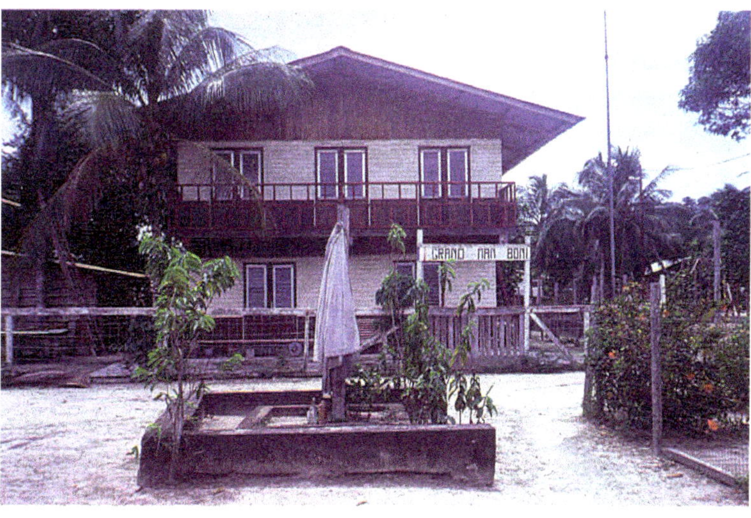

The office of Tolinga, paramount chief of the Aluku, Papaïchton, 1986.

Apatou, founded by the famous Aluku canoeman of that name in the late nineteenth century, had a population of less than 700 on the eve of the Suriname civil war, but had grown to 2,500 by its end. In 2018, it had 8,800 inhabitants, including Pamakas, Okanisis, and some 600 Alukus. So the "Aluku town" of Apatou is no longer majority Aluku! In fact, according to a recent linguistic study, only 10 percent of the children in the commune speak Aluku as their first language, and most of the population is Pamaka or Okanisi.[16] Pamakas, whose traditional territory is just across the Maroni from this commune, have long had garden camps on the French side, and many of them now benefit from French social services in Apatou—schooling, medical care, and the like. Today, the Okanisis are the second-largest population segment after the Pamakas, leaving the Aluku in third position. Pamaka territory is an active gold-mining area, and many people in Apatou are in some way involved. The commune is also home to a cultural association, Mama Bobi, which has for several decades promoted artistic products (woodcarving and painting) and medicinal plant lore, but seems less active than it once was. Since 2010, the commune has been linked to Saint-Laurent by a paved road, only an hour away by car.

Across from the mouth of the Tapanahoni, the commune of Grand-Santi, with a population of about 8,000 (including some 7,500 Okanisis), grew out of a long-standing Okanisi tradition of making gardens along the French side of the river. With an Okanisi mayor and municipal council, it constitutes a natural entry point to Guyane for the large numbers of Okanisis who live in the Tapanahoni region—62 percent of adults in Grand-Santi are not (yet) French citizens. During the civil war in Suriname, when the Jungle Commando rebel movement was based at nearby Stoelman's Island, Grand-Santi housed an especially important French military presence. As in the neighboring communes of Papaïchton and Maripasoula, it contains a military base that is now devoted to the struggle against illegal gold mining. Since 2010, Air Guyane has offered flights between Grand-Santi and the coast almost daily. Nearly all vehicles are quads (ATVs); in 2018, the commune still lacked Internet service.

The commune of Papaïchton, with its new administrative center, Papaïchton-Pompidouville, remains the "capital of the Alukus" and the residence of the paramount chief. It includes all seven of the traditional Aluku villages except the small village of Kotika, on the Suriname side of the river. Nonetheless, its population is no longer majority Aluku. Some 73 percent of adults are non-French immigrants, mainly

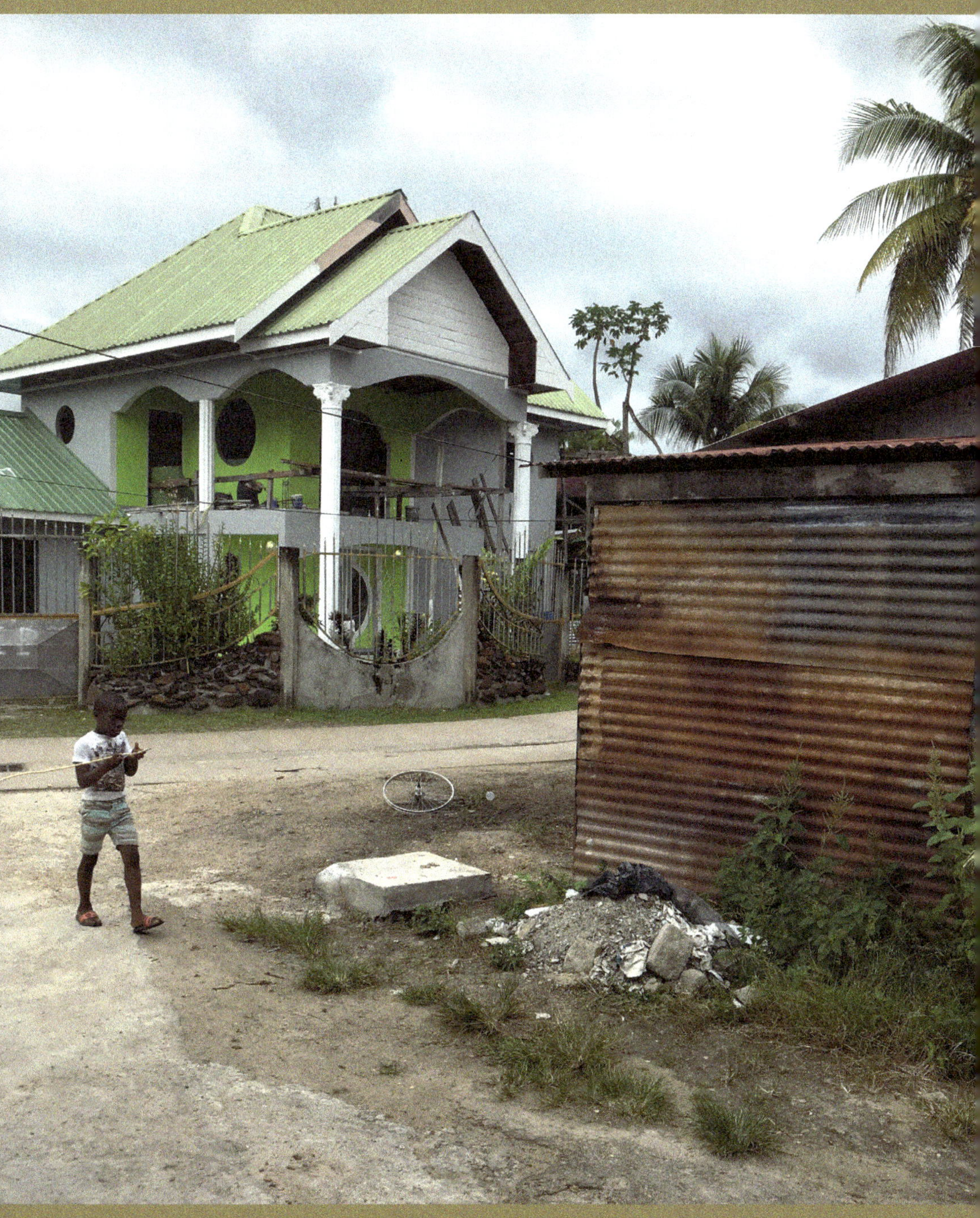

Graceland on the Lawa, 2018. The owner of this house (a teacher at the Collège Achmat Kartadinama, a junior high school in Grand-Santi) had made a pilgrimage to the home of Elvis while studying for six months at the University of Mississippi.

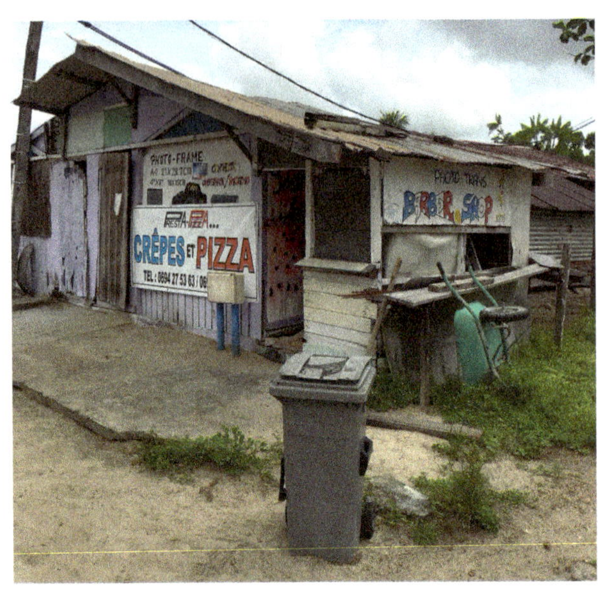

Crêpes, Pizza, and Barber Shop, Grand-Santi, 2018.

Brazilians working illegally as gold miners, along with some Okanisis from Suriname. There are only 1,200 Alukus left in the traditional Aluku villages, just 10 percent of the Alukus in the world. (The population of the commune consists of 4,500 Brazilians, 2,900 Alukus, 1,600 Okanisis, and 300 European French.) Papaïchton has a number of cars, trucks, quads, and motorcycles; it is now linked to Maripasoula by a laterite road (less than an hour by car) that gives access to the garden camps along the river between Maripasoula and Papaïchton, replacing the motor canoes that used to provide transport. The residents of Papaïchton complain about the lack of Internet service and the absence of a pharmacy—they must travel to Maripasoula to fill prescriptions written by the resident doctor. As elsewhere along the river, the decline of physical work (paddling canoes, garden work, etc.) and changes in diet (including the addition of store-bought junk food) have led to a marked increase in obesity.

The administrative post of Maripasoula, like the rest of the interior, was transformed overnight by the policy of *francisation*. It became the site of a town hall, a new school, and an expanded medical clinic, and was chosen as the main administrative center for the entire region encompassed by the Lawa and its tributaries. By the mid-1970s, Maripasoula had become the largest settlement in the Lawa River area and had the distinction of simultaneously being the geographically largest commune in the entire Republic of France and one of the least

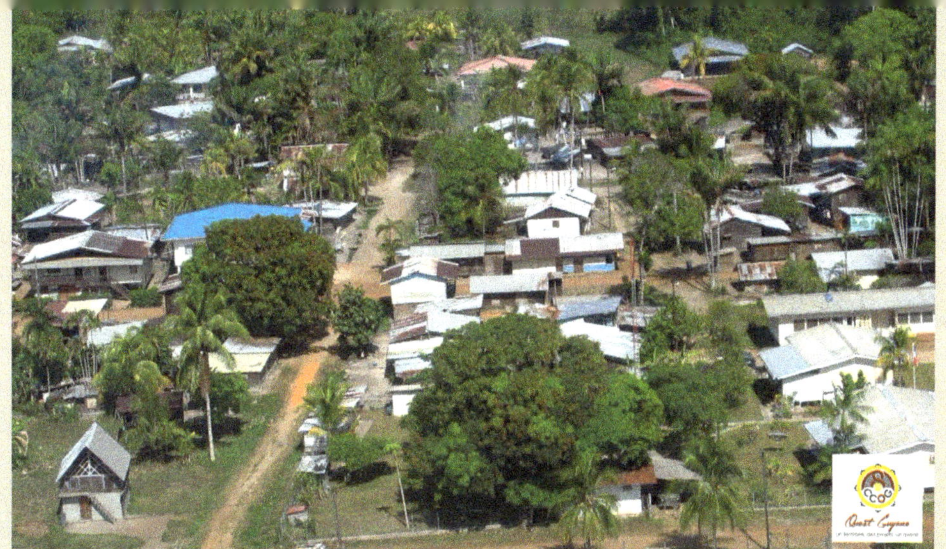

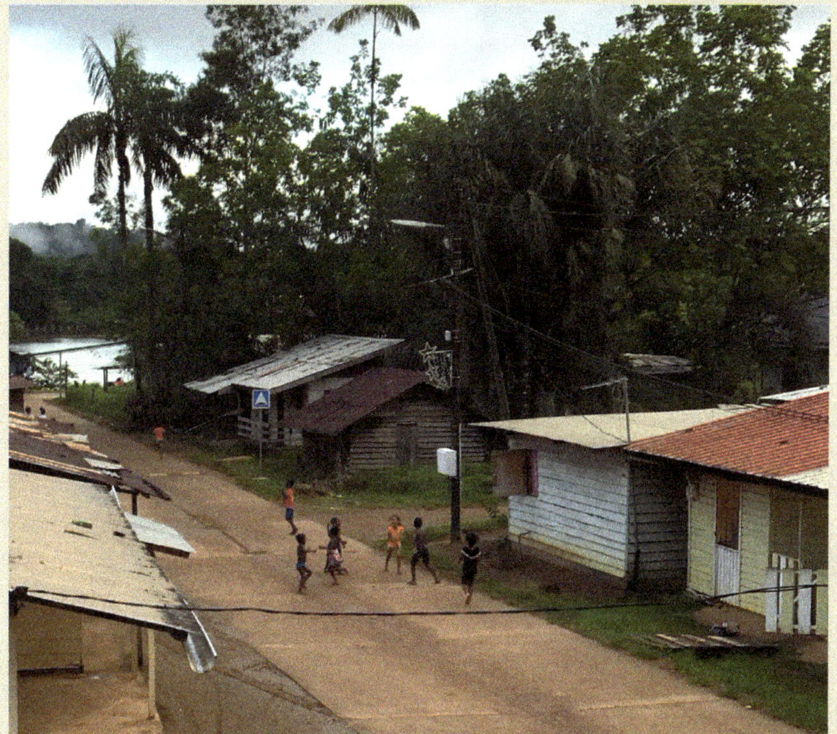

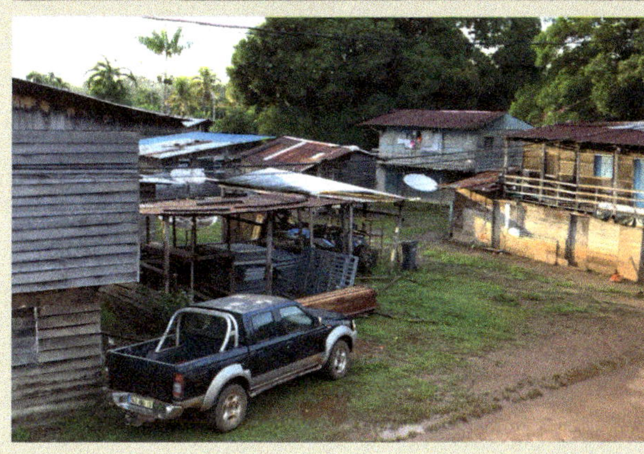

Papaïchton, 2018

populated. In 1974 it had a total population of 803—248 Wayana and Emerillon Indians, 387 Maroons (almost all Aluku), and 168 Creoles.

Today the official population is 13,000—an estimated 3,350 Alukus, 2,050 Okanisis, 50 Saamakas, 450 European French, 1,100 Amerindians, 5,500 Brazilians, and 500 others. Though a minority of the population, Alukus control the commune politically. In 2020, Maripasoula still had no high school; Air Guyane offered at least four flights a day between the commune and the coast; the post office had an ATM; the town had some 200 cars plus quads, trucks, and large construction machinery, all brought from the coast by canoe; some streets were paved, and others were of earth and mud; there were no apartment houses as on the coast; most of the population used the Suriname mobile network (Digicel) and had Suriname phone numbers because of poor service via Orange; there was scarcely any Internet service; and a handful of immigrants (mostly women) from Peru, Colombia, and the Dominican Republic played an important role in commerce and sex work.

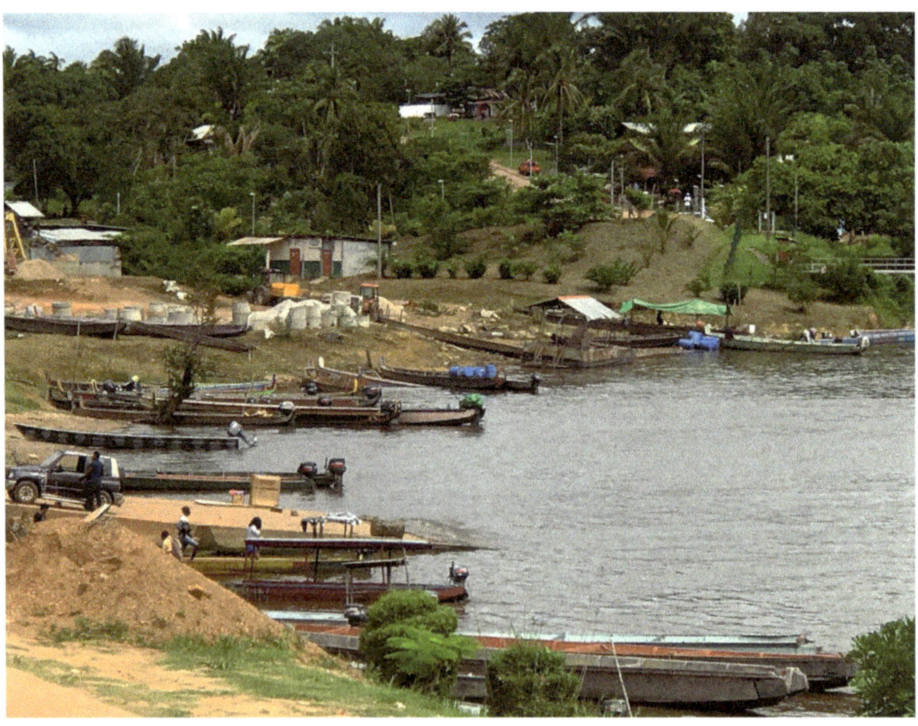

The landing place, Maripasoula, 2018.

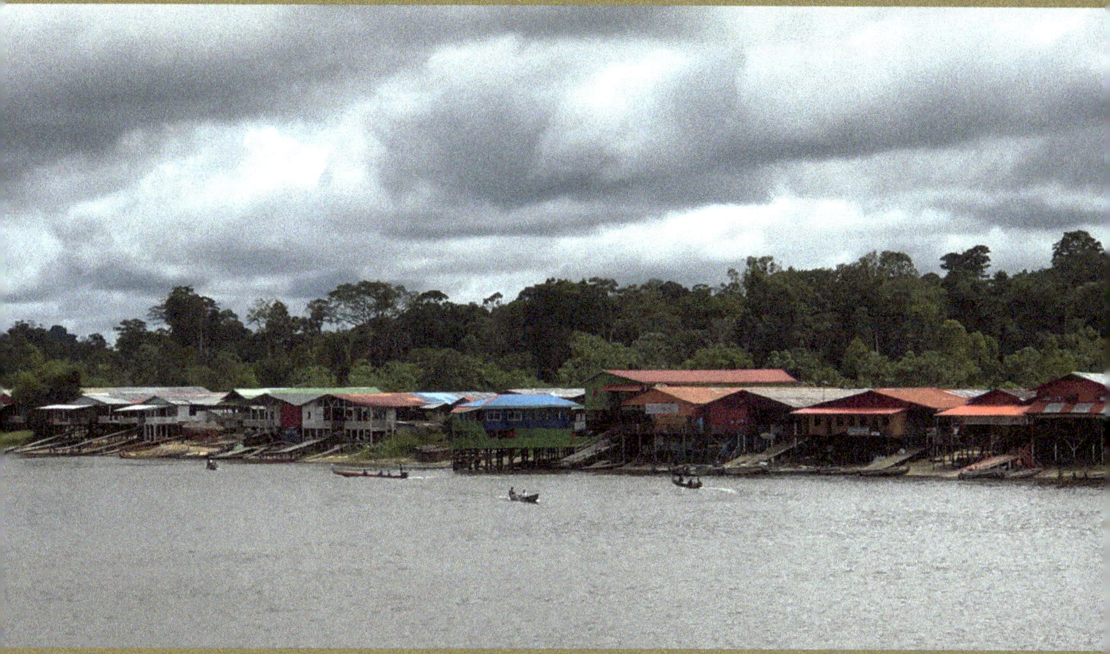

Albina II, across from Maripasoula, 2018.

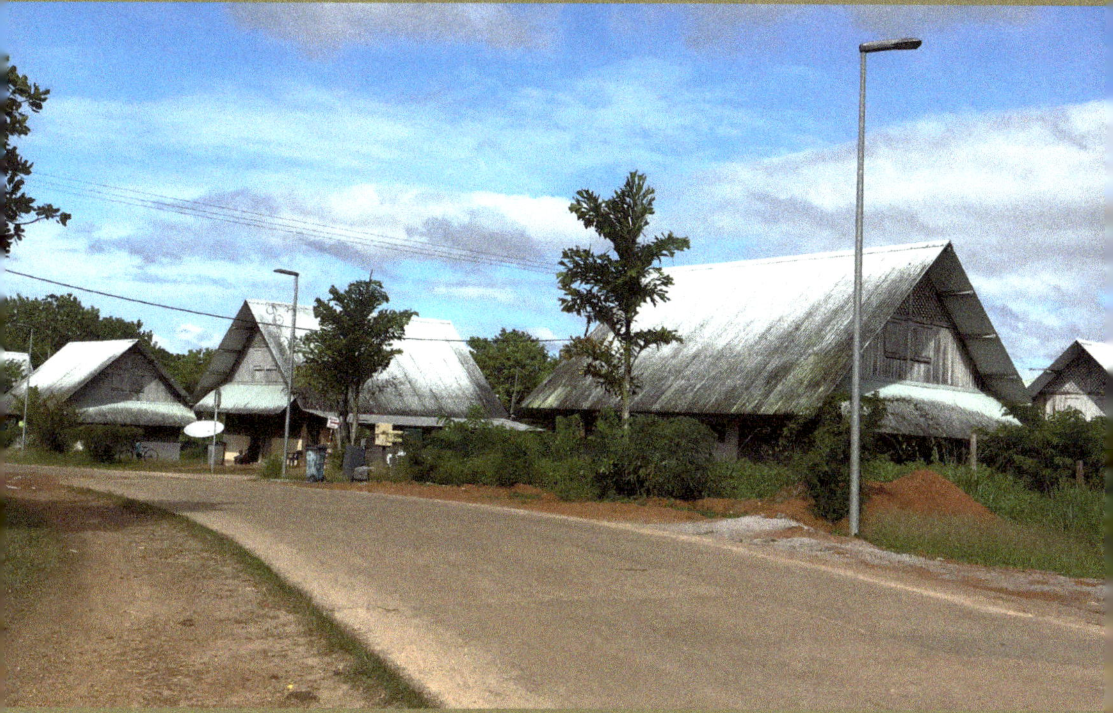

Public housing, Maripasoula, 2018.

By the mid-1980s, the amenities offered by the coastal way of life—wage-earning opportunities, Western medicine, running water, electricity, and consumer goods, to name a few—had made their way to the two new towns in the interior, Maripasoula and Papaïchton-Pompidouville, and drawn most Alukus away from their ancestral villages.[17] Roughly half of all Alukus from the Lawa River region were living in one of the two new communities, a third resided in coastal towns, and the rest (less than 20 percent), remained thinly scattered in the interior, in the old villages and the few horticultural camps still in use. Today some "traditional" Aluku villages stand nearly empty.

In the last four decades, the once-independent Alukus have become a people dependent on state welfare. In 1983, 1.8 million francs of government money made its way to the commune of Grand-Santi–Papaïchton, and since that time, yearly budgets have considerably increased. This influx of "free" (or "cheap") money has helped create an enormous appetite for financial gain and has sparked what at times seems like a frenzy of buying and selling. While before, most goods and services were exchanged or given as gifts, today almost nothing remains that cannot be bought and sold.[18]

The quality of life in these communes is strongly affected by their distance from the capital, by the indifference that many politicians show toward them, and by a general condescension to them among the general population. For the administration in Cayenne, the interior of the *département*—where services such as schooling and medical care are expected to be second-rate—remains a relatively low priority. In 2001, Dr. Flavien Rigoir, a doctor in Grand-Santi for the previous ten years, complained: "People get all upset about one case of mad-cow disease in France or three cases of dengue fever in Cayenne . . . But for a thousand cases of malaria—one-third of the population of Grand-Santi—no one cares!"[19] Today, when pregnant women in the three upriver communes reach their eighth month, they are flown to one of the three hospitals on the coast that are equipped for childbirth—in Saint-Laurent, Kourou, or Cayenne. But it is often too late.

Let's not fool ourselves. This is a society based on principles that are diametrically opposed to those of French society. Twenty years of *francisation* has just about destroyed Aluku social and political organization, while their agriculture has been abandoned, their natural resources devastated, and their family ties largely dissolved.

Instead of their wise and efficient organization, well adapted to the environment, an entirely artificial and extremely expensive substitute has been imposed that makes no one happy. The most disturbing thing, for those who knew this place in the 1950s, is that the Alukus have become totally dependent on the government and public monies for all their needs. One might hope against hope (without much confidence) that they will find some way of retrieving at least a part of their squandered independence.

Jean Hurault, "Enquêtes démographiques chez les Aluku (Boni) de la commune de Papaïchton (Guyane française), 1956–1958 et 1989–1998," in *Avenir des peuples des forêts tropicales*, ed. Pierre Grenand, volume régional Caraïbes, 1999, 11

▶▶▶

In Grand-Santi, the doctor's "office" is a single room, with a toilet and sink that don't work, which doesn't exactly make it easy to collect the urine samples needed for pregnant women. . . . There's a single refrigerator that hasn't worked since November 2000, and in spite of repeated requests, there is no thermometer to check the temperature [of stored medicines]. . . . His two current priorities: "putting the airstrip into service to permit emergency evacuations to the hospital in Cayenne, and a telephone."

In Apatou, the office of Dr. Boubacar Bondabou consists of a hallway that leads to the toilet: "People need to recognize that this is supposed to be a doctor's office!"

In Papaïchton, the municipal council wants the dispensary at Loca to be reopened. A letter was sent to the *Conseil Général* last January, but they have received no reply.

In Maripasoula, the project announced by the president of the *Conseil Général*, Jean-Victor Castor, to build a clinic with ten beds, has stagnated. The first stage of construction was completed, but the second stopped in 1994. "75% of the work had been finished . . . but once construction was interrupted, the place was thoroughly vandalized."

Daniel Saint-Jean, "Maroni: Les centres de santé malades de la scission," *France-Antilles*, September 5, 2001, 21

Gold Fever

For those Alukus who remained upriver, the 1990s witnessed a radical transformation of their lifeways as the area became engulfed—like so much of Suriname Maroon territory—by forces connected with gold mining and the unchecked extraction of forest products.[20] In 2000, many of these problems came to a head in direct clashes between Aluku Maroons who were running large gold-mining operations, Wayana (and some Emerillon) Indians who live just downstream from the mining sites, and the French state, which officially controls the territory. All the familiar elements came into play: quick money from gold, serious ecological degradation (forest destruction), and contamination of the drinking water from mercury and other pollutants. Meanwhile, the population of the once-quiet town of Maripasoula, which has an Aluku mayor (and is inhabited by Alukus and Creoles, with a large influx of Brazilian gold miners, plus a detachment of French gendarmes and a French doctor), has exploded, and gold has become "the only economic activity—other than state-supported jobs—to provide an income. Yet it brings in its wake a whole range of activities that are ruining the town—bars, prostitution, drug trafficking, arms trafficking, and nightclubs that attract adolescents. There is even an immigration of criminals—the Suriname police claim that bandits wanted in Suriname are crossing the river to Guyane."[21]

By 2000, Maripasoula—like parts of the interior of Suriname—was already being described by observers as a "Wild West" setting ("like the very worst movies about the conquest of Arizona"), with clandestine helicopters routinely bringing in black-market fuel from Suriname for the all-terrain quads used by Aluku and Brazilian miners for overland transport as well as for the bulldozers and other mining machinery.[22] Meanwhile, "Aluku children, for whom there are not enough places in the elementary school, watch the daily spectacle of miners flaunting large nuggets of gold, with bills pinned to their shirts, and with women walking around thinly or barely clad."[23] "The activity of prostitution is truly intense. A night with prostitute costs 10 grams of gold [500 French francs] and a 'quickie' goes for 2–6 grams."[24]

In other words, the combination of the physical distance of the Aluku world from Cayenne and the general indifference to (and, often, ignorance about) the interior of Guyane by the politicians has turned French plans for the smooth assimilation of the Alukus into French

It's the gold of the Bonis, with all the murders, prostitution, and misery that comes with it; it's the gold of malaria, the gold of illusions, of all things sordid, of fear, of repatriated Brazilian laborers. Invisible gold . . . But as inexperienced managers, the Boni think short-term. A liter of diesel fuel brought in by helicopter is sold for five times its value. Motors have replaced the pick and shovel, and compressed-air hoses, the sluice. They pay their workers a percentage when, and if, they wish. The Brazilians, who arrive with passports and a four-month work permit signed by the Office of International Migration, have these papers confiscated by their Boni boss until payday . . . at the end of four months. Four months with nothing, and at the end accounts are supposed to be settled. But are they?

These new nabobs of the goldfields flaunt their shiny SUVs, their stereo systems, their gold jewelry, and their outfits of VIPs or mafiosi. Their travel is sometimes clandestine. . . . They no longer use the planes of Air Guyane, but rather a chartered helicopter that picks them up at the doorstep of their elegant columned villa, preferably on the Suriname side of the river. And when they go belly-up, their automatic weapons help settle their debts.

Richard Gras, "Lettre de Richard à Baj," in "Maroni Fantôme," *Dérades* 8 (2002): 20–21

citizens, and a smooth transition from the Alukus having a semi-independent territory to being an integral part of France, into something of an ongoing nightmare. Lower down the Maroni River on the Guyane side, "large mining companies have moved into the [Okanisi-run] commune of Grand-Santi and [the Aluku-run] commune of Apatou and have forbidden the Aluku and Okanisi villagers the right of free movement in the forest to get to their gardens," which suggests that the strong-arm tactics of multinational corporations operate in the "European" legal-political context of Guyane much as they do in the postcolonial context of Suriname.[25] And in Guyane—the only territory in South America that is not subject to inter-American treaties such as the Inter-American Convention on Human Rights, since it is not a "nation"—there is a sense in which Maroons have even less legal protection than they do in Suriname.

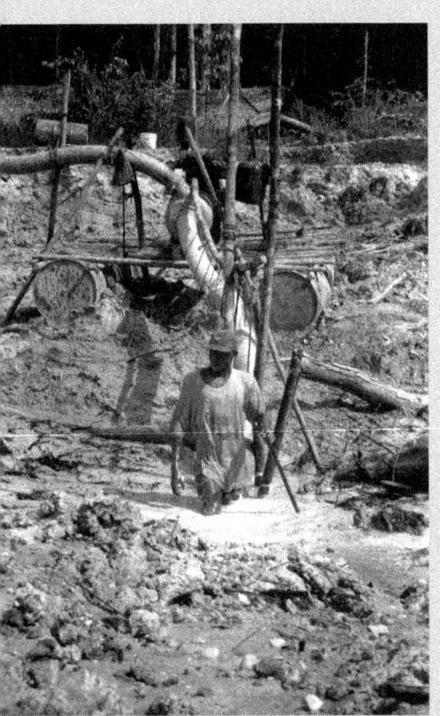

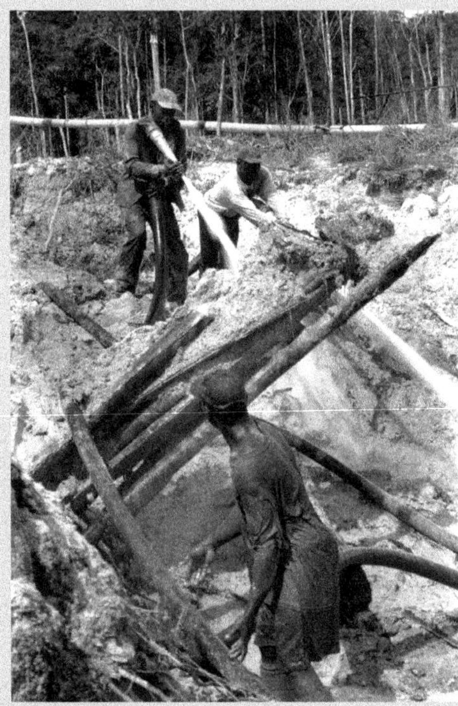

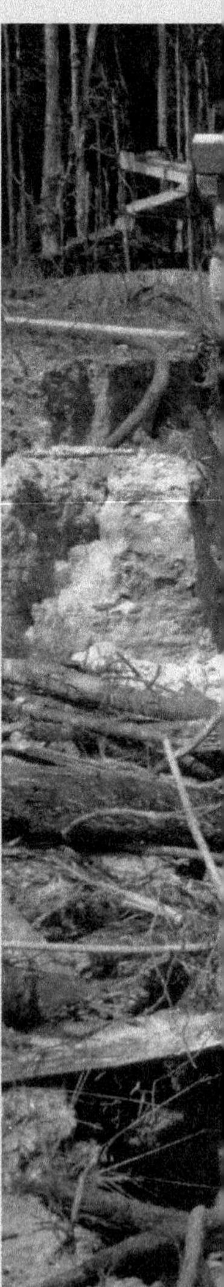

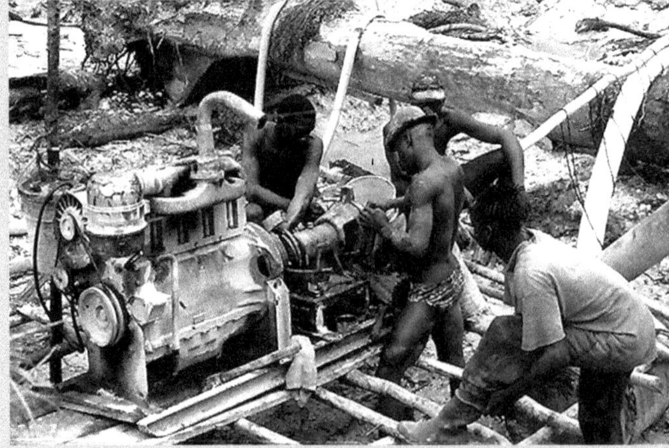

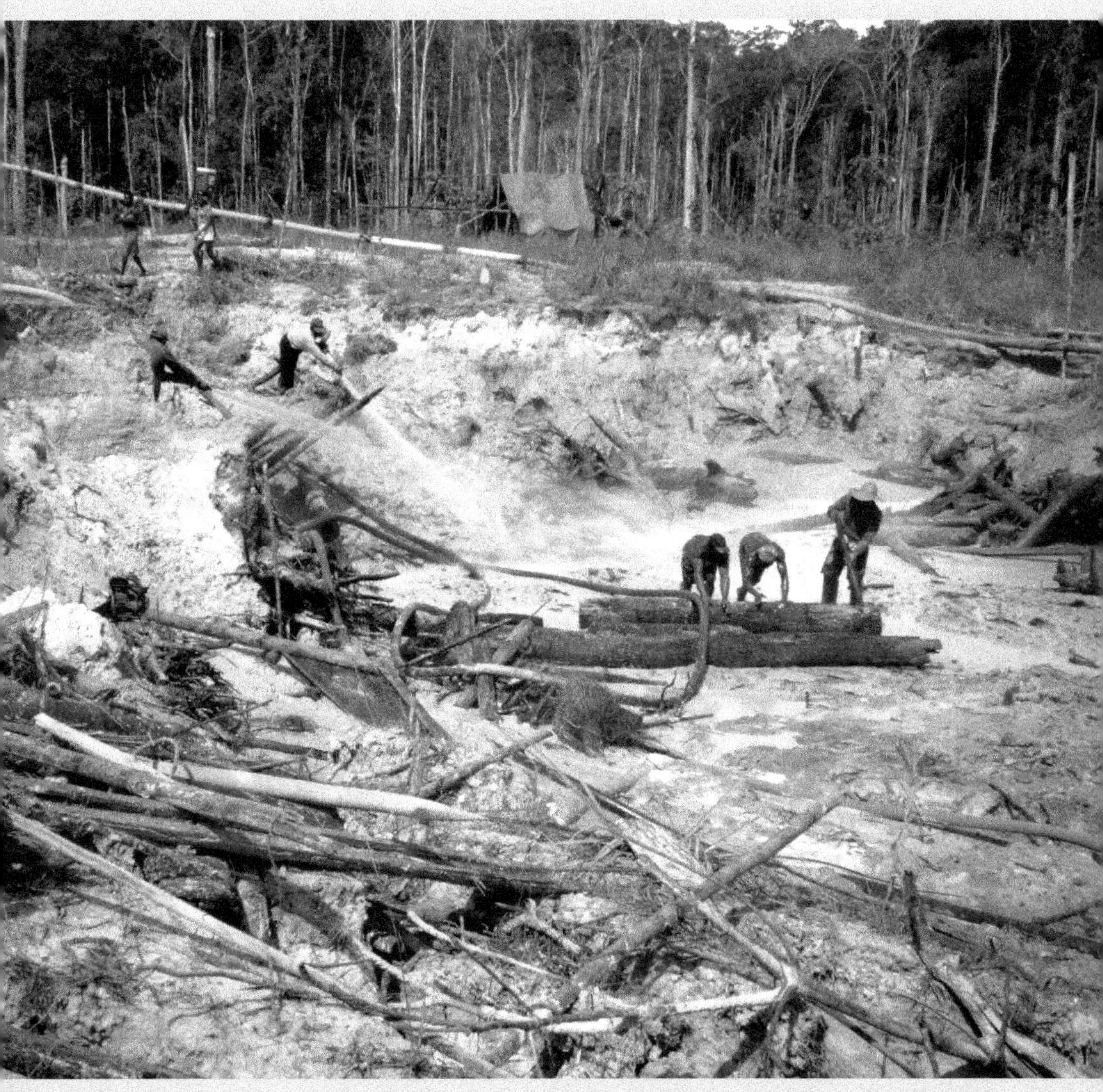

Maroon gold miners, 1990s.

The Law of the Jungle in Guyane

It is a piece of the French Republic. But people kill, torture, massacre, and lead lynching parties there. And it will soon be ten years since it all began. The state knows about it but cannot—or will not—put an end to it. It is in Guyane. The investigation that we are publishing highlights the frightening and horrible reality of lawlessness in the region of Maripasoula, where private militias and the madness of gold fever reign. . . .

The mining concessions are ceded by the state to various multinationals but also to the largest population group of the region, the Aluku Maroons. These latter hire as their laborers Brazilians who, hunger in their bellies, accept the mud, mosquitoes, and mercury. To "keep them working," the Alukus confiscate their immigration papers and, occasionally, pay them. . . . Aluku miners employ private militias to punish and keep clandestine miners in line. With the complicity of state authorities, who are simply overwhelmed by it all, the power of local potentates continues to increase.

In 1996, the state tried to limit mining but quickly reneged. Alarmed by riots in Cayenne and the threats of the independentists, France settled on a policy of "gold for the Guyanais." Very quickly, the game began anew, with witnesses recounting tortures, beatings, disappearances. The law of the jungle took over. The most powerful Aluku miners began working outside the limits of their concessions, poaching on the territory of multinationals and Amerindians, but the state still did nothing. The miners use the rivers to discharge their tailings of mercury, a metal that is highly dangerous for the Amerindians who live just downstream. The state sticks its head in the sand, fearing "ethnic war." . . .

It is time to rethink the policy of "gold for the Guyanais," which enriches only a small minority while causing tremendous human and environmental misery—and paralyzes the state.

Editorial, *Le Monde* (Paris), July 7, 2001

One important note of caution: it would be simplistic to imagine solidary, "traditional" Maroon communities standing firm against the onslaught of outside, often state, interests—either in Guyane or in Suriname. (The border between the two, especially at the level of Maripasoula and Benzdorp, is for all practical purposes fully open.) Both logging and gold mining have provided opportunities for many Maroons on both sides of the river, particularly officials and their relatives, to reap new wealth. Indeed, in some areas, most small-scale mining concessions are owned by Maroons. (Just as in others, members of the Suriname military prevail.) Maroon concession owners split profits, and in many cases get along well, with the Brazilian miners manning the shovels and machines alongside them. Likewise, a number of Maroon women—particularly Okanisis, Alukus, and Pamakas—have been willing entrants into the sex-work arena, and Maroon men frequent the Brazilian women who also follow the miners and rent rooms in makeshift brothels throughout the mining regions. In a sense, these Maroon and Brazilian miners temporarily share a culture—almost all carry guns (pistols, shotguns, or automatic weapons), make use of the same sex workers (both Brazilian and Maroon), and expose themselves to the same dangers, from AIDS and malaria (this region of Suriname and Guyane now has the highest rate of infection in the Americas) to everyday violence. This situation engenders innovative arrangements: Pamaka Maroon mining-concession owners along the Maroni have often hired ex-members of the French Foreign Legion as security guards.[26]

The past fifteen years have seen tremendous changes in illegal gold mining, particularly along the Lawa, where residents on the French and Surinamese sides of the river have come to share a way of life dominated by mining and its supporting services—commerce, transport, and prostitution.

The Suriname government began distributing gold-mining concessions to politicians and their friends in the 1990s and instituted arrangements in which Brazilian miners (Portuguese: *garimpeiros*) as well as Aluku and Okanisi miners (Okanisi: *gowtuman*) pay 10 percent of their gold to the concession holders. Indeed, by 2011, gold had become the major export of Suriname, and by 2015, 10,000–20,000 Brazilians were working in the goldfields and in related services there. The state's hands-off attitude toward artisanal mining (no intervention from the police) stems, in large part, from the tremendous profits that politicians—including the president and his friends and family—gain from it.[27]

The explosive growth of the once-tiny village of Benzdorp, across the river from the communes of Maripasoula and Papaïchton, dates from the late 1990s, when a Brazilian immigrant, Dona Maria, quit her job as a cook in a mining camp.[28] With the World Cup of 1998 fast approaching, she bought a large satellite dish and began selling drinks and snacks. This soon turned into a restaurant, to which she later added a brothel. The town of Benzdorp was reborn, becoming the commercial and recreational center of the whole region. Today's vast lineup of bars, brothels, and supermarkets all stem from these beginnings, and the population is now 1,000, some 90 percent of it Brazilian.

Between 2007 and 2010 there was an upheaval: Chinese entrepreneurs arrived and quickly monopolized commerce along the Lawa. By 2012, there were fourteen Chinese supermarkets, all selling pretty much the same products, in Benzdorp alone, and only a handful of Brazilian clothing stores and beauty salons had survived. Today, directly across from Maripasoula, the settlement known variously as Antônio do Brinco or Albina II (and the nearly contiguous settlement of Ronaldo, just upstream) boasts some thirty Chinese supermarkets lined up in a row, frequented not only by the region's gold miners but also by the population of Maripasoula, Papaïchton, and other towns in Guyane. For the past several years, the Chinese proprietors have provided free transport by motorized canoe between Maripasoula and the supermarkets (as well as the neighboring restaurants, discos, and brothels). In these stores, the price of everything—beef, toys, toilet paper—is less than on the French side, and they also sell everything one might need to set up and maintain a gold mine—giant motor pumps, diesel generators, and plastic pipes of every length. The Chinese proprietors rent out space under their stores to Brazilians who have barbershops, cloth and shoe stores, and sandwich shops; *garimpeiros* also hang their hammocks under the stores while taking a break from mining.

On the French side of the river, there are now between fifteen thousand and twenty thousand Brazilian miners. Most are employed by Alukus, the traditional owners of the land. Relations have not always been pacific. In the early 2000s, there were murders, frequent thefts, confiscation of passports, and debt peonage. The residents of Grand-Santi, Papaïchton, and Maripasoula, like those of Benzdorp and other sites on the Suriname side, cross and recross the river at will, depending largely on the pressure of police operations against illegal mining on the French side. The French forestry service estimated that there were 173 sites on the French side in 2004 and over 1,000 in 2019.

Since the construction of Albina II (around 2007), the once violence-ridden town of Maripasoula has become far calmer as the *garimpeiros* tend to go directly from the mining camps to the Brazilian village. There is barely any other economic activity in the region—90 percent of the households in the villages along the Tapanahoni, Maroni, and Lawa Rivers are financially dependent on small-scale gold mining.[29] In most parts of this region, on both sides of the river, commerce is conducted routinely in both gold and euros.

Along the Lawa, the amount of petroleum products needed to keep the machines running for transportation and gold extraction defies belief—about 15 million liters of diesel and 50,000 liters of oil and grease are used in small-scale mining each year. And fuel transport brings big profits. A 200-liter barrel of fuel costs 2.5 grams of gold in Albina but 50 or more in the illegal mines along the Lawa in Guyane. Almost all food and drink for the many thousands of residents is also imported from the coast, mainly by canoe from Albina. Okanisi canoemen hold a virtual monopoly on transport from the coast for all these products.

The prices in the gold camps are exorbitant. The markup between the supermarkets of Benzdorp and the mining camps in Guyane is four times for cooking oil, five times for rice, and between six and twelve times (or more) for a can of beer or Coca-Cola. (A beer that costs the equivalent of one-half euro in Paramaribo often sells for 12 euros in a mining camp, reflecting the cost of transport but also the serious risks along the route.)[30] And a night with a prostitute that costs 60 euros in Paramaribo goes for the equivalent in gold of 200 euros in the mining camps.

In 2002, the French launched Operation Anaconda, which included gendarmes, the French Foreign Legion, and the French Army, aided by helicopters—some 100 military operations a year designed to destroy mining sites and equipment (burning or exploding them), but in general not to capture or expel the miners, because the cost of repatriation was judged too high. The largest of these assaults found 1,000 Brazilian "illegals" (4,000, according to some sources), as well as a church, a dental office, and a large number of stores, bars, and brothels. After a lengthy exchange of gunfire, the site was destroyed, including large quantities of *cachaça* (Brazilian sugarcane liquor), and 106 *garampeiros* were captured and expelled to Belém by plane (at a cost of 1,500 euros per person).[31]

Between 2002 and 2006, Operation Anaconda confiscated or destroyed "more than 935,000 liters of fuel, some 1,400 motor pumps, 61 kilometers of pipes, some 6,700 small buildings, 363 guns, and more than 65 tonnes of food. But seized only 42 kilos of gold."[32] In 2006, the use of mercury was banned in mining, but despite the serious danger it poses to the health of residents all along the river, especially Amerindians, it continues to be used exactly as before.[33] In 2008, Operation Anaconda was replaced by Operation Harpie, which involved some 1,000 soldiers. (There was also Operation Penelope,

Marjo De Theije reports that substantial new settlements are continuing to spring up along the Lawa. Kabana-vo on the Suriname side, for example, morphed from an Aluku garden camp in 2008 to a settlement of several hundred Brazilians and Surinamers today. While it slumbers during the day, "at night or during the early morning, Kabana-vo bursts with activity as it is the departure point for smuggling people and goods into the Waki Creek on the French side of the river. Boats filled with merchandise and mining gear leave before dawn to cross the part of the river that is controlled by the French police when it is still dark. Jaw Pasi is a similar place, further up the Lawa, in the customary territory of the Wayana. . . . In the last eighteen months, several Chinese entrepreneurs have set up supermarkets there, and they have now forced the Brazilian shop owners out of the market, just as happened a few years ago in Benzdorp."[1]

1. Marjo De Theije, "Small-Scale Gold Mining and Trans-Frontier Commerce on the Lawa River," in *In and Out of Suriname: Language, Mobility and Identity*, ed. Eithne Carlin, Isabelle Léglise, Bettina Migge, and Paul Tjon Sie Fat (Leiden: Brill, 2015), 73–74

a special-forces operation that borrowed troops from the Foreign Legion and employed helicopters, chainsaws, incendiary bombs, etc.) In his report for 2016, the prefect signaled that there had been 1,700 military operations and that 1,894 illegal mining sites had been destroyed.[34] But the *garimpeiros* and their employers are doing just fine. According to the estimates of the gendarmerie, the miners extract about 10 tonnes of gold each year, worth about 500 million euros. And in 2016, the various military operations seized a grand total of "a bit more than 3 kilos of gold."[35] In 2017, there were still some fifteen thousand Brazilians (without French papers) working at 1,000 illegal gold-mining camps in Guyane. And in 2019, the 1,220 military operations against more than 500 mining sites destroyed 5,254 small buildings, 290,000 liters of fuel, 1,092 motor pumps, and 273 vehicles—mostly quads—but seized only 9 kilos of gold.[36]

In 2016, in the commune of Maripasoula alone, there were at least ninety-one gold camps and twelve mining barges along the Waki and Tampok Creeks. Officials from the national park (Le Parc Amazonien de la Guyane), in which gold mining is prohibited, warned, "The situation in the basin of the Waki-Tampok-Liki is catastrophic."[37] And according to the prefecture, in 2016 there was "an increase of 28.51% in active gold-mining sites."[38] At the height of the 2020 coronavirus pandemic in Guyane, the prefect announced that Operation Harpie 2 (the updated name since 2018) was now in full swing, with some 600 military troops active in the struggle, at a cost of 70 million euros annually.[39]

Along the Coast of Guyane

Since 1980, the collapse of the economic, social, and moral fabric of Suriname has led to large-scale immigration of Maroons to the coastal areas of Guyane, where some 76,000 now live—a significant number of them without residence papers of any kind.

The largest influx came as a result of the civil war in Suriname. Beginning in 1986, some ten thousand Okanisi refugees—almost all from the Cottica region—were placed in a half-dozen camps in Saint-Laurent and Mana. These camps, surrounded by heavy barbed-wire fences and guarded and staffed by the men from the Foreign Legion and other military personnel, held Maroons for years at a time. Many of these refugees were women and children who had been twice traumatized—first by the arrival of war in their villages and again by their incarceration. Although these people satisfied all international criteria for receiving refugee status (including the Geneva Convention of 1951), France steadfastly fought against granting them this status, along with its rights and privileges.

At the end of the war, in 1992, the French government decided to close the camps, to force the refugees to return to Suriname, and to destroy all signs of the camps' former existence.

In the course of the civil war, many other Maroons (mainly Saamakas and Pamakas) arrived as "illegals" and attempted to make a new life out of sight of the French forces responsible for their expulsion. For the thousands who have remained in Guyane, the quality of life generally rises and falls with immigration policy decisions made in Paris. In 1997, for example, Saamaka men in a number of rural settings in Guyane told us that they'd sent their women back to Suriname because the women couldn't run away fast enough when teams of gendarmes raided their woodcarving stalls and set fire to their houses. During a visit in 2001, we were told that the situation had improved and that many of the women had come back. Since that time, many of these immigrants have received papers, but a large number remain "illegal."[40]

Condemned, Without Rights

For more than two years, in a French *département*, Guyane, many thousands of Surinamers have been "parked" in camps under the control of the French Army, without rights of residence, the right to work, the right to attend school, any guarantees that they won't be sent back to the land they fled because of persecution, the right of free speech, and so forth, without rights of any sort. . . . These Maroons have been placed outside the law . . . without the official refugee status to which both normal French law and international law entitle them.

Jean Quatremer, *Libération*, May 9, 1989, 25

▶▶▶

France has never wanted to grant the status of "refugee" to the Surinamese, whom they consider simply "people who have been temporarily displaced"—because refugee status brings with it almost all the rights of citizenship, for example, the right to work and the right to receive various welfare benefits. A second reason is to discourage the flood of new arrivals in order to ensure the calm and security so important to the smooth functioning of the space center at Kourou. And finally, there would be a violent political reaction in Guyane if France suddenly granted the status of refugee to 10,000 immigrants.

This refusal to grant refugee status, linked with a wish to remain master of its own territory, has led France to bar the U.N. High Commissioner for Refugees from taking over the camps, and to allow the H.C.R. only to act as one of three parties in an ongoing and difficult dialogue with Suriname and France.

Sophie Bourgarel, "Migration sur le Maroni: Le cas des réfugiés surinamiens en Guyane" (master's thesis, Université Paul Valéry, Montpellier, 1988), 71–72, 112–115

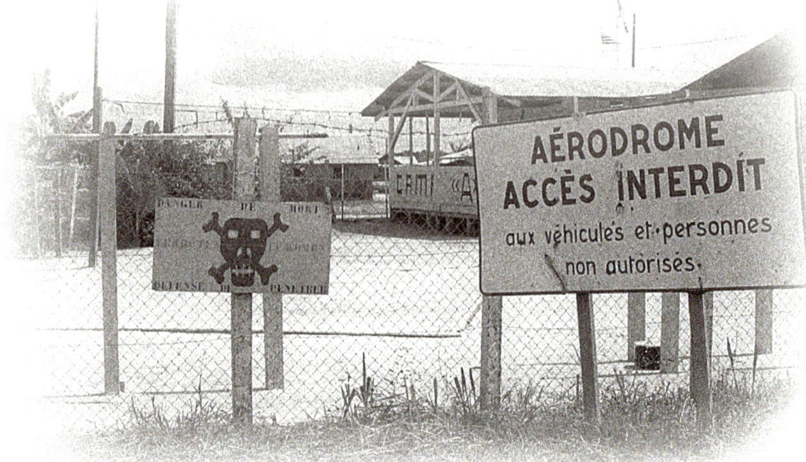

Entrance to Camp A, a refugee camp near the center of Saint-Laurent, 1990.

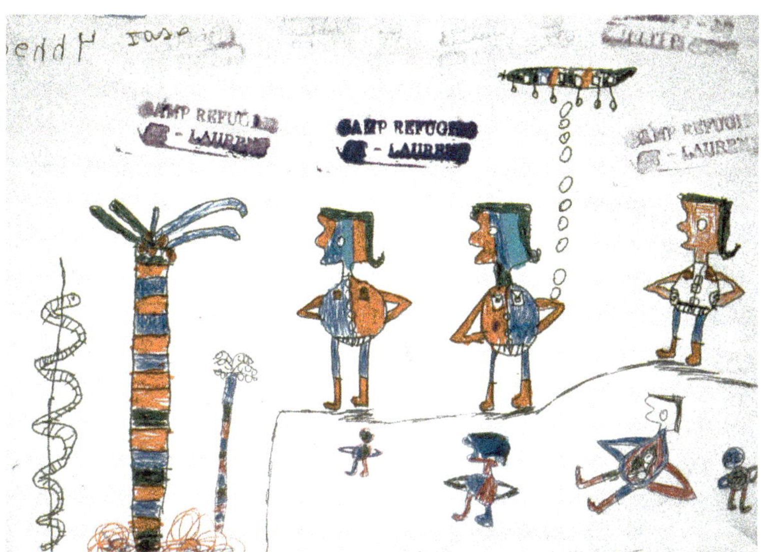

Drawing made by an eight-year-old survivor of the Moiwana massacre, living in a refugee camp in Guyane, 1990. Four years after the killings, a nurse gave the child a felt-tip pen and asked him to draw a picture of anything he wished. His response: a Suriname army helicopter raining down bombs on three women and, under the ground, dead, two small children, an older girl, and a woman with a baby in her belly. To decorate his artwork, he used the ink stamp of the establishment in which he had been parked for half his life, "CAMP RÉFUGIÉS ST-LAURENT."

Nevertheless, the opportunities for adequate health care and schooling are proving extremely attractive to a whole generation of young Maroons, whose prospects in Suriname offer little hope for the future. Maroons, both men and women, play an active and important role at the lower ends of the labor market throughout the coastal region of Guyane. The great majority live in the communes of Saint-Laurent, Mana, and Kourou or in Greater Cayenne. Scattered in other parts of the coastal region, however, there are significant and long-standing clusters of Maroons, particularly Saamakas—outside Iracoubo off the Saint-Laurent highway, along the Cayenne-Régina highway, and elsewhere.

Saint-Laurent-du-Maroni

The last fifty years have seen enormous changes for Maroons in and around the town of Saint-Laurent-du-Maroni, once the heart of the French penal colony. Soon after the Second World War, Maroons

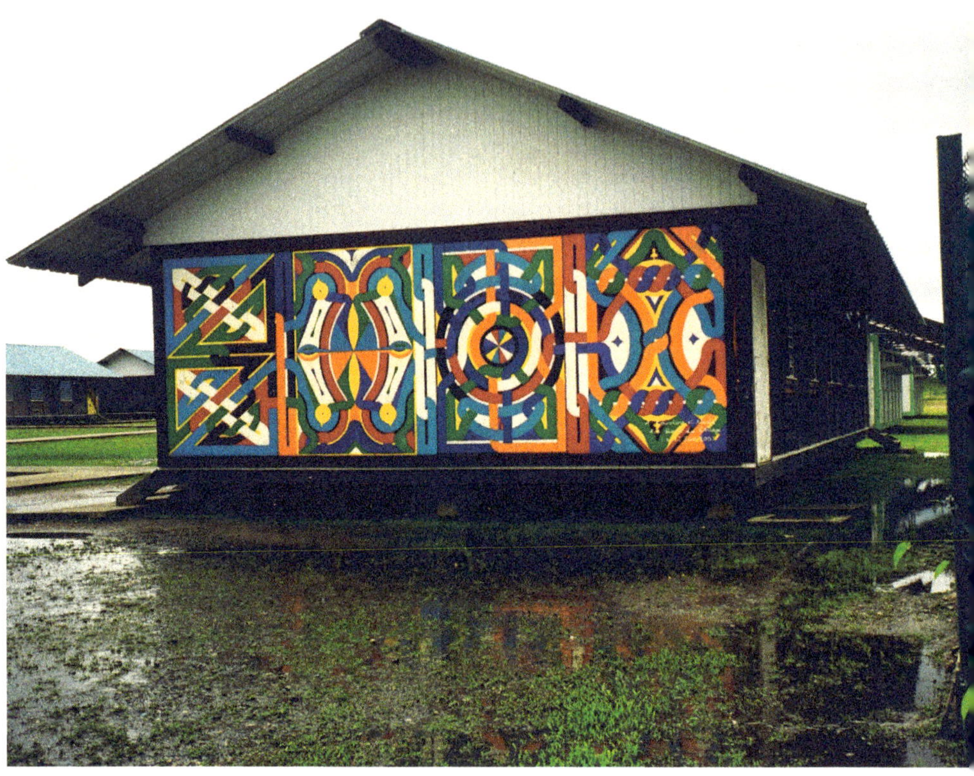

A junior high school (Collège III) in Saint-Laurent-du-Maroni in 2002, with a mural painted by Maroon students in 2000, when the school was located on the site of Camp A.

had begun settling in the thin strip of unoccupied land between the Camp de la Transportation and the river—first Alukus, then Okanisis and Pamakas, and eventually Saamakas. By 1980, more than 1,200 Maroons of different groups were living in this riverside fringe.[41] And in the mid-1980s, just before the arrival of thousands of refugees from the civil war in Suriname, Ken Bilby counted some 2,300 Maroons residing in the town of Saint-Laurent (about 52 percent Okanisi, 19 percent Saamaka, 17 percent Pamaka, and 12 percent Aluku)—roughly half the entire population.[42] By that time, the Maroon riverside shantytowns were being demolished, and Maroons were being offered residence in public housing (in a development called La Charbonnière) that segregated them from the rest of Saint-Laurent on the southern fringe of the town. The housing was specifically designed to segregate Okanisis, Saamakas, Pamakas, and Alukus in neighborhoods separate from one another.[43]

In the late 1980s, the civil war in Suriname brought more than ten thousand Maroons to Saint-Laurent, and substantial numbers remained. In the wake of the war, many Pamakas and Okanisis, who had long frequented Saint-Laurent, established residence on the French side of the river, having witnessed the decline in services in Suriname and the possibility in Guyane of receiving medical benefits and schooling for their children. Indeed, in 1987, Pamaka Granman Forster made an official request to the French government to change the status of his whole people from Surinamese to French.[44]

The population of Saint-Laurent has risen dramatically over the past three decades, due partly to the abandonment of Okanisi villages on the Tapanahoni River and a birth rate among Maroons that is among the highest in the world. Today, the official population is 50,000, but our research suggests that the real figure is more like 60,000, including at least 46,000 Maroons—24,200 Okanisis, 17,300 Saamakas, 3,000 Pamakas, and 1,500 Alukus.[45]

More than half of the adults are non-French immigrants, three-quarters of them from Suriname and mainly Okanisi. The population is

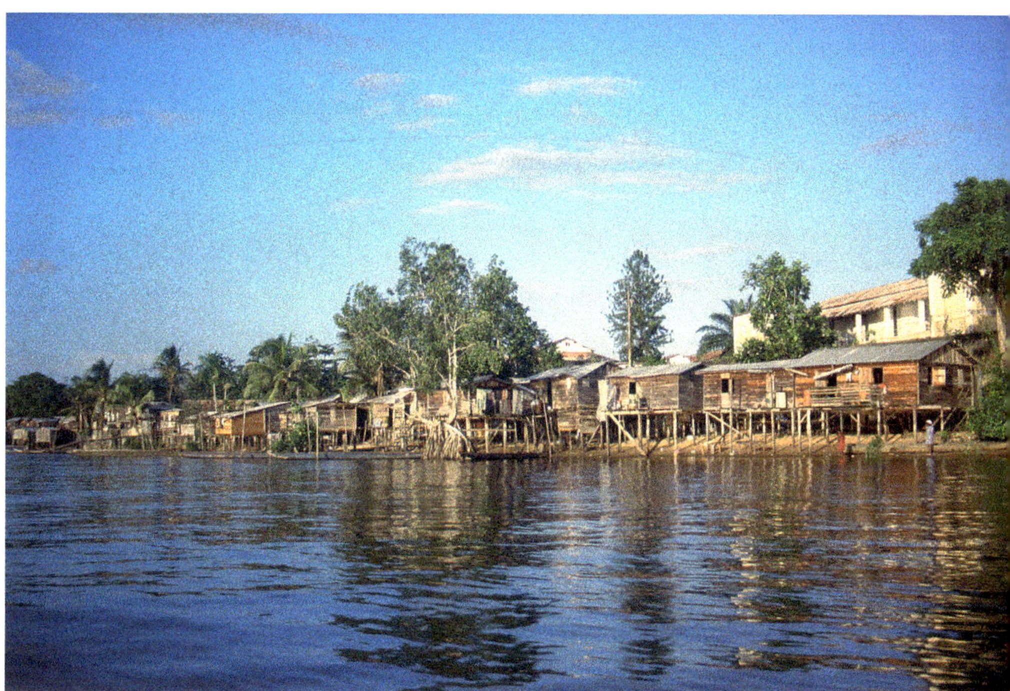

Maroon houses, Saint-Laurent, 1984–1985.

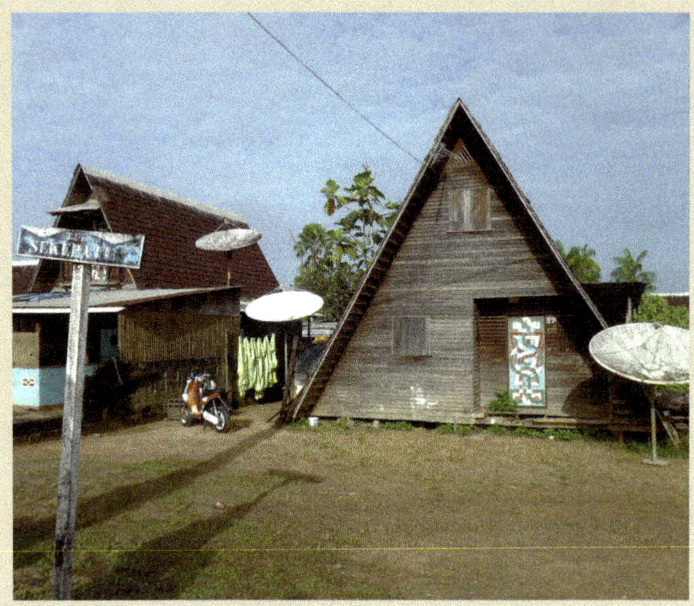

Public housing in La Charbonnière, 2011.

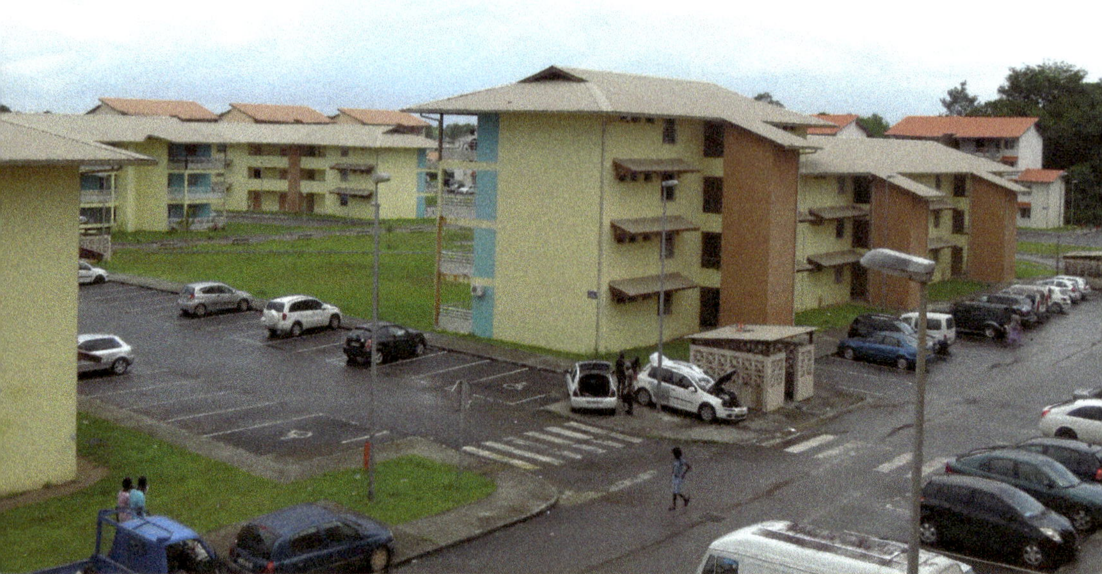

The public housing project called Résidence Écoles 5, 2016.

very young; 40 percent are less than fifteen years old and 66 percent under thirty. Saint-Laurent ("Soolan" in all the Maroon languages) has become the largest majority-Maroon city in the world.

Some Maroons still live in houses they built in neighborhoods that could be considered shantytowns or ghettos; many others own small houses in the extensive public-housing areas, often enlarging, repainting, and renovating the originals and adding cinder-block reinforcement to the wooden walls.[46] Yet others manage to get a highly desired apartment in one of the new public-housing projects built by the state, located along streets with names evoking French culture-heroes (rue Jean-Paul Sartre, rue Denis Diderot, and so forth); many of these apartment residents are women with children, who pay the rent with welfare money, supplemented by earnings from housekeeping jobs in a school or from caring for the children of non-Maroons.

Since the 1980s, the city (like the state) has been struggling, unsuccessfully, to keep pace with the needs of the fast-growing population by building public housing and schools and expanding social services. By 2018, Saint-Laurent had five junior high schools and four high schools, but the mayor told us he felt frustrated that even after he'd built a new school each year, he still needed four more high schools. The state has mounted numerous campaigns against "spontaneous housing" in Saint-Laurent, bulldozing self-constructed houses and sometimes relocating residents—at least those with French papers—in public-housing units: the "Maroon-style" houses built in the 1980s in La Charbonnière, the vast tracts of small houses spread across the neighborhood called Sables Blancs/Vampire twenty years later, or the three-story apartment blocks, symbols of modernity and urbanity, that are being built all around the periphery of the town today.

Watching their houses being bulldozed, struggling for years in the hope of being granted a temporary residence card, dealing with the bureaucracy of the welfare system and the hospital—Maroons living in Saint-Laurent never forget that their world is governed by the Other, that is, Creoles and people from metropolitan France. This is even true of Saamakas who live along the roads and earn their living by selling woodcarvings: in 2018 the National Forestry Service warned woodcarvers that their chainsaws and shotguns would be confiscated if they cut their own wood (rather than buying it from the state) or hunted certain animals that were part of their traditional diet. In this sense, the quality of life for Maroons living in Saint-Laurent is quite different from that of those living in the four interior communes

(Maripasoula, Papaïchton, Grand-Santi, and Apatou), where the state is less omnipresent and the local government is run by Maroons.

The rapid expansion of the Maroon population in Guyane has created a gap between young people, who have learned French in school, and their parents, who, in many cases, speak only their Maroon language as well, often, as languages they learned in Suriname, whether Sranantongo or Dutch. In 1987, a survey of Maroon adults in Saint-Laurent found that 87 percent had never been to school and that only 15 percent were officially employed.[47] Today there are young Okanisis and Alukus (and a few Saamakas and Pamakas) who work for the city, but most adults who have jobs are manual laborers, domestics, or shop assistants.

Junior high and high school teachers complain about the low academic level and truancy rates, and the fact that the largest junior high, with 1500 students, has only a single social worker. Three hundred meters from the front door of that school, in an area known locally as "Chicago," drugs are sold openly. And teachers report that their students are serving, more and more, as mules for drug dealers from Suriname, swallowing as many as one hundred balloons or condoms filled with cocaine before taking the flight to Paris and returning four

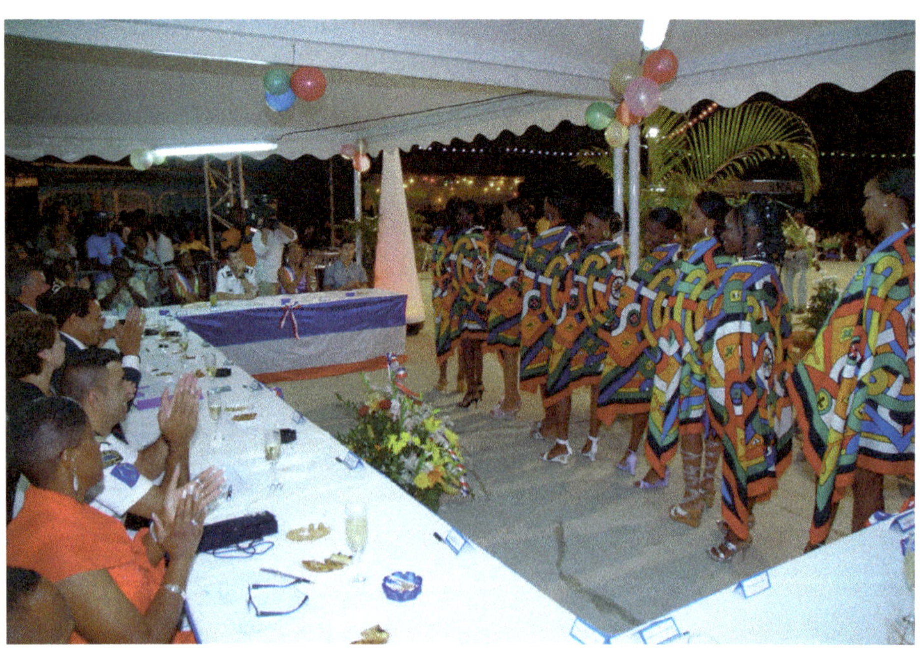

Miss Saint-Laurent competition, 2007.

or five days later wearing the latest fashion in sneakers and showing off big wads of bills.[48]

But at the same time, there are success stories. We know of three Maroons (an Aluku, an Okanisi, and a Saamaka) who have earned degrees from the prestigious Institut d'études politiques (Sciences Po) in Paris, a Saamaka woman from Iracoubo who earned her degree from the Medical School of Caen and works in the hospitals of Caen and Lisieux, and an Aluku historian born in Boniville who teaches at the University of the Antilles in Guadeloupe. More and more Maroons from Saint-Laurent are pursuing degrees at the university in Cayenne; some estimates put their number at 30 percent of the student body. Other Maroons are studying in France, from Montpellier to Rennes. And several thousand others, despite never finishing high school, have moved to France in search of a better life.

The population of Saint-Laurent includes many "transnationals," both men and women, who go back and forth to Suriname. There are also children who were born in Saint-Laurent and go to school there (thus acquiring the right to request French citizenship when they are older), but live mainly in Albina (across the river in Suriname). They register for school with a Saint-Laurent relative's address and then commute across the river each day by motor canoe. And upon the death of someone who grew up in a village "on the river" (whether the Tapanahoni or the Suriname), the family often repatriates the body, despite the high cost and bureaucratic complexities, in order to conduct a proper funeral.

Protestant churches, mainly evangelical or Baptist, have made great inroads, and many Maroons in Saint-Laurent and Mana (and elsewhere) have joined either universal churches such as Jehovah's Witnesses or small congregations such as Les Combattants de la foi, Source de Vie, or La mission biblique de l'Église Baptiste Genezareth du Mexique. The outlying Mana neighborhood of Charvein, which includes 2,500 people (all Maroons), now has churches of fifteen denominations. This upsurge in church membership brings with it a rejection of traditional values and beliefs; Okanisi converts in Grand-Santi told us that they no longer return to their "pagan" villages upriver, just a half hour away by motor canoe, even for the funeral of a family member, because they fear being "bewitched." Clearly, this development carries deep consequences for the future.

The first Maroon to be recognized as captain in Saint-Laurent was an Aluku, Pierre Neman, in the 1970s; he died in 2015 and has not been

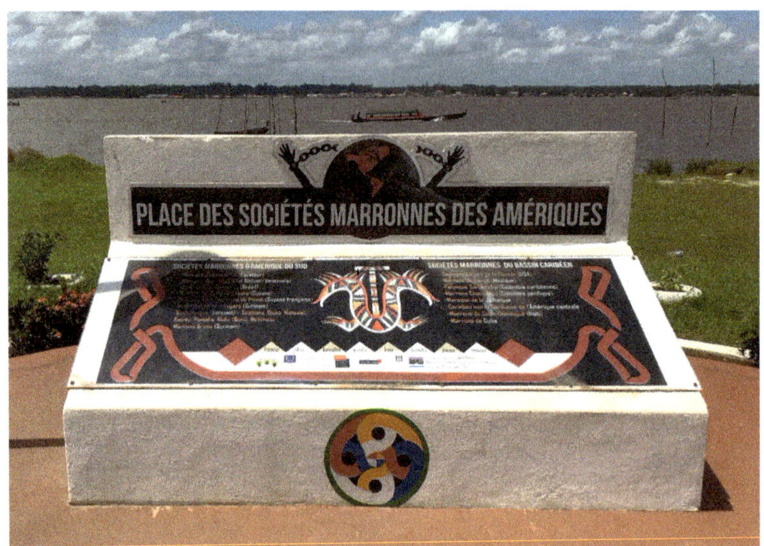

Monument honoring Maroon societies in the Americas, inaugurated in 2013 in La Charbonnière.

replaced as of this writing. The second, in 1984, was a Saamaka, Antonisi Anakaba, who died in 2021. Today there is also an Okanisi captain, Sony Poïte, and a Pamaka captain, Mafoo André Siko, but these authorities no longer play an important role in the life of residents.

Some 500 Saamakas live in small houses along the roads that link Saint-Laurent, Mana, and Saut-Sabbat to Saint-Laurent, doing their best to survive on the sale of carvings made by the men and produce from the gardens cultivated by the women. Many have not been able to get residence papers and travel back and forth to their home villages in Suriname, leading a truly transnational life.

Mana

After the refugee camps were closed at the end of the Suriname civil war, some 1,200 Cottica Ndyukas were taken in by the mayor and given residence papers as well as land at Charvein, the site of one of these camps. (The Charvein refugee camp was built on the site of one of the most infamous sections of the penal colony—"The camp of the incorrigibles," also known as "the hell of hell," where the prison administration sent, in the words of the French journalist Albert Londres, "the most exquisite products of the prison colony's scum.")[49] This new Okanisi community has a captain, Eddy Pinas (who had first become "village chief"

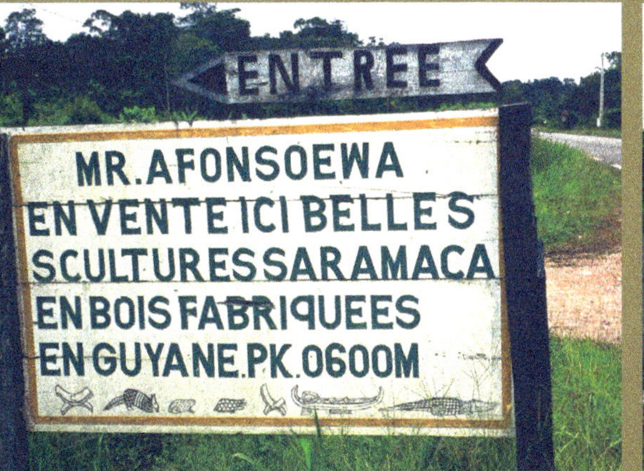

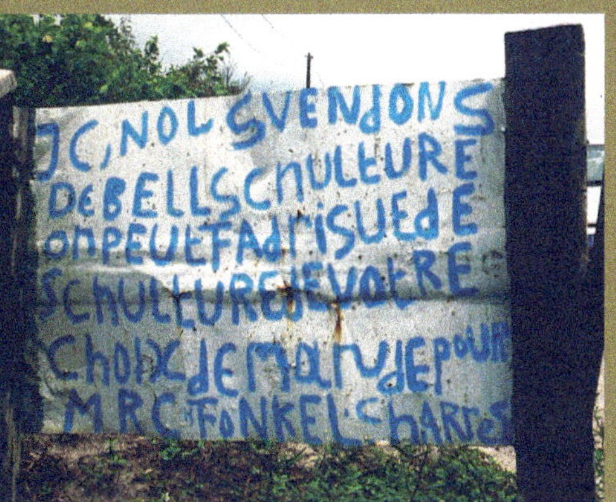

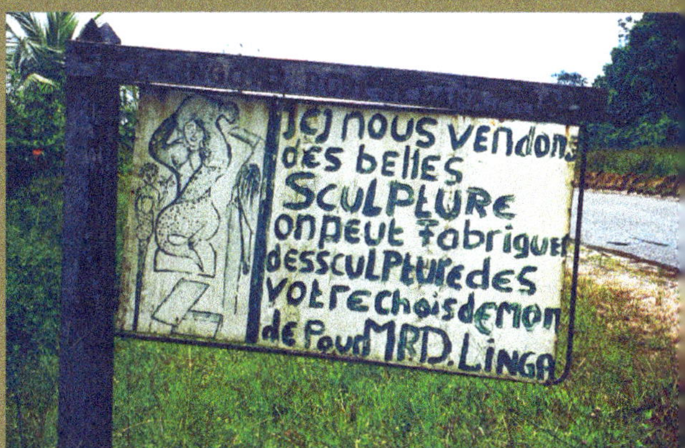

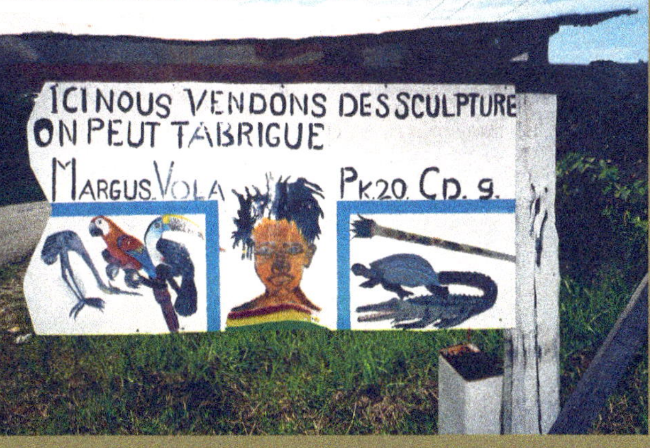

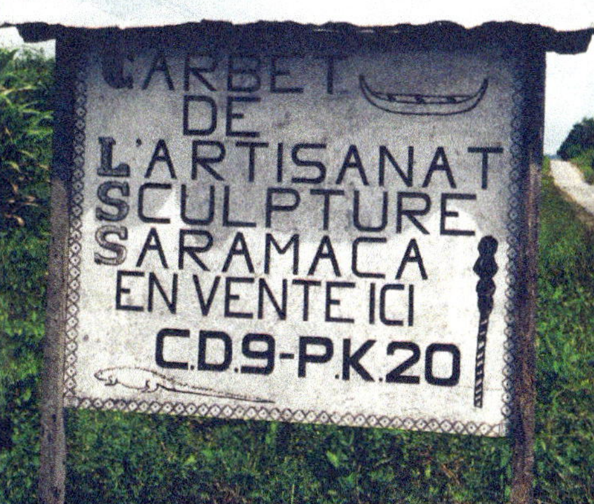

Some of the roadside panels put up by Saamaka woodcarvers, Route de Mana, 2002.

in the refugee camp in 1987). Today there are some 2,500 Okanisis in Charvein (despite the fact that an increasing number of young people have left for France) as well as 400 others along a nearby road.

By the side of the road that links Saint-Laurent to Mana, young residents of Charvein have set up a series of stands filled with tourist art. Their offerings are varied; some they make themselves, but most are bought from Saamaka carvers who live along the same road closer to Saint-Laurent and, as "illegals," have poorer access to the market. Of generally mediocre quality, these pieces range from standard folding stools and walking sticks to carved phalluses and other knickknacks.

Mana is also the headquarters of the "Chercheurs d'art" association, which promotes the work of a deliberately multicultural Maroon and non-Maroon mix of artists. It has created a computerized database of all artists in the communes of Saint-Laurent, Mana, and the Amerindian village of Awala—Maroons, Kalin'a, Hmong, and others—and published it in a lavishly illustrated guide describing their wood sculptures, calabash carving, textiles, ceramics, ironwork, performance arts, and so forth.[50]

Kourou

In the 1960s, urban planners converted the little Creole village of Kourou into a large planned city in preparation for the opening of the adjacent space center. The Maroons (mainly Saamakas) who provided much of the labor were permitted to build a shantytown from leftover materials on the construction sites, and soon it became known as the "Village Saramaka," even though it included Maroons from the other groups as well. During the 1970s, most of the initial Aluku and Okanisi population drifted away to Cayenne or Saint-Laurent; and in 1992, the 2,500 Saamakas made up 87 percent of the city's Maroon population.[51]

Today in Kourou there are about 9,000 Saamakas, 2,900 Okanisis, 225 Alukus, and 100 Pamakas. Over the past several decades, the jerry-built structures of the old Village Saramaka have been largely replaced with state-built public housing—individual houses that are rented to Maroons with an option to buy. Many Maroons have moved to the other end of town, where apartment buildings have been constructed to accommodate the fast-growing population, but they still spend time in the Village Saramaka, which continues to be the center of their social life. Saamakas in Kourou also keep up with life in their home villages in Suriname, making frequent trips back for several

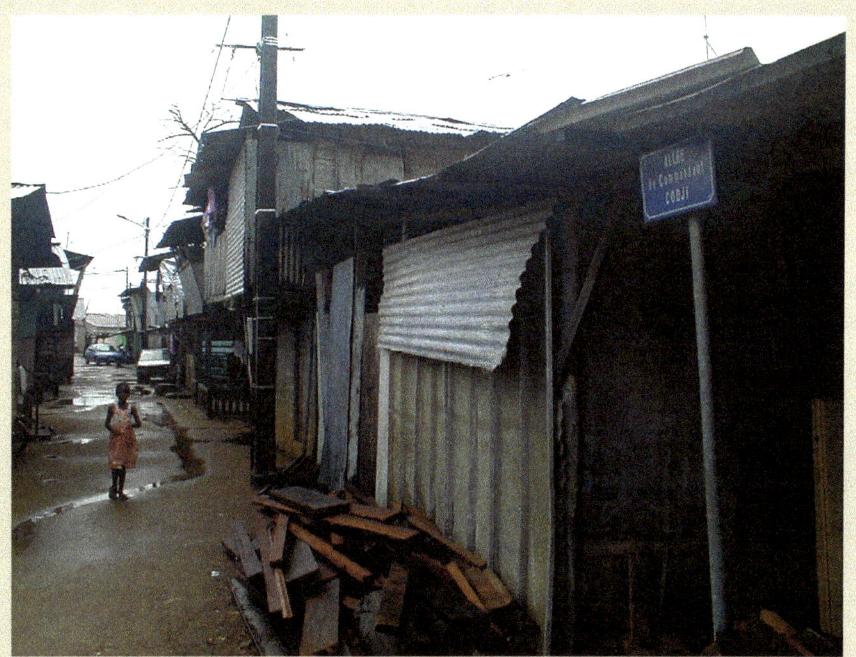

Street in the (now largely razed) Village Saramaka, Kourou, 2002. The street is named for Kodyi (junior), captain of Tampaki, 1923–1972.

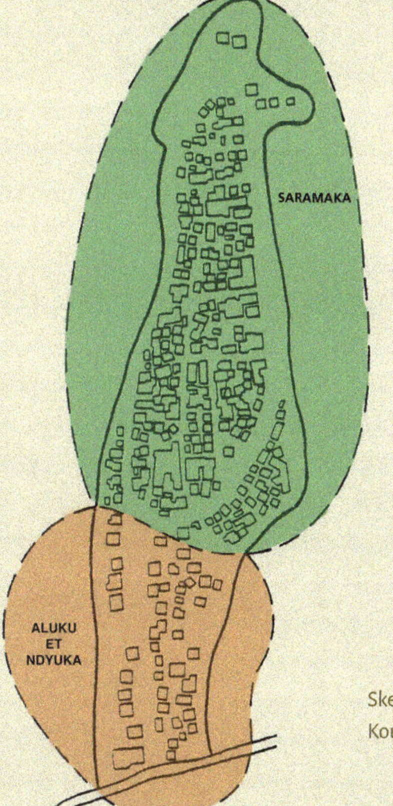

Sketch of the Village Saramaka, Kourou, 1980s.

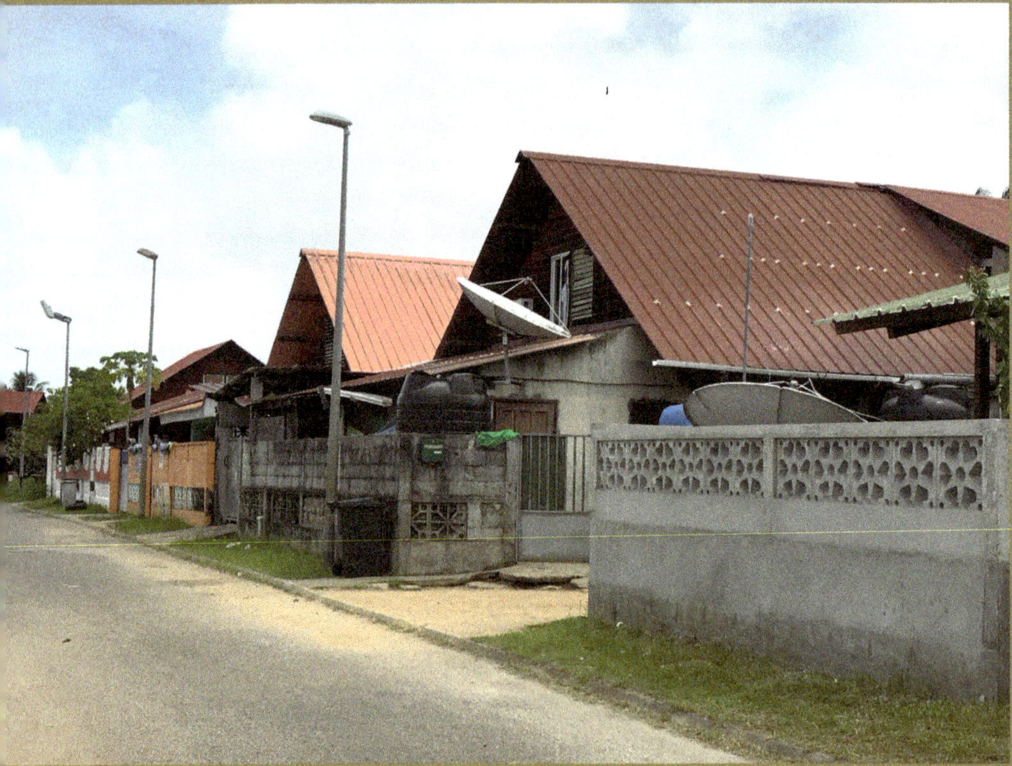

The new Village Saramaka, 2018.

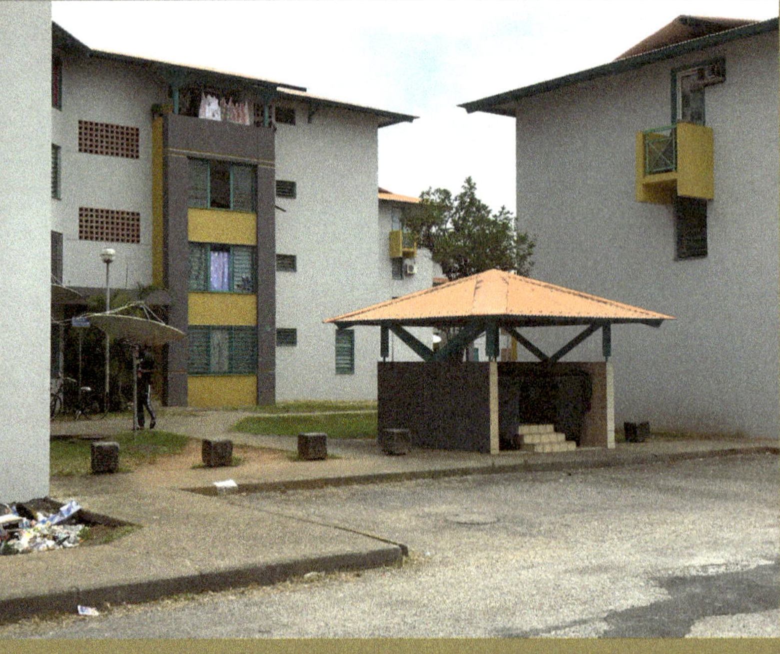

The neighborhood of L'Anse, Kourou, where many Saamakas now live, 2018.

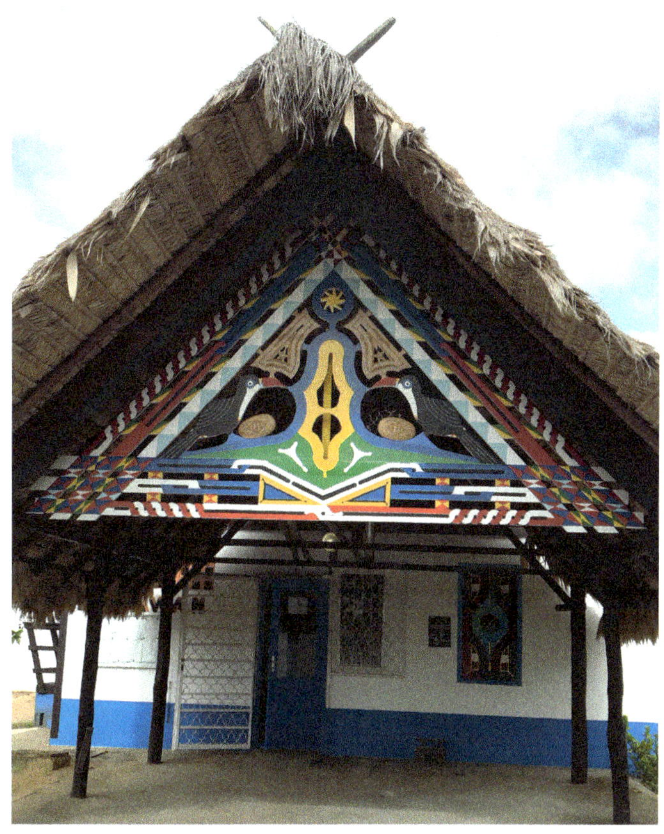

The office of the Libi Na Wan association, 2018. The façade was a collaboration by Aluku, Okanisi, and Saamaka artists.

weeks at a time. Like Okanisis in Saint-Laurent, they are real transnationals. Some Saamaka men still have jobs at the space center, while others work in forestry, do woodcarving, or find temporary jobs in construction and gardening.

Libi Na Wan, founded in 1994, began as a cultural and artistic association for Saamakas, Okanisis, Alukus, and Pamakas, but depends heavily on the metropolitan French members who have played a central role in its operation since the beginning. Once a lively organization, hosting exhibitions and publishing glossy catalogues, it has become less active in recent years. The neighboring Papakai association, founded in 1994, is smaller but seemingly more active, and focuses on facilitating the adaptation of Saamakas to Guyane in terms of both residence status and employment.

Kourou remains an important port of arrival for young Saamaka men making their first solo trip to Guyane. Many support themselves by woodcarving while they are seeking a better job and, eventually, residence papers.

Since 1977, the French administration has acknowledged the importance of the Saamaka community in Kourou by recognizing an official captain. Until his death in 2018, the post was held by Adaïsso Ngwete. For reasons of political parity, similar posts were created for the smaller communities of Okanisis (whose captaincy is now held by Paul Kago Afoeja) and Alukus (Bruno Apouyou).[52] Today the new Village Saramaka has a street named after each one of these captains. Just days before his death at age eighty-nine, Captain Adaïsso shared rich memories with us of his childhood in Mana, where he had gone with relatives working as canoemen—for example, the excitement caused by the arrival of the first bicycle and later the first car, and the fact that travel to the last gold-mining site upriver required three months and the negotiation, with a *takiri* pole, of ninety-nine rapids.

Cayenne and Matoury

In Cayenne and the neighboring commune of Matoury there are some 6,200 Saamakas, 1,500 Okanisis, 1,000 Alukus, and 300 Pamakas. In 2001, recognizing the size of the Saamaka presence in the region, the French government created the first post of captain of Cayenne, installing Alexander Tooy in a gala ceremony on the Place des Palmistes.[53]

There is considerable variation in the employment of Maroons in Cayenne. Many Saamaka men work, legally or off the books, in the construction industry; others work as cooks in pizzerias or other restaurants or as shop assistants in Chinese-owned stores; and others work full-time as sculptors for the tourist trade. Saamaka and Aluku men have a long tradition of employment as assistants to researchers from French scientific institutions such as ORSTOM (Office de la recherche scientifique et technique d'outre-mer, which became the IRD, Institut de recherche pour le développement), the CNRS (Centre national de la recherche scientifique), or the Institut Pasteur, providing their expertise in tropical flora and fauna. Other Maroons have developed work in tourism, particularly ecotourism, along the Sinnamary and other rivers, where visitors can experience a few days of tranquil camping and forest life.

Most women devote full time to family responsibilities. Many of those who have regular jobs work as cleaning women or look after the children of non-Maroon families. But other kinds of work are

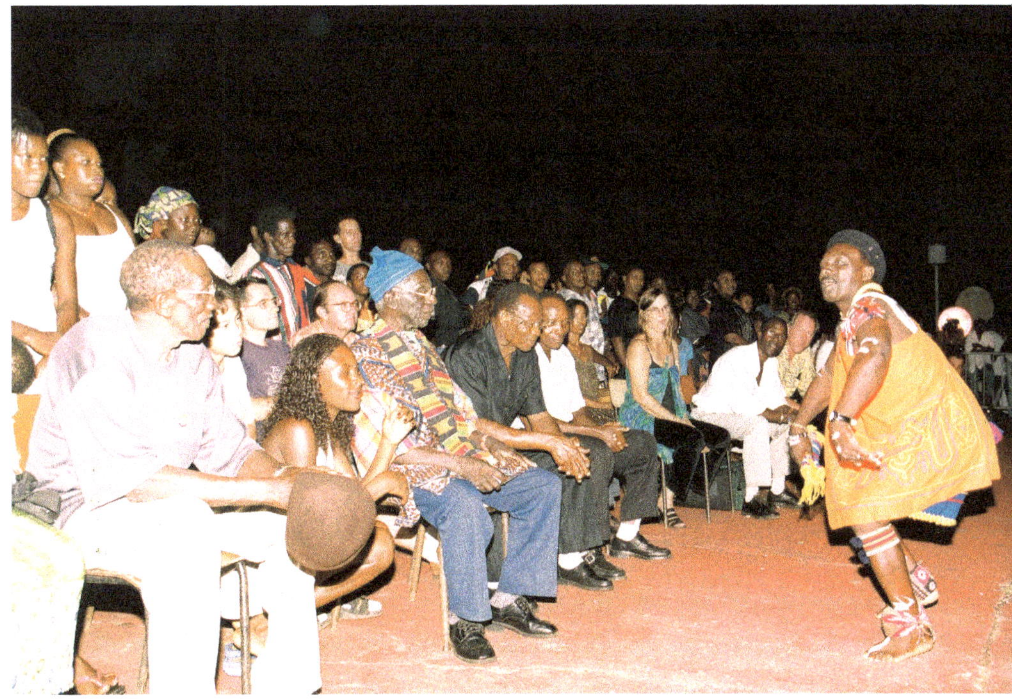

Dyangili, star dancer of the group Denku, which came from Suriname for the installation ceremony honoring the new Saamaka captain of Cayenne, 2001. *Left*, Alexander Tooy; *center with a blue cap*, Anikei Awagi, head captain of the Saamakas in Suriname; *in a black shirt*, Saamaka Captain Adaïsso of Kourou.

becoming increasingly common. One Saamaka woman sells her appliqué textiles at the Family Plaza shopping center in Cayenne; another runs an online beauty-and-fashion site; and the streets bordering the Cayenne market are lined with Okanisi and Pamaka women selling the *kwaka* and cassava cakes they produce with manioc grown in their gardens. Many young Maroons are enrolled in the university and are as comfortable in French as in their native languages. And like Maroons in Suriname who have moved to Paramaribo, those in Cayenne and surrounding areas live shoulder to shoulder with other segments of a multiethnic society. For example, the Saamaka captain Tooy lived, until his death in 2015, in an almost exclusively Brazilian neighborhood at the edge of the city; the largely Haitian settlement of Cogneau, which has sprung up without municipal water or electricity in Matoury, includes a number of Saamaka and Okanisi families; and there are Aluku families living alongside Creole households in the bourgeois suburbs of Rémire-Montjoly.

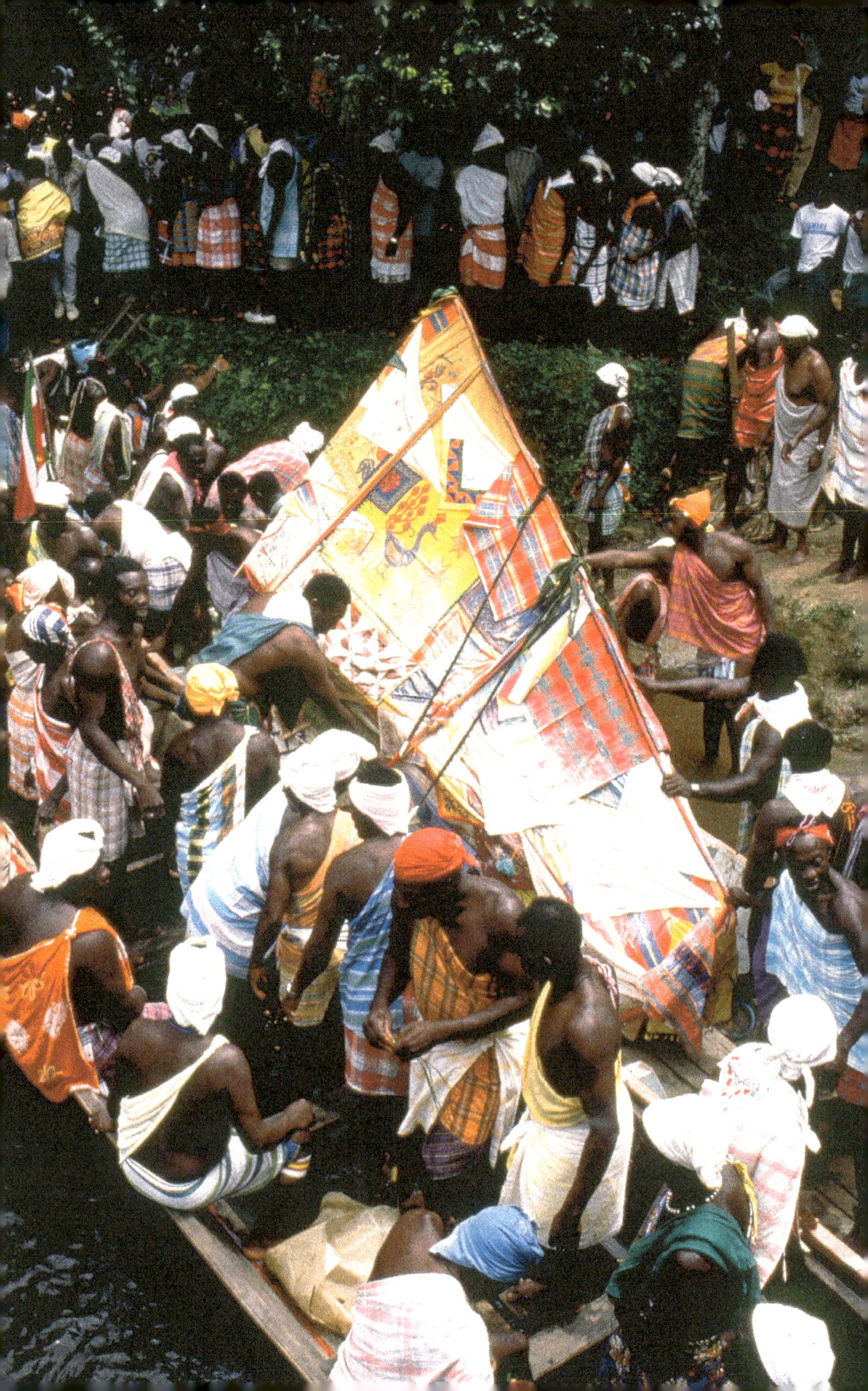

Looking Back, Looking Ahead

Until 1986, when war broke out in Suriname, the very great majority of Maroons—Okanisis, Pamakas, and Saamakas—lived in "traditional" villages along the rivers of the interior.[1] Except for those Saamakas who had been forced to relocate in the 1960s because their villages were flooded by the hydroelectric project at Afobaka, they all lived in houses they had built themselves, using materials from the forest—wood from trees felled by the men using axes or chain saws, and palm fronds for the side walls and roofs. When they visited a relative in another village or went to work in a garden camp, it was by paddling small canoes. Women washed laundry and dishes at the riverside and brought water back to the houses in buckets on their heads. Tiny clearings just outside the residential areas served as toilets, though men preferred to go to the river at night. Meals were based on the fish and game provided by men and the garden produce provided by women. Rice was the staple for Saamakas, and manioc for Eastern Maroons, each supplemented by bananas and plantains, tubers of various sorts, okra, corn, and forest fruits. Hunting kills were never sold (they were shared), and more generally, money rarely made its appearance in the villages. Women cooked on wood fires and used palm oil that they made themselves. The houses were furnished with hammocks bought in Paramaribo and small stools carved by the men. Men and adolescent boys wore breechcloths and shoulder capes, and women wore a double layer of wrap-skirts ("breasts outside," as one elderly Saamaka man put it, approvingly). Adolescent girls wore a frontal apron hung over a cord, and children had a waist-tie, sometimes embellished with beads for girls.

Except for villages where missionaries had converted people to Christianity, all women had body cicatrizations designed to enhance the tactile pleasure of sex (on the face, chest, back, and inner thighs for older women, and at least some "under the skirt"

Opposite: The coffin of Agbago Aboikoni, paramount chief of the Saamaka, covered with cloths he owned, being placed in a canoe for its voyage to the cemetery, 1989.

designs for teenage girls), and women observed the rules of menstrual seclusion that protected ritual powers in the village. There were ritual activities of one sort or another virtually every day—prayers to ancestors, oracle consultations, rites for possession spirits, and more. Men were the ones who had experience with coastal society, spending several years at a time doing wage labor to buy shotguns, machetes, cloth, cooking pots, sugar, and other products to bring back to the villages. Women generally stayed home in the villages, though some got permission from their lineage leaders to join a husband on the coast. There were no tourists, and many children had never seen a white person except at a school or clinic run by missionaries. Very few people knew how to read. This general picture lasted for most Maroons into the 1980s.[2]

It's shocking, but not necessarily surprising, that many Westerners—even in Paramaribo and Cayenne—viewed Maroons as "primitives," and that even today the prestigious American Museum of Natural History in New York classifies its rich Maroon materials from Suriname and Guyane as part of its "African Continent" collections.

Today 53 percent of Maroons live in Suriname, 38 percent in Guyane, and 9 percent in Europe and elsewhere. More than 40 percent of Okanisis, almost a third of Saamakas, and the great majority of Alukus and Pamakas now live in Guyane.

A scant 1 percent of the Maroons in Guyane now live in traditional villages. That said, the majority of today's adults grew up at least partly in these villages and return from time to time to visit relatives or participate in ritual events, most frequently funerals. Their past experiences in the villages, regarding beliefs, relations with ancestors, physical comportment, or other aspects of living, continue to mark their lives in more or less subtle ways. For example, women do not sleep with their husbands or cook for them during their periods, even while living in urban apartments, and many houses with a TV and a washing machine also have a small ancestor shrine. But the world that an earlier generation knew while growing up on the river is becoming increasingly distant for younger people, who see it in an almost folkloric light. We are often contacted by high school students in Saint-Laurent asking for information for papers they are writing on traditional rites of passage or marriage customs. Not surprisingly, today's teenagers are primarily concerned with school, social networks, popular music, sports, and other aspects of life that their parents and grandparents never knew.

Table 4. Maroon Residence, 2018

	Suriname	Guyane	Europe, USA, etc.	Totals
Okanisis	58,000	47,000	10,500	115,500
Saamakas	70,000	35,500	10,000	115,500
Alukus	500	9,800	1,300	11,600
Pamakas	2,100	6,900	2,000	11,000
Matawais	8,100	—	400	8,500
Kwintis	1,050	—	150	1,200
Total	139,750	99,200	24,350	263,300

Maroons who have moved to coastal Guyane from villages on the river, even those that have recently been partially transformed by electricity, running water, or evangelical churches, often harbor nostalgic feelings for their earlier lives, even though they have opted for "modernity." The advantages are all too clear: better medical services, schools for their children, and various other conveniences such as washing machines and supermarkets. But access to such things varies, depending on their civil status, and those without French residence papers spend enormous amounts of time and energy on the bureaucratic struggle to obtain them.

The lives of Maroons in Guyane are strongly influenced by the kind of residence where they live. In some urban neighborhoods of apartment blocks in Saint-Laurent, Kourou, and Soula, for example, many Maroons hardly know their neighbors, while in others, family members live in close proximity. There are jerry-built single-family houses in areas with no municipal services and other places where a whole kinship group manages to live together. Some Maroon-built agglomerations have as many as 20–100 dwellings—La Flèche (near Iracoubo) and Gotalikonde (near Saint-Laurent) are among the largest. In the communes of the interior, large modern concrete houses stand side by side with single-family public housing and rudimentary self-built dwellings.

As mentioned earlier, Saamakas think of Kourou as their town. In the 1960s it was mainly Saamakas who cleared the forest next to the small and somnolent Creole village and who were the mainstays of the

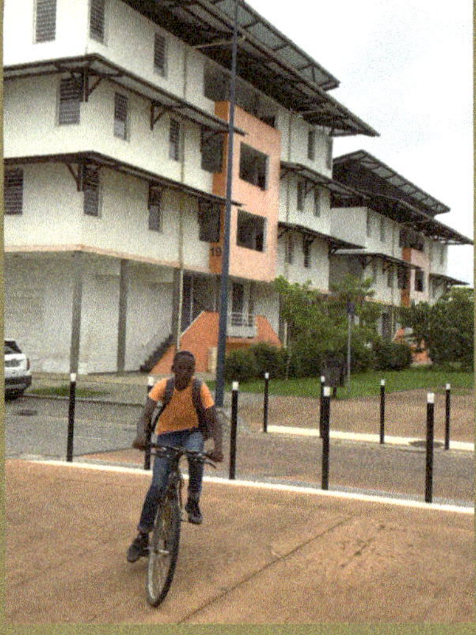

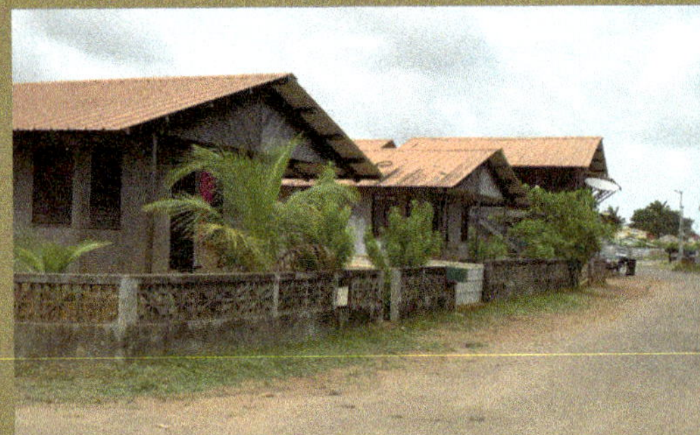

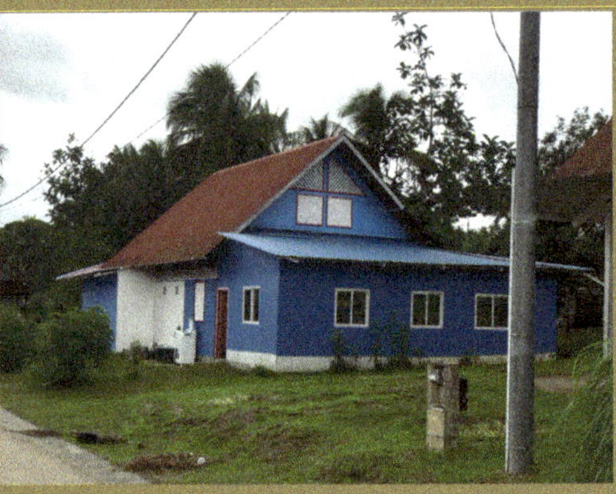

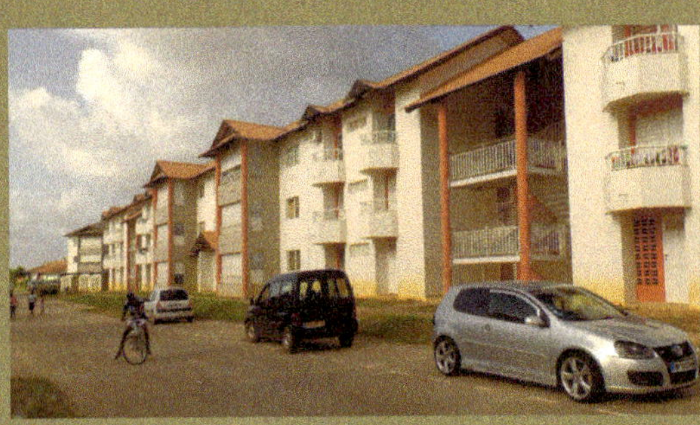

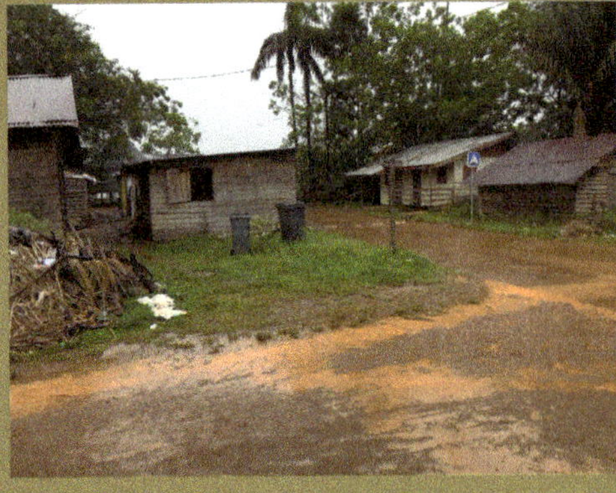

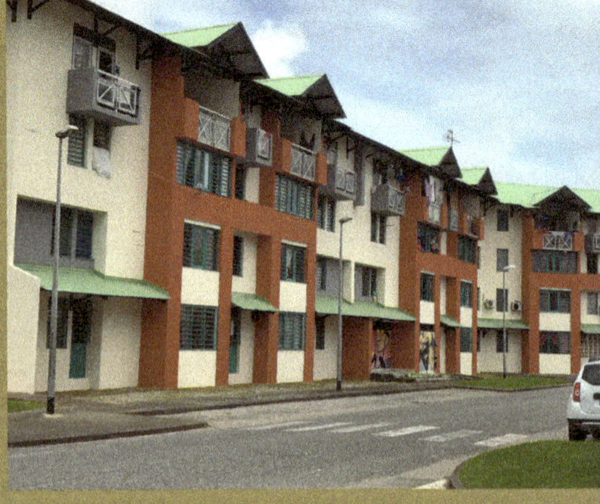

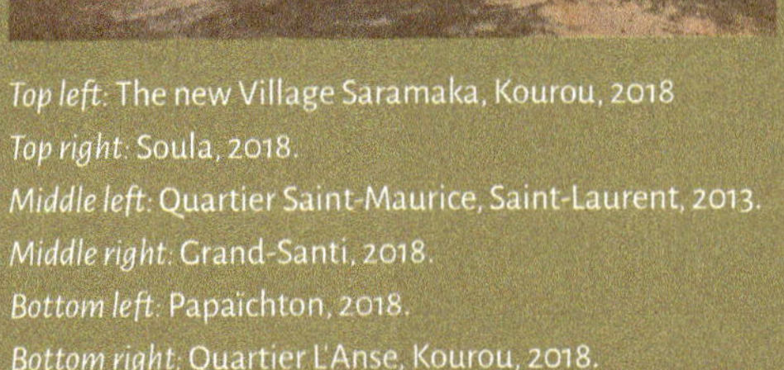

Top left: The new Village Saramaka, Kourou, 2018.
Top right: Soula, 2018.
Middle left: Quartier Saint-Maurice, Saint-Laurent, 2013.
Middle right: Grand-Santi, 2018.
Bottom left: Papaïchton, 2018.
Bottom right: Quartier L'Anse, Kourou, 2018.

construction crews for both the residential areas of the new city and the space center itself.

In contrast, the city of Saint-Laurent, which is dominated by Okanisis and includes nearly half of Guyane's Maroons, is multicultural. The Saamakas who live there speak the Saamaka language at home, but Okanisi (the language of Okanisis, Alukus, and Pamakas) serves as a lingua franca, varying slightly in its vocabulary and pronunciation depending on the social context.[3]

Many hundreds of Saamakas and a lesser number of Okanisis have built houses along the roads around Saint-Laurent, with or without authorization from the government. A good number of these people are featured in *La Route de l'Art*, the guide to the work of artists living in this area that serves as a richly informative catalogue for tourists and others in the market for local art and handicrafts (see above).

In the interior, the communes along the Lawa, neither fully urban nor fully rural, have a very different feel from both the traditional villages (in spite of the gardens that some people maintain there) and the coastal towns (in spite of daily flights to Cayenne and Saint-Laurent). Some of the roads are paved, others are pure mud. And in spite of several areas of single-family public housing, most Maroons live in houses they've built themselves. There are no supermarkets like those in Kourou and Saint-Laurent, the Internet barely functions, and education is limited to elementary and junior high schools. Okanisi is the near-universal language.

To give a better idea of the various situations of Maroons in Guyane, we have constructed twelve vignettes, altering the details of each to protect the anonymity of people whom we visited in the course of our 2018 research, but trying our best to convey the variety of their experiences and the nature of their feelings about their situations.

- One Saamaka family lives in Kourou's new Village Saramaka, in one of the concrete houses built by the government after it razed the "insalubrious" structures of the old Village. The couple, both in their fifties, arrived from Suriname during the civil war of the 1980s. They have ten children, from three to twenty-eight years old. Two adult daughters and their four children live with them. Together, the three mothers receive about 3,500 euros monthly in government child-support payments (CAF), and the CAF pays the rent. The husband works in construction, one son is a car mechanic in France, and one of the daughters is a university student in Cayenne. The younger children go to school in Kourou and can get along in French, though Saamaka is always spoken at home. The well-furnished kitchen includes a large freezer and a refrigerator, a microwave oven, two rice cookers, a deep fryer, and hundreds of plastic and enamel bowls and plates. This large family eats its main meal at a large table once the husbands of the three women return from work in the afternoon. There's also a sewing machine, used mainly by one of the daughters to make appliqué skirts that she sells through a cultural cooperative, and a large flat-screen TV that is on from morning till night. The hospital, where one of the children is treated for hearing problems, is fifteen minutes away on foot, as is the largest supermarket in town. In general, the parents feel that they've created a promising future for their children.

- A sixty-year-old Saamaka man lives in one of the four-story apartment blocks at the other end of Kourou, in a public-housing unit. He arrived from Suriname in 1990 and lived in the old Village Saramaka until it was destroyed as part of the state's cleanup efforts. He has a French residency card, receives child-support money from the CAF, and does odd jobs, working with a machete, a chain saw, or a grass trimmer. His wife left him a couple of years ago, but two sons and three daughters have stayed on in the apartment, along with the baby that one of the girls had with a Haitian boyfriend. The TV is on all day, but the girls also spend a lot of time in front of a laptop playing Black music videos—they've mastered the American accents of the performers and sing along at full voice. The social life of these younger members of the household centers on their new urban neighborhood, but for their father, the old Village Saramaka is where he hangs out with his friends. The children show little interest in school; to us, their future seems to point to marginalization and poverty.
- An Okanisi woman in her fifties lives in an apartment in the three-story public-housing blocks of the Saint-Maurice neighborhood of Saint-Laurent. She grew up in a village on the upper Tapanahoni River and went to school in Paramaribo, where she learned Dutch. She came to Guyane with her second husband, living for the first several years just outside Saint-Laurent in a small house with neither electricity nor running water. After a twelve-year-long struggle with the authorities, the couple received French residence papers and the right to live in a public-housing unit, which they have furnished and maintained impeccably. Most of her neighbors are Saamakas. She's just bought a large washing machine, which allows

her to earn some money by taking in laundry; her husband has a job in the local rum distillery. Several years ago, after she and her husband were baptized in an evangelical church, they bought a large sound system on which she plays gospel music almost non-stop, sung in English, Sranantongo, Okanisi, and Saamaka. They have six children, all French citizens, one of whom is in the army, another at the university. Their rent is 700 euros a month, of which the CAF pays 550. She considers the quality of life in Saint-Laurent pretty good.

- An Okanisi woman lives in a single-family modern house at the edge of Saint-Laurent. Her mother was born in Saint-Laurent, as she was, so she is a French citizen. (The law of *double droit de sol* makes a child born in France of a parent born in France automatically a citizen.) She is well educated and works as a nurse at the hospital. Her husband, of Chinese heritage, works for the municipality. She speaks French with her four children, though they can understand Okanisi. She has never visited the villages upriver and never wears a traditional wrap-skirt. She stays in close contact by telephone with her lycée friends who are now in France.
- A seventy-year-old Saamaka man who arrived in the Sables Blancs neighborhood of Saint-Laurent in 1994 has periodically built additions onto his house, which now is home to an older sister, six children, and one of his wives. The other two live ten minutes away by foot. He also has seven adult children, three in Saint-Laurent, one in Kourou, two in Cayenne, and one in France. Thanks to money he earned from gold mining and various illicit activities, the house is well furnished: leather armchairs and sofas, a large TV, a large freezer, and a washer-dryer. The shells of two cars rust by the side of the house. When we visit one morning, three of the late-adolescent girls come out of the house dressed like prostitutes. One of their aunts who lives nearby scolds the eldest for her daring décolletage, but the girl laughs her off scornfully and pulls the zipper down even lower.
- An Okanisi woman crossed the river to Guyane in 1989 and now lives in one of the original public-housing units in the La Charbonnière neighborhood of Saint-Laurent. She had four children before coming to Guyane, and then five more, with a new husband, in Guyane. Her husband eventually took a second wife after their arrival in La Charbonnière, and the couple has frequent arguments. She maintains a garden across the river near Albina with her sister, who lives

on the Suriname side, and visits there several times each month. She shows us a beautiful wrap-skirt that one her sisters had embroidered for her, and explains that she is saving it as the garment she will someday be buried in. Three of her children remain at home, and she watches over their homework with diligence, feeling handicapped that she doesn't speak French, but convinced that their schooling is the key to a better life. Speaking with us, she expresses disgust about a neighbor's son who has served as a drug mule between Cayenne and Paris three times in the past several months.

- A thirty-five-year-old Saamaka woman who lives in the Petit Paris neighborhood of Saint-Laurent has three children between the ages of five and ten and is raising a niece who is in her final year of vocational high school. Flip-flops are left at the door, and the apartment is furnished with cheap chairs and sofas. The TV is always on, usually showing cartoons for the kids. She was born across the river in Albina but managed to get a residence card ten years ago. She speaks Saamaka at home but can get along in French. She works as a housekeeper in a nearby elementary school, but returns to her family's village on the Suriname River each summer. After the birth of her last child, her husband took a second wife, so she threw him out and hasn't seen him since.
- There's a Saamaka man who lives next to the Saint-Laurent highway and has a small diesel generator that allows him to make furniture such as cabinets and bedframes in precious woods, usually on commission. When we visited, he was completing a rack, ordered by a Creole man, to stock fifty pairs of shoes. He had six children with several women before taking his present wife, with whom he's had four; all of them are now attending school. His wife does cross-stitch embroidery on hammocks, bedsheets, and wrap-skirts for sale. Neither of them has residence papers or receives any aid from the state, despite their many requests over the years. Solidary as a family, they live in real poverty.
- Another Saamaka woodcarver and his wife live beside the road to Saint-Laurent. Both are from the lower Suriname River. Shortly after their arrival in Guyane in 1993, he found work with a Frenchman who raised cattle. That man helped them with administrative matters, and once they got residence papers, he began paying the Saamaka man the minimum wage. The eldest of the couple's five children was trained as an electrician but has recently become a schoolteacher in Sinnamary. The wife complains that her husband's

There are many Maroons along the roads in the West who live under daily threat of expulsion. Consider, for example, the case of the Vola family, who have lived in the same place along RN9 since the 1980s. "This site includes important artists of the Route de l'Art and makes available, depending on what the woodcarvers are working on, some of the best pieces on the whole Route."[1] The men sell their carvings to tourists; the women take care of their gardens. Many of the thirty-some members of the family have residence papers, and "in 1995 the family began the necessary administrative procedures at the *mairie* and the Établissement public d'aménagement de la Guyane to gain title to the land." Nevertheless, in March 2018, the gendarmes, armed with a judicial order, destroyed all their houses, claiming that a photocopy of a person's identity papers and a cadastral map had not been furnished as requested—a charge that the family denied. "Fifty-seven people in total were expelled . . . The expulsion operation was successful." Meanwhile, the prefect reminded people in a statement of his firm stance against illegal residence anywhere in Guyane, "without regard to distinctions among the kinds of people who are concerned." (For a 1968 photo of the head of this large family, today a captain of the Saamaka village of Bofokule in Suriname, see page 27 [the boy standing with his mother].)

See *France Guyane*, March 30–31 and April 18, 2018

1. *La Route de l'art: Artistes de l'ouest Guyanais* (Guyane: Édition ONF, 2014), 125.

work doesn't allow him time for hunting, which means that wild boars constantly threaten her garden produce. She has tried to learn French, but it's been hard to take the classes in Saint-Laurent, since transportation is expensive. The two eldest children in the household have joined a Baptist church, but the parents, even though they no longer maintain an ancestor shrine, say they're "not yet ready" to follow their example.

- On a muddy street in Matoury, hidden from view by walls of rusting sheet metal, there are two substantial cement houses. The sixty-four-year-old Saamaka man who lives in the largest one came to Guyane at the age of fifteen to work in Kourou, machete and axe in hand. He loves to tell how he shot a howler monkey out of the great mango tree that stood where the Banque Nationale de Paris sits today. Later, he moved to Cayenne, married a Creole woman whose father was a Saamaka canoeman on the Oyapock, and had seven children with her (all trilingual in Creole, Saamaka, and French). They later parted ways, and he moved to Matoury. The second house on the site is occupied by the daughter of one of his brothers, who lives there with her five children and Creole husband. Perfectly bilingual in French and Saamaka, she is a certified social worker, taking care of an elderly French man for 500 euros a month. As in all the homes of the Maroons we visited, the TV is on all day long. In front of the two houses are various fruit trees and a cement platform for a swing set, a bicycle, and other playthings for the children.

- An Okanisi woman in her thirties in Maripasoula who was born in a village on the Tapanahoni originally came to the town to visit her sister but met an Aluku with whom she now has children who are ten, seven, and four years old. Her husband serves in the army in France and visits occasionally. Having been to school in Paramaribo, she can get along in Dutch and now is trying to learn French. She still doesn't have French residence papers, but her husband receives child support from the CAF and pays the rent. The house, a stand-alone public-housing unit, is minimally furnished—downstairs is a large open room with an old, tattered armchair and several plastic children's chairs; upstairs, several mattresses rest on the floor. In the kitchen there's a table, as well as a gas stove with two of four burners that don't work, a half-size refrigerator, and a deep freeze. There is no hot water. Unlike all the neighbors, who have satellite dishes, she has a TV that uses a rabbit-ears antenna. She does not complain about her life; indeed, she seems to take real pleasure in raising her family.
- An Okanisi family in Grand-Santi. The woman, in her fifties, was born in a garden camp just upstream from the present town—her mother's village was on the lower Tapanahoni. Today, she has her own garden near her birthplace, now accessible by dirt road. She lives in a large concrete house, still unfinished (like many of those in the town), with her four sons, ages fifteen to twenty-four. Her other six children live elsewhere: two work in France, two are at the university in Cayenne, one lives in Saint-Laurent, and another lives in Paramaribo. Her husband works for the *mairie* and drives around town in a quad. For the past two years, the family (except for two sons who are Rastas) have belonged to the Jehovah's Witnesses, which means that they no longer visit the villages of their parents and grandparents, less than an hour away by motor canoe, even for funerals, fearing "sorcery" by their "heathen" relatives.

The people of Guyane feel seriously neglected by France, as evidenced by the massive, general strikes of 2017. But at the same time, people in the west of Guyane (Saint-Laurent, Mana, and the towns upriver) feel seriously neglected by the Creole politicians in Cayenne. Despite forming only 30 percent of the total population, the Creoles control all political decisions for Guyane, and their vision for its future privileges their own interests. Although they no longer (for the most part) speak of "primitives" when referring to Maroons, they still tend to view them as "belonging to the lower classes that are too numerous, dangerous, and implicitly racialized behind the label of 'Buschinengué.'"[4]

Let us be absolutely clear: The Creoles of Guyane have nothing but disdain for the tribal populations, about whom they know next to nothing and for whom they use the blanket term "Bosch," that is, "forest people." They hesitate between two possible scenarios: either to destroy them by assimilation or to exploit them for purposes of tourism.

Jean Hurault, *Français et Indiens en Guyane, 1604–1972* (Paris: Union Générale d'Editions, 1972), 300

Among those Maroons who shared their thoughts with me, there was not a single one who had not felt the smart of Creole scorn. All of them had had to endure ethnic slurs and negative insinuations, if not outright insults, while living on the coast. From the young schoolchildren to those working toward the *baccalauréat*, all were accustomed to being treated as inferiors . . . Once I was standing in a shop in Saint-Laurent, looking at magazines, when a Creole woman walked in; seeing a group of Ndjuka women in one corner of the store, she said out loud, "Bosch, c'est la *dernière* nation!" (Bosch, it's the *last* [i.e. lowest] "nation"!); she then did a rapid about-face, and walked out.

Kenneth M. Bilby, "The Remaking of the Aluku: Culture, Politics, and Maroon Ethnicity in French South America" (PhD diss., Johns Hopkins University, 1990), 448, 456

No minority escapes this racist gaze, but some hold a privileged place. We would single out those officially called "tribal," that is, the Maroons and Amerindians. In speaking of them, most Creoles say "the primitives." True, they have adopted an old term used by whites (who nonetheless continue to use it), but it is always used in a pejorative sense. "Primitives," in contrast to those who call them by the term, are not part of the civilized world. This prejudice runs very deep. In Cayenne, the feelings of the Creoles in this regard lose any hint of ambiguity.

Marie-José Jolivet, *La question créole: Essai de sociologie sur la Guyane française* (Paris: ORSTOM, 1982), 403–404

At the same time, the role models of those Maroons who do well in school are European French (who are the great majority of teachers, doctors, and so forth) rather than Creoles. And while Maroon men who worked as laborers or canoemen in Guyane a half century ago learned enough of the Creole language to communicate with their bosses and shopkeepers, Maroons in Guyane today find it far more useful to learn French. This means that Maroons today often prepare themselves better for a future in metropolitan France than in Guyane, and indeed, more and more young Maroons are now settling in France. In general, Alukus (and to a lesser degree Okanisis and Pamakas) experience less difficulty than Saamakas in adapting to life in coastal Guyane. But one thing they all share: being the target of discrimination by Creoles and European French.

In fact, discrimination is part of daily life for Maroons in Guyane and a frequent topic of discussion among them. Both the Aluku and Saamaka captains of Kourou have told us, with bitterness and emotion, of a whole series of discriminatory acts against family members in school, at work, and elsewhere. Maroon university students in Paris tell us that they frequently hear the word *sauvage* used to taunt them, just as they did in Cayenne. Much like the attitudes of many Americans today toward foreigners seeking a better life in the United States, many Creoles and European French people in Guyane let nationalism and xenophobia come to the fore in their attitudes toward Maroon immigrants from Suriname. Such widespread sentiments and practices run against both the model of multiculturalism that has for some time been officially voiced in Guyane, and the valorization of the historical "*nèg mawon*" adopted by intellectuals and politicians in the Antilles.

The local system of justice confronts daily the challenge of how to recognize cultural difference within the context of the French Republic. The further individuals are from French norms in terms of language, beliefs, and education, the less chance they have of defending themselves before the courts in Guyane.[5] Maroons are frequent victims of this situation, especially the young, who are incarcerated in large numbers. In 2002, we estimated that some 80 percent of the prisoners in the central penitentiary were foreigners who could not speak French. And a more recent study found that only 10 percent of the patients in the Saint-Laurent hospital could express themselves in French.[6] It seems clear that the particularities of immigration in Guyane need radical solutions despite republican norms, as well as Creole attitudes, that create a formidable challenge to reform.

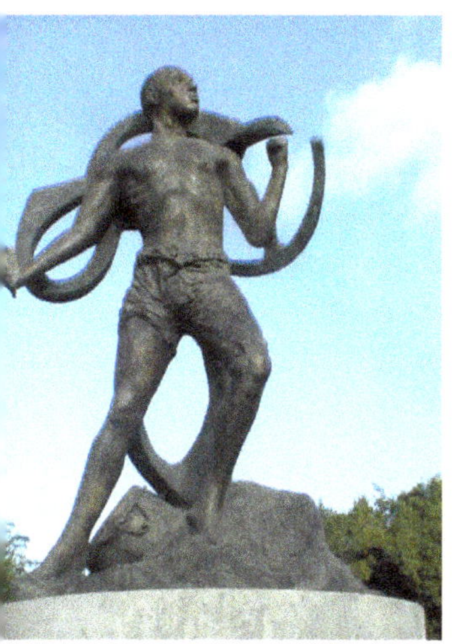

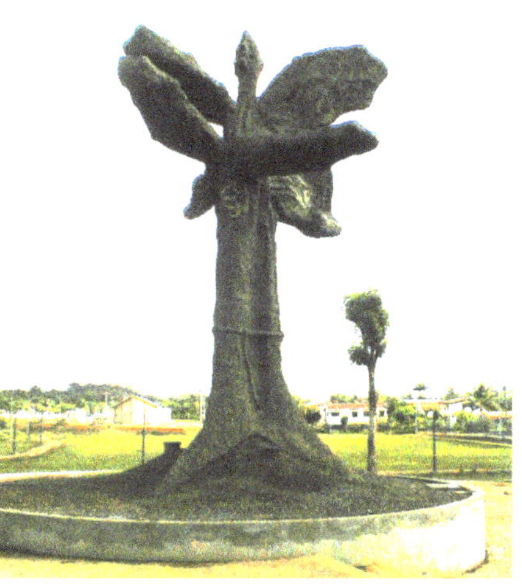

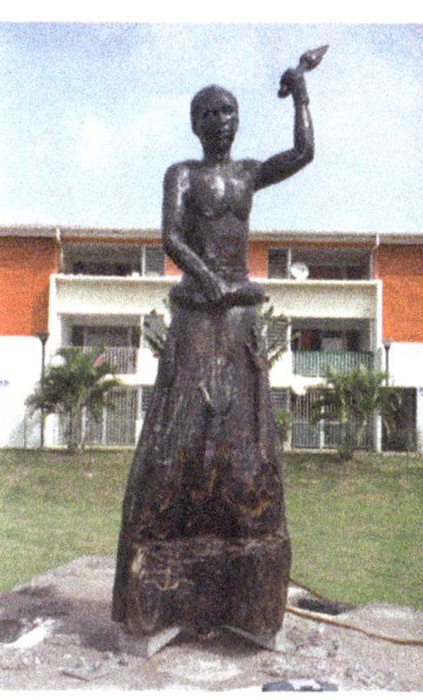

Monuments to the *Nèg Mawon* erected in Martinique during the commemoration of the 150th anniversary of the abolition of slavery: (a) H. Charpentier, *Place du Nègre Marron*, Diamant, Martinique, 1998; (b) Khokho René-Corail, *Nèg Mawon, Arbre de la liberté*, Place d'Armes, Lamentin, cast by Alberto Lescay (Cuba), 1998; (c) Narcisse Ranaresson, *Nègre Marron*, Trois-Ilets, Martinique, 1998.

The Social Security agents who deal with medical services invent rules stricter than those required by law when dealing with foreigners. Their stereotypes include behaviors: "Maroons are like children, . . . Amerindians drink their welfare checks," etc. These stereotypes are used to justify imbalances in power.

The case of Maroons in Saint-Laurent is interesting. They make up the majority of the city, but the professionals who control access to medical services are Creoles and European French. When these latter describe the behavior of their clients, they speak of "the history of the Maroons" and their lack of readiness for modern life . . . Some Creoles insist that Maroons "have left their forest" solely to get the benefits of the French welfare system. They contrast this with their own position as tax-paying citizens. Foreigners and all Maroons are the main victims of this administrative debacle. This combination of racist and territorial inequality is far from being random. It is the clear product of centuries of history in Guyane.

Estelle Carde (author of *Discriminations et Accès aux soins en Guyane française* [Montreal: Presse de l'Université de Montréal, 2016]), in *The Conversation*, April 6, 2017, https://theconversation.com/guyane-quand-le-racisme-empeche-lacces-aux-soins-75739

> The mayor of Cayenne, Marie-Laure Phinéra-Horth, who participated in 2018's carnival in the Neg' Mawon group, asked in an interview on Guyane 1ère [the country's main radio/TV station]: "Don't we need a law to limit the number of births?" targeting "the minorities who arrive in our land" and "the insecurity [crime] caused by youths on our territory."
>
> *France-Guyane*, January 24, 2018

Alukus, who make up only 10 percent of Guyane's Maroon population, continue to speak on behalf of all Maroons in Guyane, and they have the backing of their Creole political allies. To cite only the most recent example: the Grand conseil coutumier des populations amérindiennes et bushinengué (Great traditional council of Amerindian and Maroon populations), established with considerable pomp by French law under the aegis of the prefect in February 2018, consists of eight Maroon leaders (six official "captains" and two leaders of Maroon "associations"). All are Aluku men—there isn't a single Okanisi or Saamaka or Pamaka representative. How much longer will the other three groups, who are ten times more numerous in Guyane than the Alukus, accept this political anomaly (some might say "oppression")?

In the first edition of this book (2003), we evoked the possibility of a future time when the attractions of a pan-Maroon identity might gain supremacy among the different groups in Guyane, citing the increase in "mixed" marriages and the growth of popular music groups that included Maroons from different groups. "A pan-Maroon identity, based in part on such shared cultural tastes and practices," we wrote, "is a genuine possibility for the future."

Today we feel less sure. We wonder whether the historical rivalries and differences among the four Maroon peoples in Guyane aren't perceived as sufficiently important to put a brake on the development of a collective politics or identity as *marron* or *bushinengué*. Among Okanisis, for example, the differences between those who identify as "Opo" (coming from villages on the upper Tapanahoni) or "Bilo" (on the lower Tapanahoni) or "Cottica" (from the Moengo region of Suriname) remain important. And the differences between Alukus, Okanisis, and Pamakas are yet stronger—without even considering the fierce communal pride of Saamakas, who often use the pejorative term *Dyuga* to refer to the other three peoples collectively.

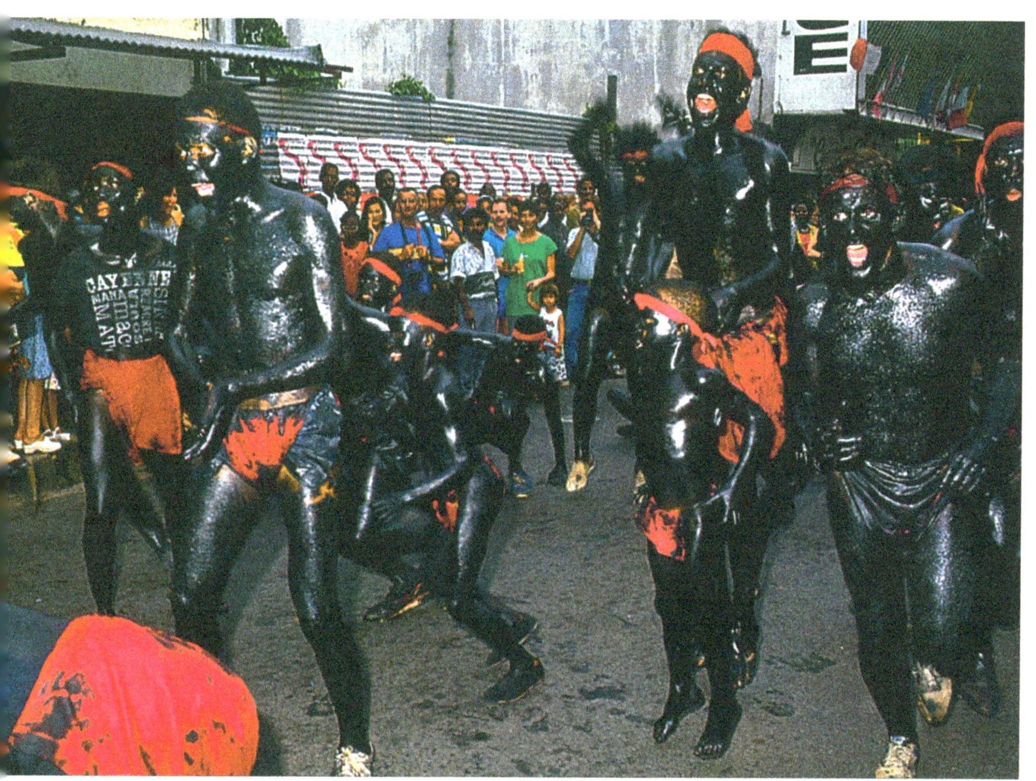

Carnival: *Les Neg' Mawon* (postcard, 1990s). In a venerable Cayenne carnival tradition, bands of Creoles (and more recently, European French) smear themselves with used motor oil and soot, don breechcloths and red kerchiefs, and paint their lips red with annatto juice. In the guise of stereotyped Maroons, they menace the crowd, holding it back to keep the parade route clear. This tradition is not appreciated by real Maroons—whether Alukus, Okanisis, Pamakas, or Saamakas—who take it as a serious insult.

That said, the prejudice that Maroons experience from Creoles, together with their position at the bottom of Guyane's class system, probably unites them more significantly than do any cultural traits they may share. One cannot deny a certain sense of Maroon "nationalism" on occasion, for example, in the 2018 victory of the young Okanisi Lénaïck Adam, who was elected *député* to the National Assembly in Paris.[7] Schoolchildren and many parents in the west of Guyane expressed pride that "one of their own" had won (the Barack Obama effect), but that has not yet changed the system.

In 2018, when Maroons already made up 77 percent of the population of Saint-Laurent (poised to surpass Cayenne in population),

According to the American Convention on Human Rights, which applies to Indigenous peoples and Maroons: First, it is well established in the Inter-American system that indigenous peoples have been historically discriminated against and disadvantaged and, therefore, that special measures and protections (affirmative action) are required if they are to enjoy equal protection of the law and the full enjoyment of other human rights. These special measures include protection for indigenous languages, cultures, economies, ecosystems, and natural resource base, religious practices, "ancestral and communal lands," and the establishment of an institutional order that facilitates indigenous participation through their freely chosen representatives. The Inter-American Commission of Human Rights (IACHR) characterized the preceding as "human rights also essential to the right to life of peoples." Protection of these rights, then, amounts to a broad prohibition of assimilation and ethnocide.

Fergus MacKay

1. See, among other resources, *Report on the Situation of Human Rights of a Segment of the Nicaraguan Population of Miskito Origin*, OEA/Ser.L/V/II.62, doc.26. (1984), at 76–78, 81; *Report on the Situation of Human Rights in Ecuador*, OEA/Ser.L/V/II.96 doc.10, rev.1 (1997), at 103–104; *Case 7615 (Brazil)*, OEA/Ser.L/V/II.66, doc 10 rev 1 (1985), at 24, 31; and *Third Report on the Situation of Human Rights in the Republic of Guatemala*, OEA/Ser.l/V/II. 67, doc. 9 (1986), at 114.

2. *Human Rights in Guatemala*, 114.

3. Fergus MacKay, "The Rights of Maroons in International Human Rights Law," *Cultural Survival Quarterly* 25, no. 4 (2001): 11.

we asked ourselves how long the Creole mayor (in office since 1983) and his party could expect to hold onto political power.[8] For now, the answer is uncertain, as the local forces that weigh against a single Maroon identity and any sort of what the French call communautarisme remain strong.

In Suriname, things are different, since there remain at least some efforts among Maroons to continue the struggle for collective rights. Having organized themselves and presented their case to the Inter-American Commission of Human Rights in 2000, the Saamaka People demanded collective title to their territory and a strong degree of sovereignty, and the Inter-American Court ruled fully in their favor in 2007.[9] But in Guyane, it looks as if it's already too late (absent the rise of a nativist movement, which seems unlikely to us).

France, invoking the country's centuries-old commitment to that particular version of secularism called *laïcité,* has always opposed international conventions or declarations that grant individuals special rights on the grounds that they are members of a minority group. Moreover, invoking constitutional justifications, France has never signed International Labor Organization Convention 169, which deals with "the rights of indigenous and tribal peoples in nation states . . . who differ from the rest of the national population by their social, cultural, and economic conditions and whose lives are ordered, wholly or in part, by customs and traditions that are their own." France's position runs counter to the resolution of the European Parliament adopted in 1994 that "recognizes the rights of indigenous peoples [and Maroons] to be masters of their own destiny in choosing their political status and their territory, in defending their collective property, in maintaining their usage of customary law for judicial matters, and in respecting the treaties they have made in times past."[10] It is hard to

It is true that in New Caledonia, the French Republic has finally come to grips with the demands of the Kanak people. But those of the Amerindians [and Maroons] of Guyane remain forgotten. These people should, however, be able to have recourse to International Labor Organization Convention No. 169, which recognizes the right of autochthonous and tribal people "to control their own institutions, way of life, and economic development, and to work out their identities, languages, and religions within the context of the nation states in which they live." Alas! France has not yet signed on to this convention. . . . Today, very serious problems confront the Amerindians and Maroons of Guyane. . . . The traditional customary rights to collective land ownership on the part of kin groups—involving gardens, hunting, and fishing—have never been recognized by French law. The government in fact foresees a process of individualization of land ownership which will lead, in the case of Amerindians and Maroons, to the breakup of their communal way of life and the disappearance of a mode of exploitation that, for centuries, has preserved the Amazonian forest and its fragile soils. In fact, in regard to customary law, it is time to change the laws of France.

Simone Dreyfus Gamelon, "Les Indiens de la République," *Le Monde,* January 16, 1999

imagine that Alukus, the only Maroon people who could claim a traditional territory in Guyane, would have the will or desire to organize themselves to fight for such rights. And given their status as immigrants in Guyane, the Okanisis, Pamakas, and Saamakas can have no hopes in this regard.

If Guyane (and France) truly wished to acknowledge the contributions of Maroons to the colony (and later the *département*) in both cultural and economic domains, it might begin by publicly recognizing that Maroons have played a key role in the development of Guyane, by granting residence papers to the thousands of Maroon "illegals," and by injecting a large amount of money and other resources to bring the schools, hospitals, clinics, justice system, and other social services that serve Maroons up to the same level enjoyed by the residents of Cayenne.

The Maroons who now make up more than a third of the population of Guyane can never return to their traditional villages. In this sense, France has "won" its gamble of forced *francisation*. But at what price for Maroons? Mightn't it be time to make a much more serious effort to promote equal opportunities for young Maroons? Such an effort would require money, personnel, and, especially, political will.

With the passage of time and the succession of generations, the assimilation of Maroons into the society of Guyane continues apace. (If a few militants with whom we've spoken prefer to speak of "integration" rather than "assimilation"—a way of life that would maintain a double identity, in the mode of current U.S. identity politics—we would counter that the policies of France continue to push against such practices.) Those young Maroons who succeed in school are becoming increasingly "French." Those who do not—and, unfortunately, they remain the great majority—enter society at the lowest level: marginals, the unemployed, day laborers, drug dealers, and single mothers living on welfare.

The future of Maroons in Guyane depends on political decisions made both in France and in Guyane. (To a lesser degree, it also depends on the shifting political and economic situation in Suriname.) But the people of Guyane may sooner or later be forced to acknowledge the importance of Maroons in Guyane—the extent of their demographic expansion and their many contributions to the economy, culture, and history of the territory. A little respect might be a good beginning.

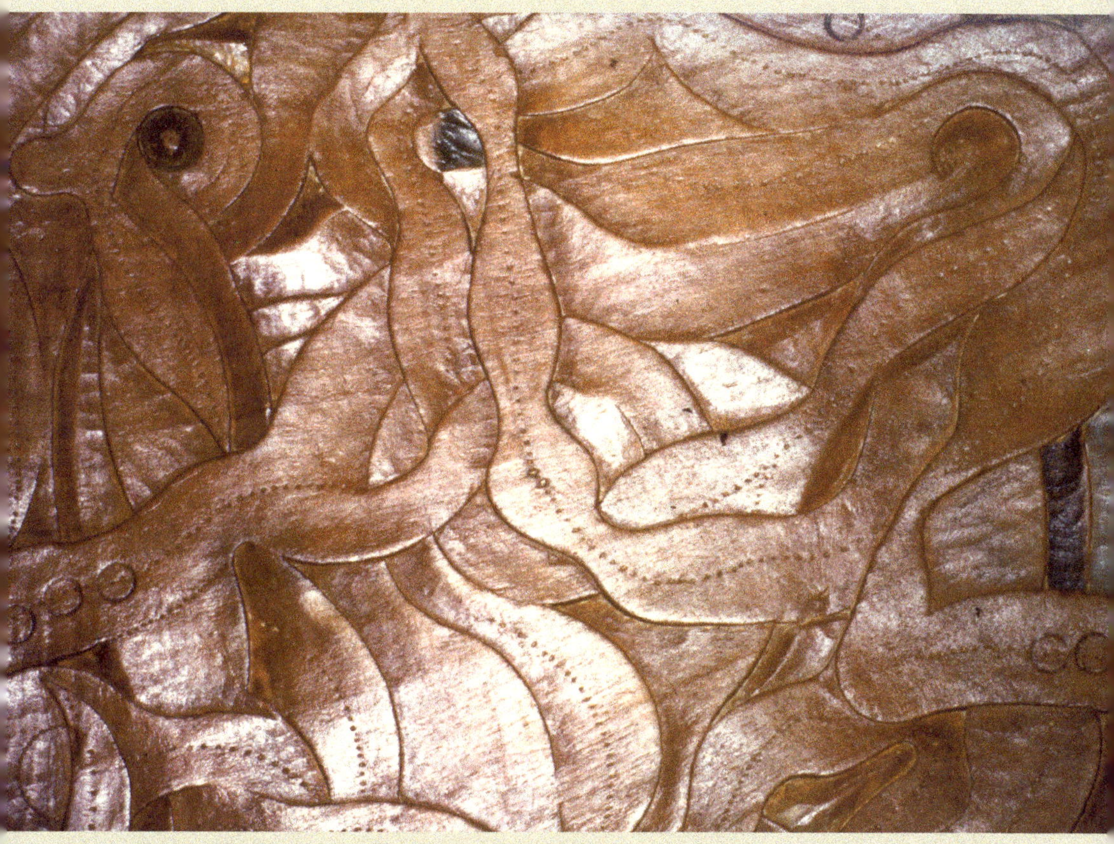

Detail of an Okanisi winnowing tray, collected on the Tapanahoni, 1960s.

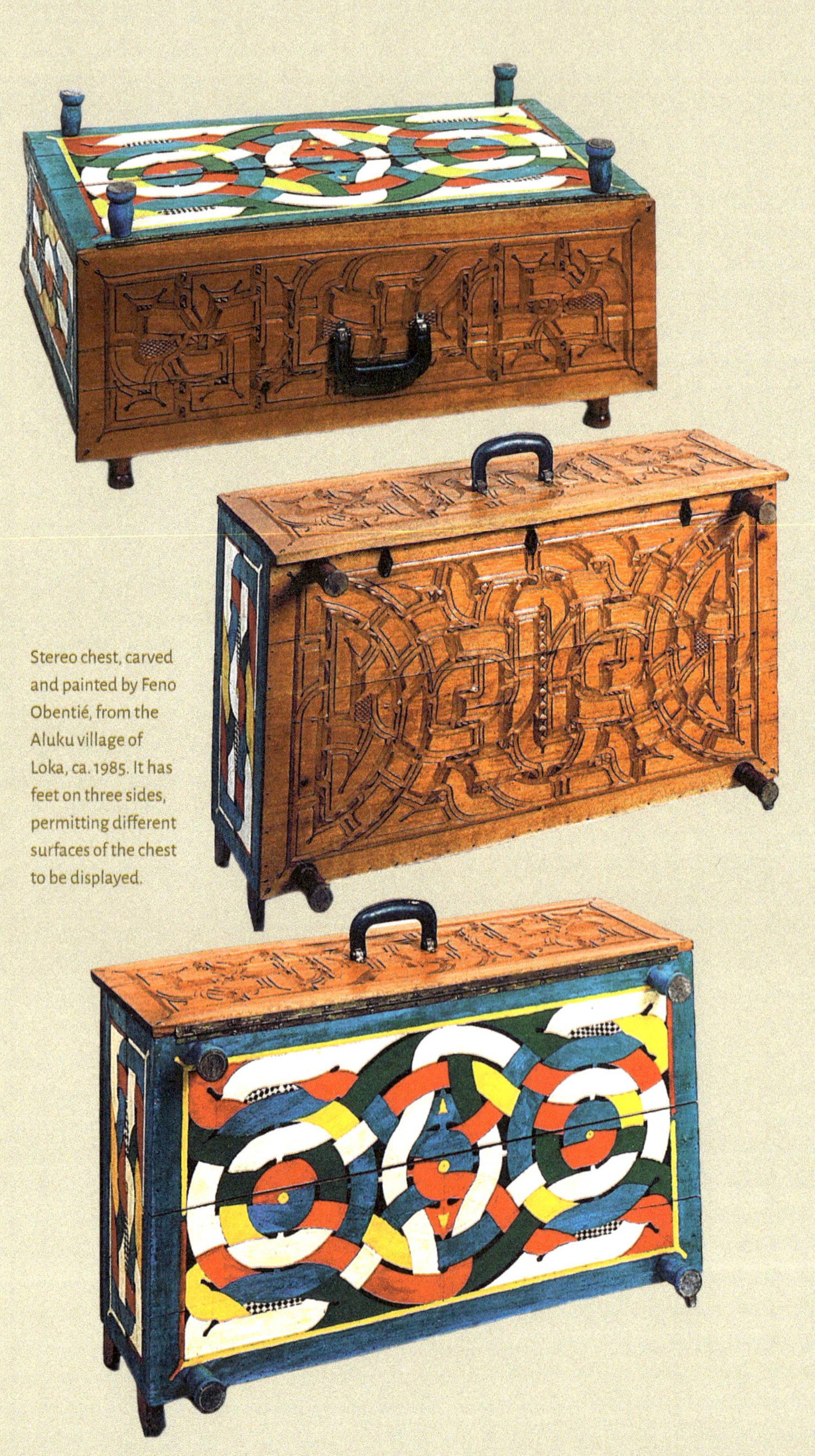

Stereo chest, carved and painted by Feno Obentié, from the Aluku village of Loka, ca. 1985. It has feet on three sides, permitting different surfaces of the chest to be displayed.

Art Gallery

Maroon Men's Woodcarving

The Maroons of Suriname and Guyane are known worldwide for their woodcarving, an art practiced only by men. Until recently, every Maroon man was expected to be able to produce and decorate a whole range of objects in wood, both for his own use and as gifts to wives and lovers. The repertoire included canoes, paddles, doors, house façades, stools, combs, kitchen utensils, laundry beaters, and many other items.

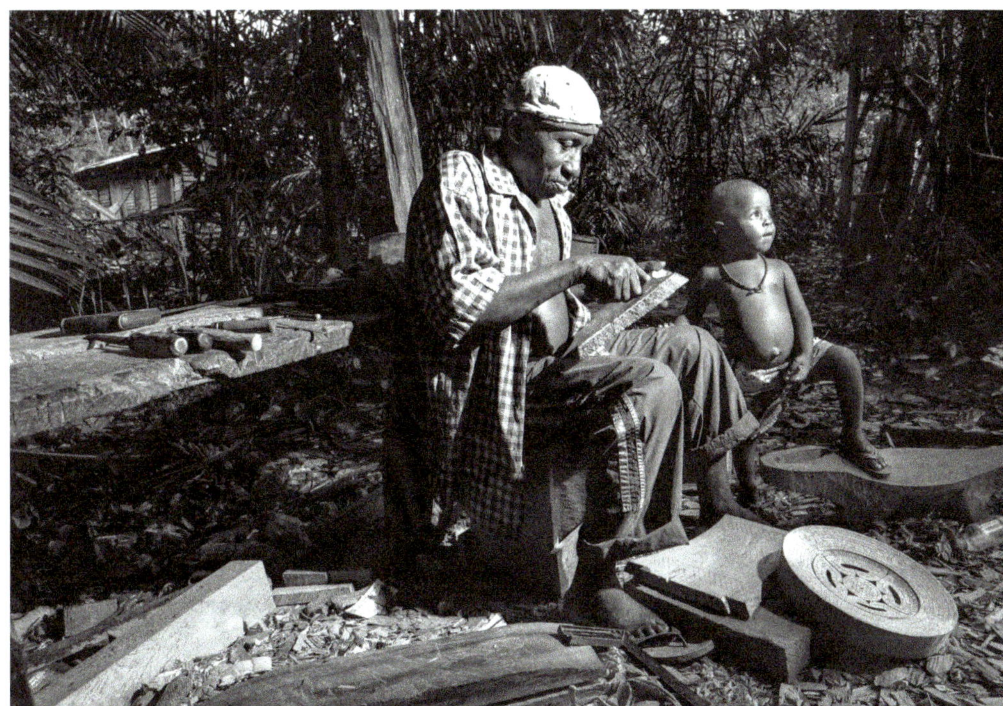

Adelison Amimba, from the Saamaka village of Kambaloa, carving the foot of a mahogany stool, RN1, Saint-Laurent, 2012.

Most objects serve some practical function, but there are also elaborately decorated objects that are purely aesthetic, carvings to be hung with pride on the wall of the house.

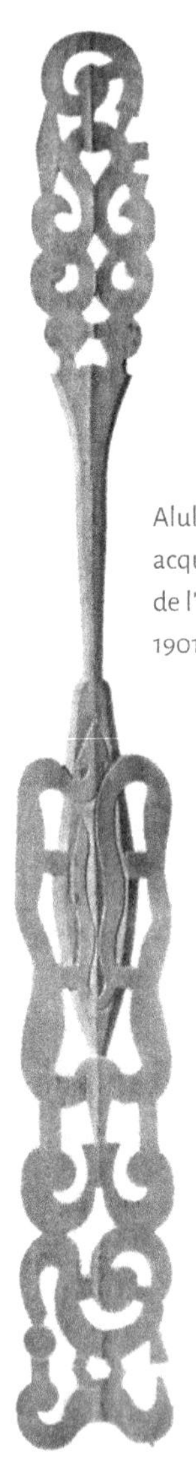

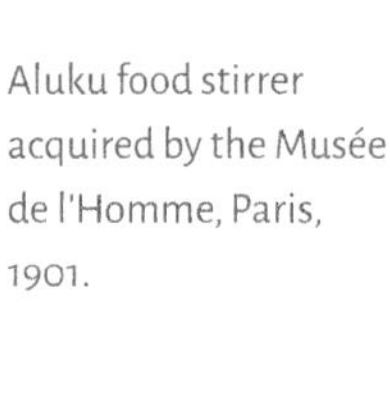

Aluku food stirrer acquired by the Musée de l'Homme, Paris, 1901.

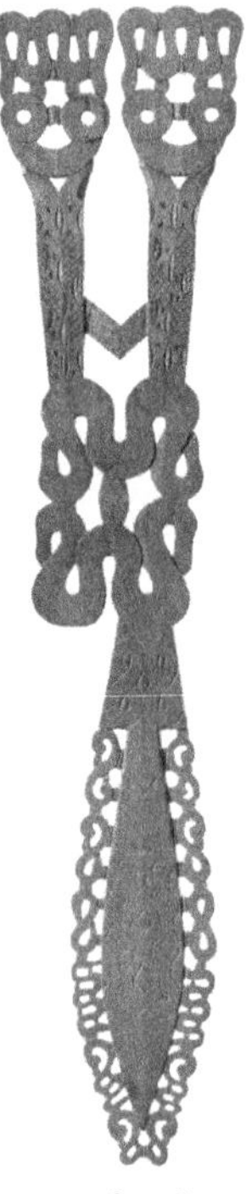

Okanisi food stirrer, collected in the village of Pisiang, 1920s.

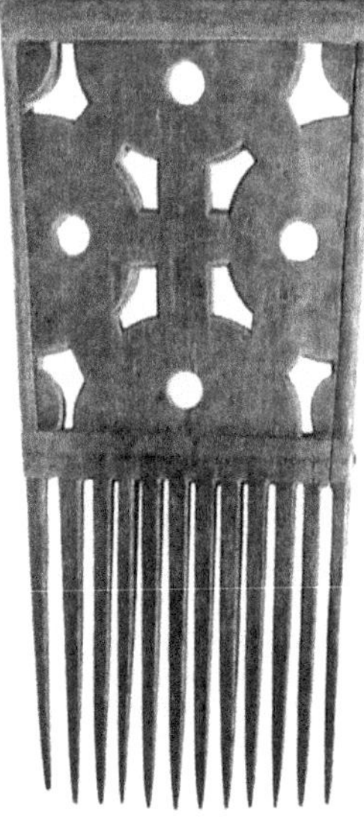

Okanisi comb, collected in the village of Pisiang, 1920s.

In spite of superficial resemblances to various artistic traditions found in Africa, Maroon woodcarving was developed in the Suriname rain forest in the nineteenth century by people many generations removed from the last people to be brought from Africa. Early examples were centered on simple forms such as cutout circles or semicircles, concentric arcs incised with a compass, or cross-hatchings, and large parts of the surfaces were left undecorated.

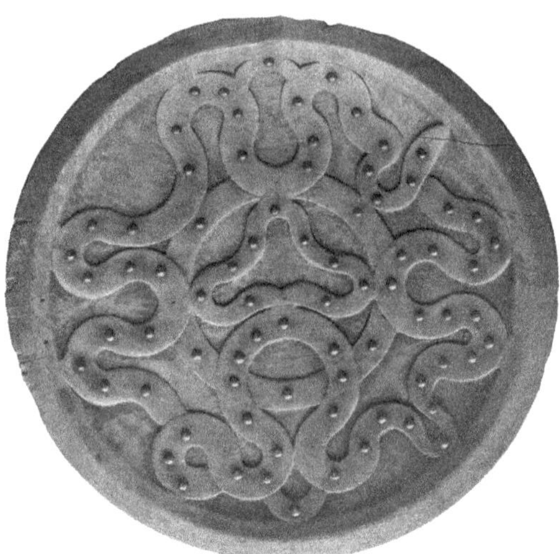

Aluku winnowing tray, carved at the beginning of the twentieth century.

Since then, each generation has introduced its own innovations, stylistic shifts, and virtuosic touches. By the early twentieth century, woodcarvers were already displaying an impressive technical mastery and producing aesthetically sophisticated designs.

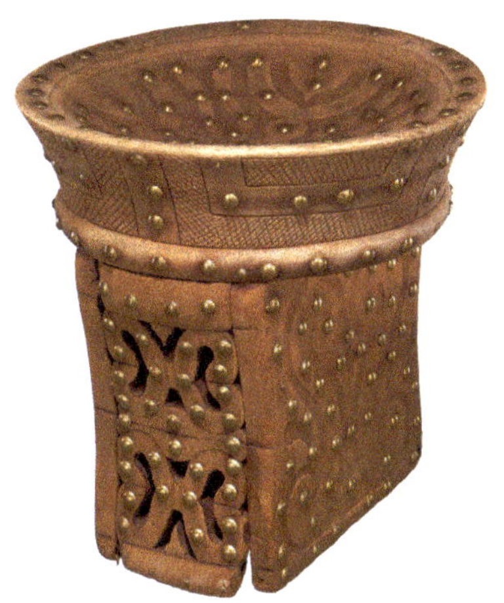

Stool carved by Seketima, from the Saamaka village of Godo, ca. 1915–1920.

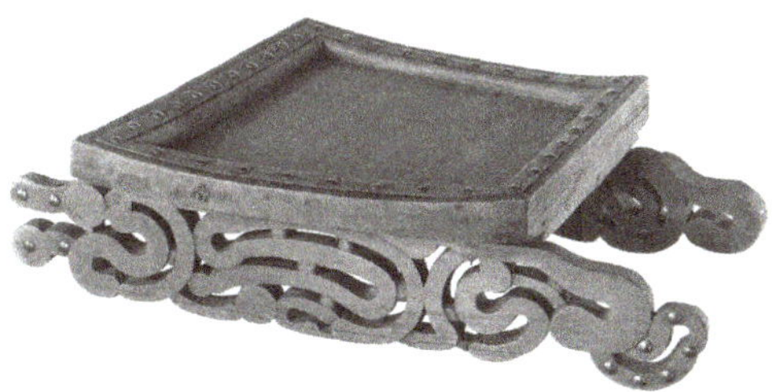

Peanut-grinding board, collected at the end of the 1920s in the Okanisi village of Moompusu.

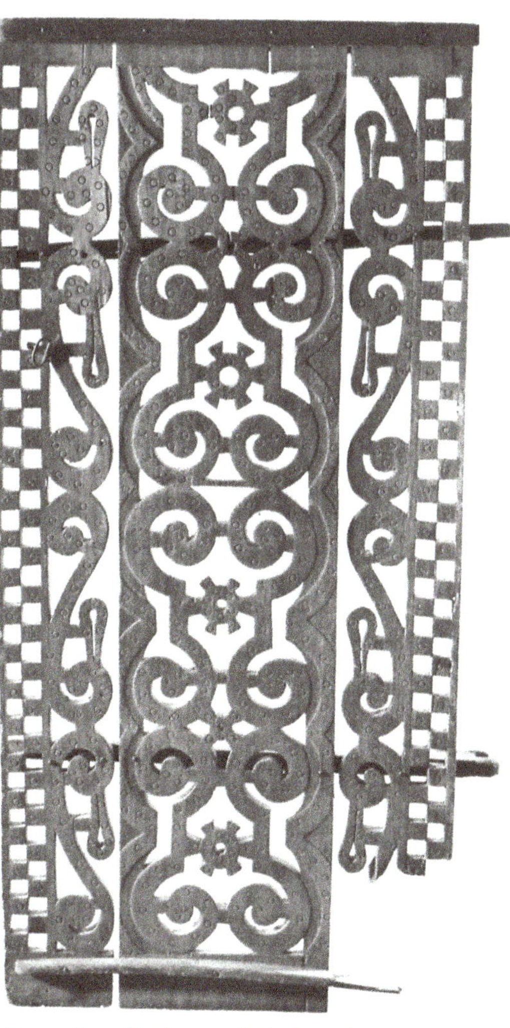

Door, collected in the 1960s in the Saamaka village of Semoisi.

The technique of interlaced ribbons, introduced around 1900, came to dominate both bas-relief and openwork carving for much of the twentieth century.

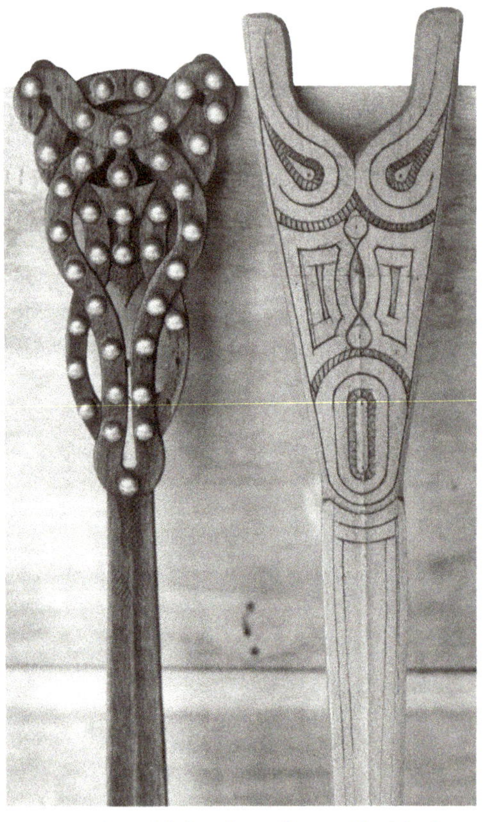

Two Saamaka paddle handles. *Left*, carved by Seketima, from the village of Godo, ca. 1920; *right*, carved by Kondemasa, from the village of Dangogo, ca. 1965.

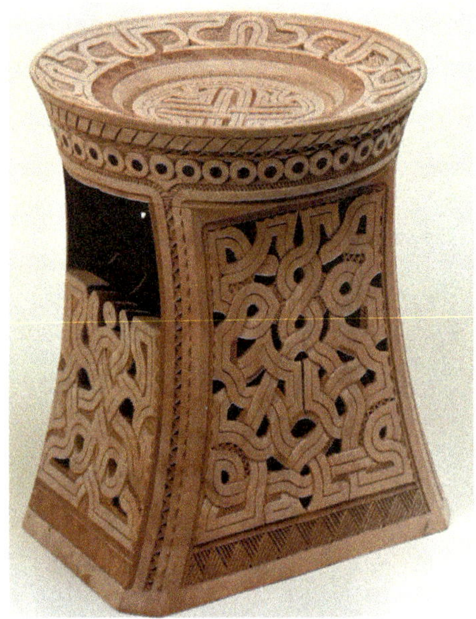

Stool carved in 1997 in Cayenne by Menie Betian, from the Saamaka village of Kambaloa, for his wife.

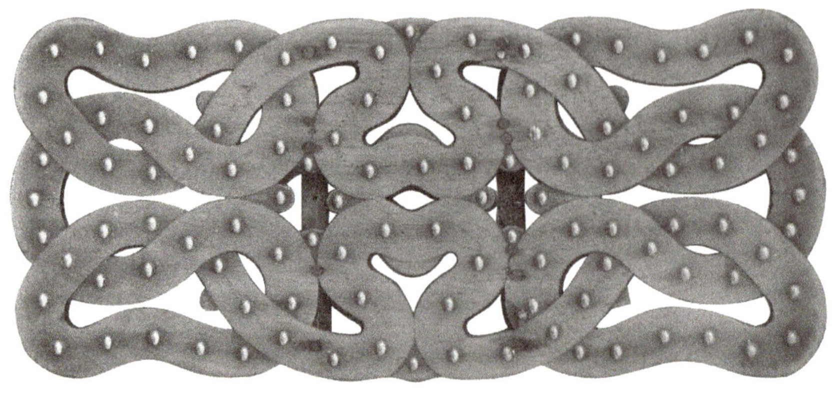

The seat of a stool carved by Seketima, from the Saamaka village of Godo, ca. 1920.

Among Eastern Maroons, bas-relief carving sometimes created undulating compositions of overlapping, layered ribbons.

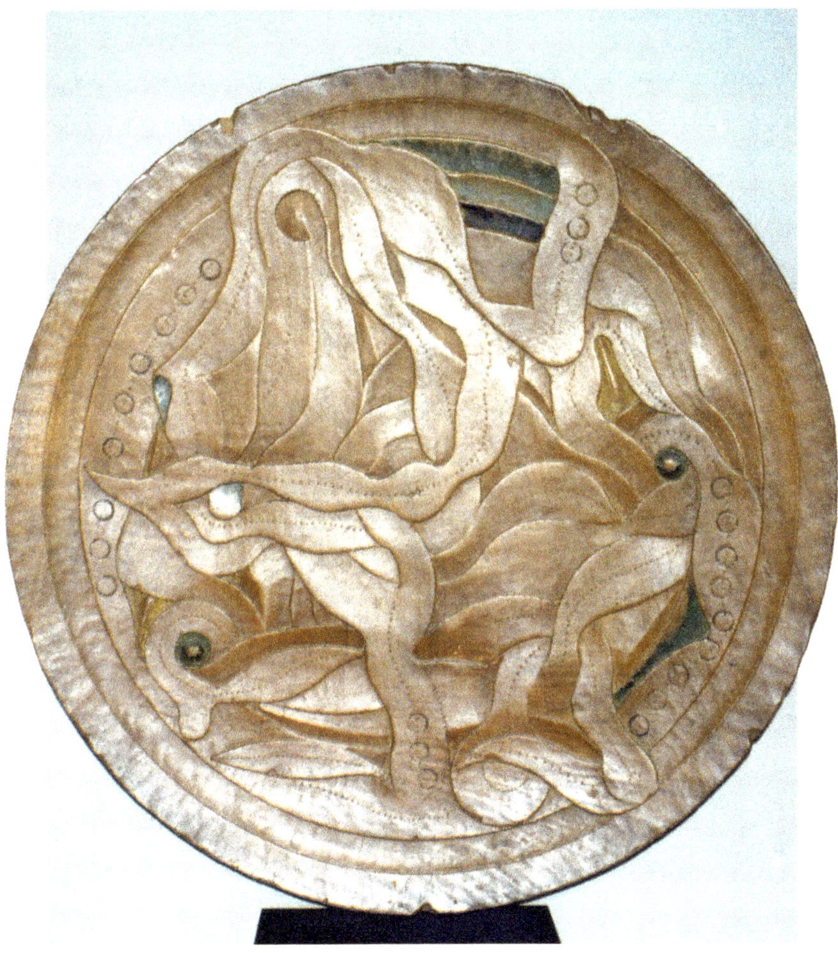

Okanisi winnowing tray, collected in the 1960s on the Tapanahoni (see detail, p. 139).

Saamakas embellish their woodcarvings with inlays, branding, and tacks bought on the coast. Among Eastern Maroons, paint is used to complement the carving. At first the colors were subdued, but they became progressively brighter as acrylic paints became available on the market. Today Eastern Maroons work much more in paint than in carving and call their style *art tembé*.

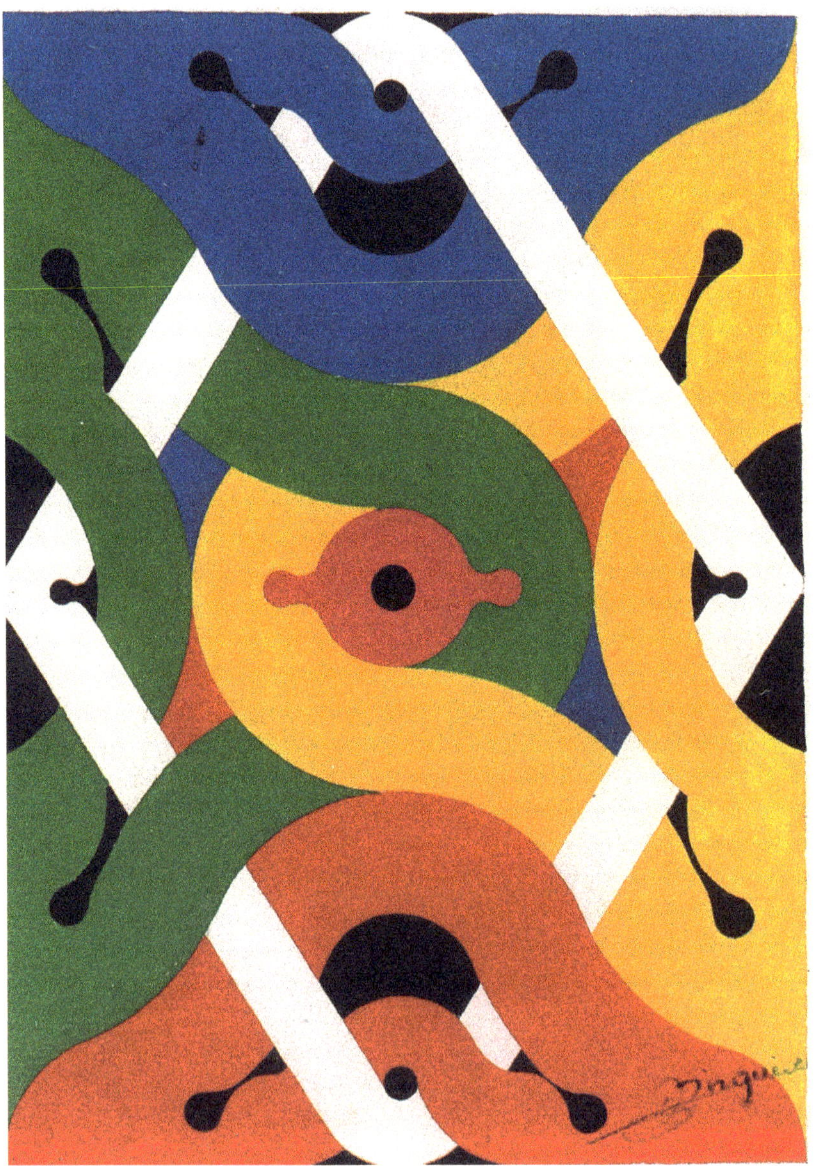

Painting on canvas, by Antoine Dinguiou, from the Aluku village of Papaïchton, 1990. This was around the time that Maroon painting on canvas began.

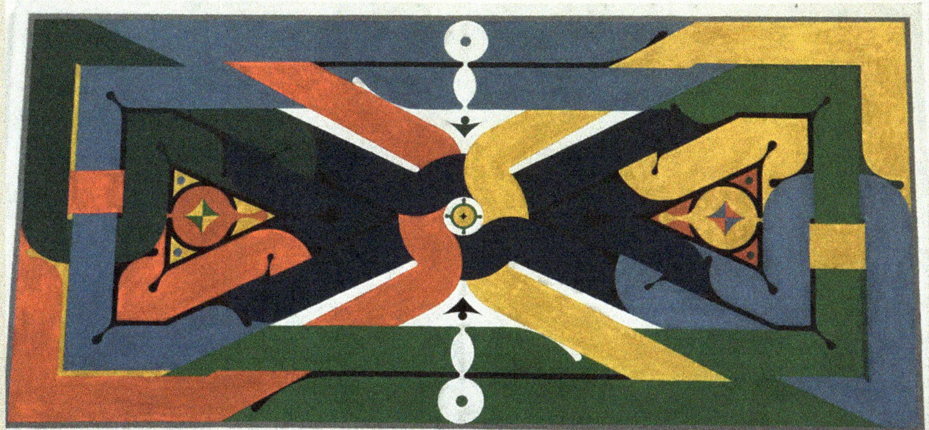

Painting by the Okanisi artist Sawani Pinas, 2011, now on permanent display in the entrance hall of the Hôtel de la Collectivité Territoriale de Guyane, Cayenne.

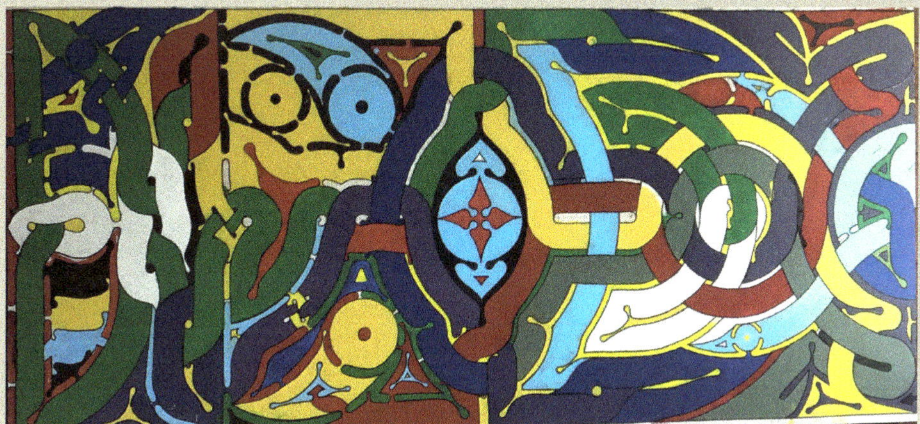

"Fresco made by guests at the Festival Mapa Buku Festi 2015, under the direction of Franklin Amete and Carlos Adaoude," now hanging in the office of the municipal library in Maripasoula.

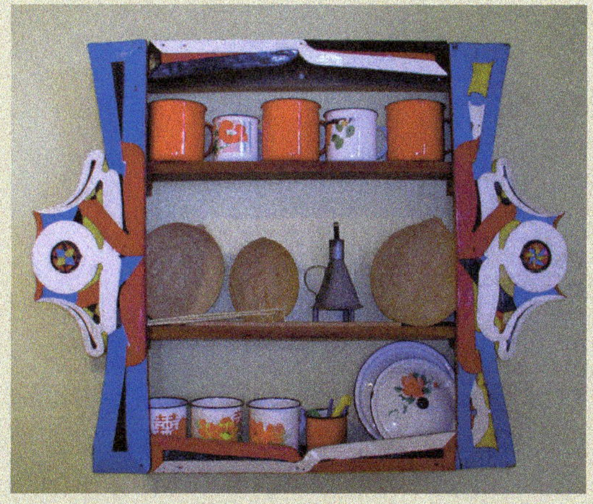

Cupboard made by the Pamaka artist Jozef Obentie Ameikan, Langatabiki, late twentieth century.

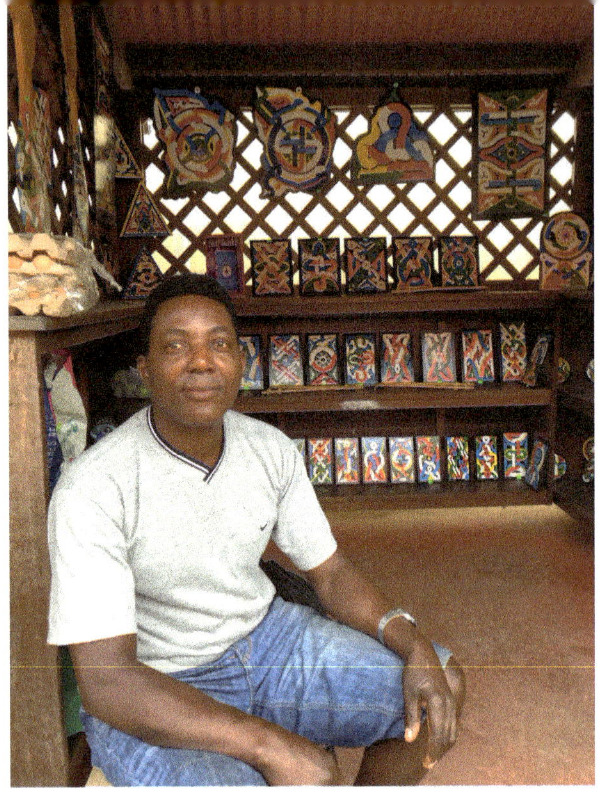

The Okanisi artist Thomas Adiejontoe in his stall at the market in Saint-Laurent, 2018.

The Market for Maroon Men's Art

In the interior of Guyane, there has been a significant decline in woodcarving, especially among Alukus, where it has nearly disappeared. But on the coast, the tourist market (dominated by Saamaka carvers since its beginnings in the 1960s) is increasingly active. The "classic" forms made by Saamakas—folding stools and chairs, combs, and end tables sculpted in cedar—continue to be popular items.

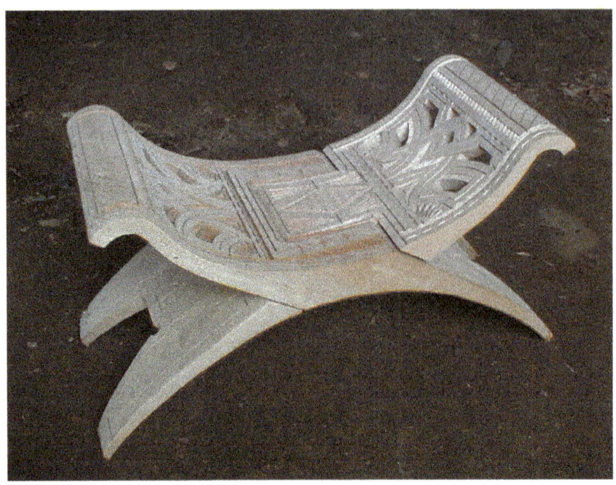

Folding stool, carved in the workshop of Mando Amimba, from the Saamaka village of Kambaloa, Cayenne, 2002.

Cedar is also used for a whole range of knickknacks, for example, small figures of anteaters and caimans, or the Ariane rocket.

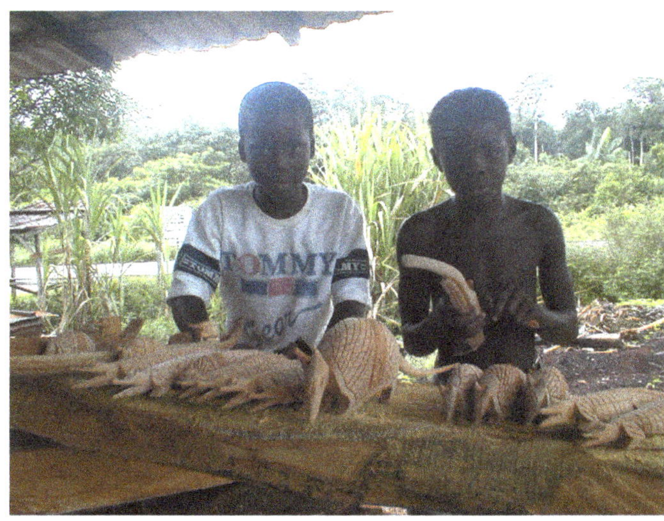

Young Saamaka woodcarvers, Route de Régina, 2002.

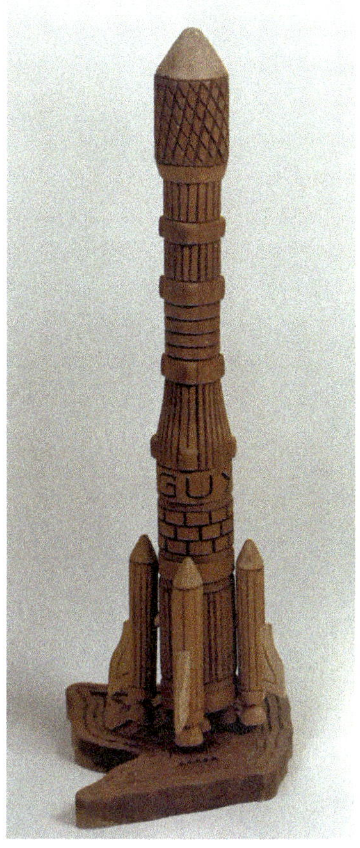

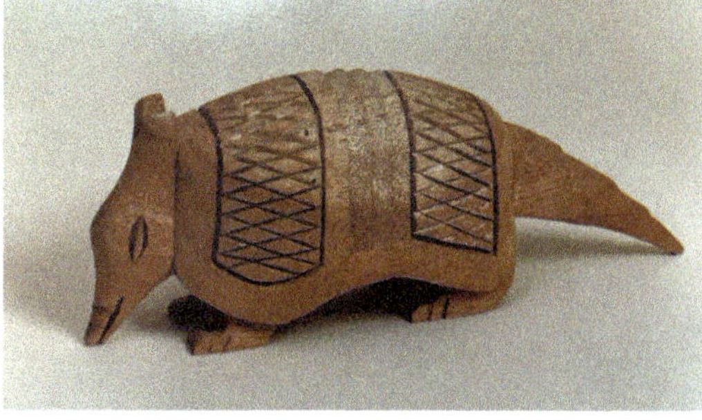

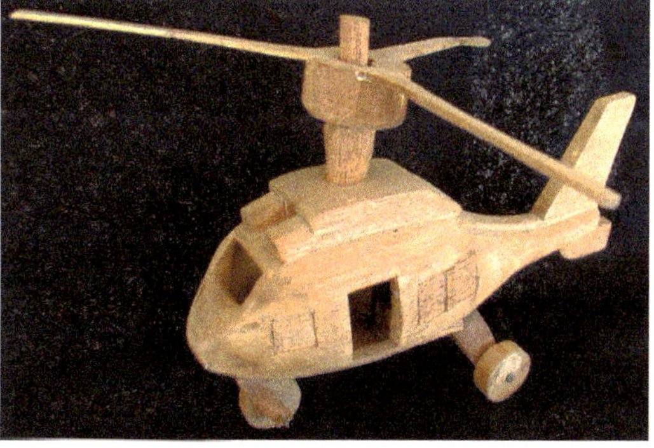

Carvings made in 1990 by Saamaka boys in the workshop of Mando Amimba: an Ariane rocket by Apindagoon, from the village of Kambaloa; an armadillo by Miseli, from the village of Dangogo; and a helicopter made by Mando for his six-year-old son.

During the 1990s, woodcarvers began working with letterwood, producing familiar forms in highly polished variants, but also adding new items to the repertoire, such as salad servers, jewelry boxes, and large animal statues.

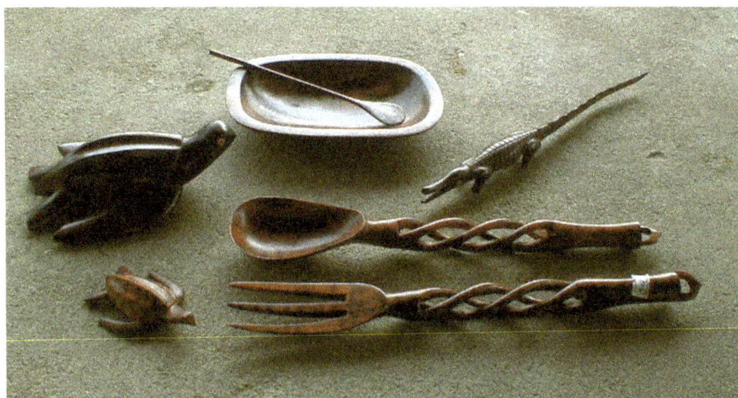

Objects in letterwood (Saamaka: *pauletu*), carved in the Saamaka workshop Ici Vola on RD9.

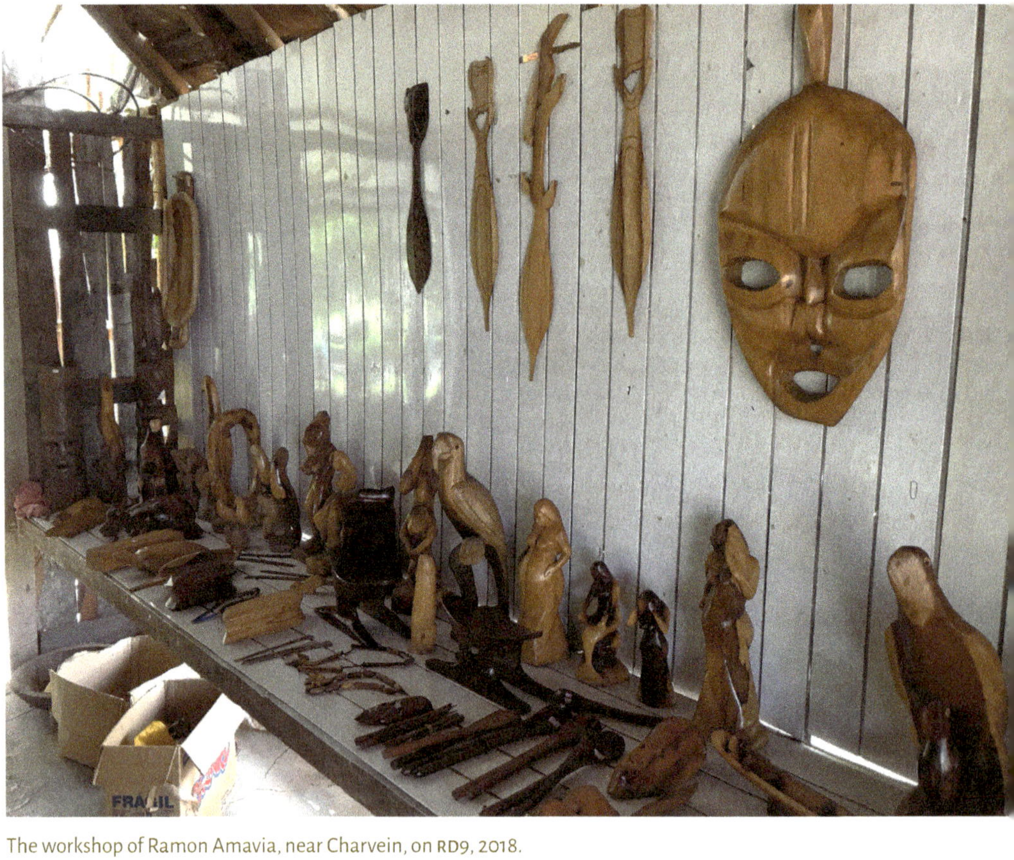

The workshop of Ramon Amavia, near Charvein, on RD9, 2018.

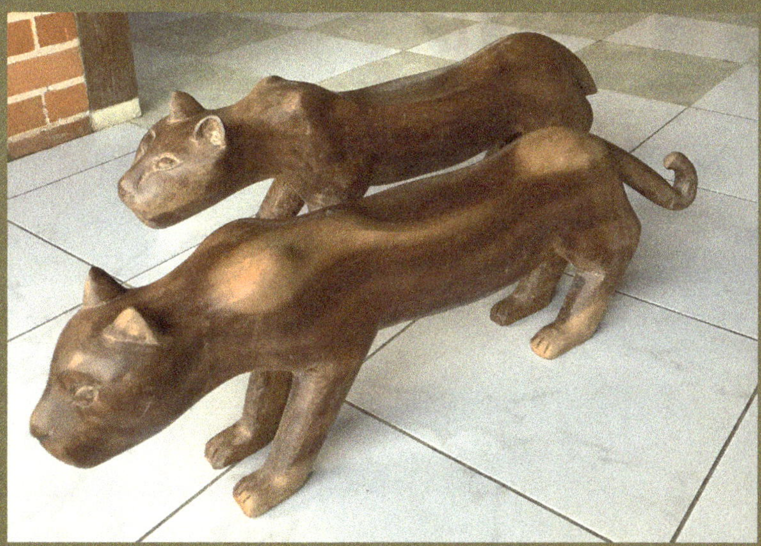

Two jaguars carved by Adelison Amimba in basralocus wood (French: *bois angélique*; Saamaka: *sindyapeetu*).

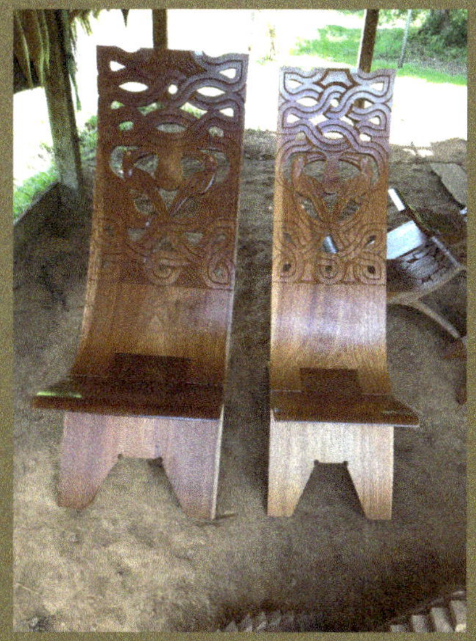

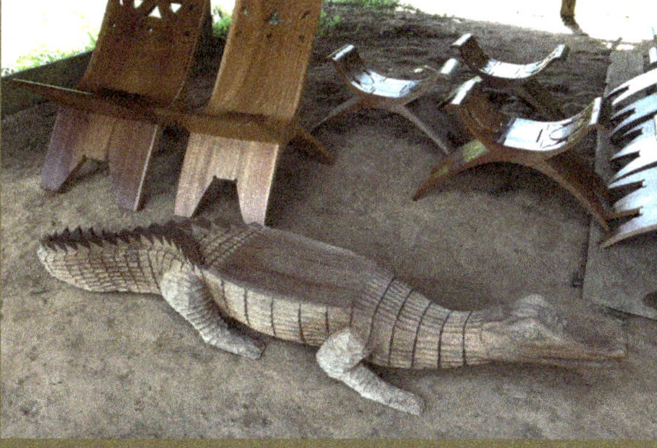

Carvings by John Zoli, from the Saamaka village of Kambaloa, in the workshop of Madjo Kampu, on National Route 1.

Toward the end of the twentieth century, woodcarvers began consulting illustrated books on Maroon art for inspiration, reproducing forms and styles that their fathers and grandfathers had created, but adapting them in subtle ways to a more current aesthetic. A comb made in the 1960s that we illustrated in a 1980 book, for example, inspired a number of copies in the 1990s.

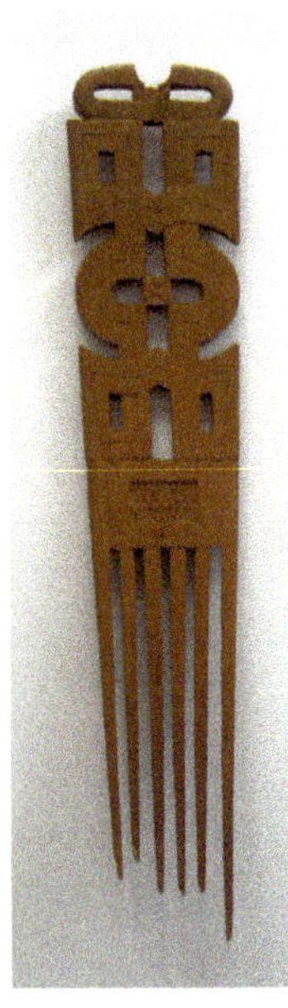

Comb carved in 1963 in a Saamaka village on the Pikilio and illustrated in a 1980 book.

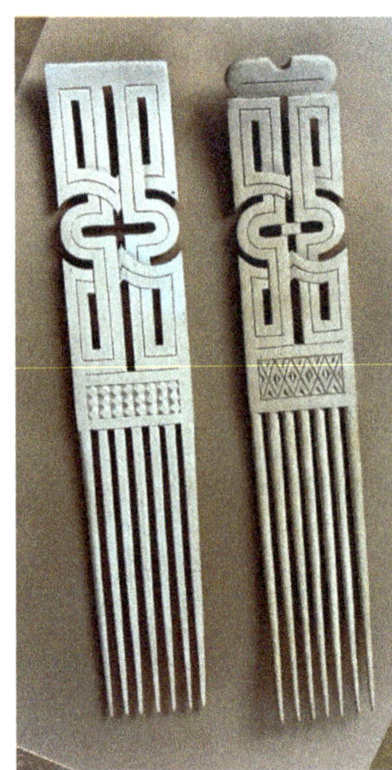

Left: Comb carved near Saint-Laurent by Georges or Simeon Paulus, from the Saamaka village of Botopasi, 1995. *Right*: Comb carved near Saint-Laurent in 1990 by Soni Bodji, from the Saamaka village of Semoisi.

Today a number of Maroon artists have become full-time professionals, with Facebook pages and websites, and they are exploring innovative outlets such as coloring books for children. Governmental funding facilitates the diffusion of their work both in Guyane and elsewhere. In 2014, for example, the city of Toulouse devoted its annual Rio Loco festival to "the discovery of *art tembé*" (especially the vibrantly colored paintings of Franky Amete); Saamaka carvers collaborated on a sculpture with students from Paris's School of Fine Arts in a project organized by the Chercheurs d'art association of Mana; and Lobi Cognac contributed a statue to the Changchun World Sculpture Park in China (the country where he sculpted a representation of "a couple, resistors to oppression," that was installed in 2008 in a traffic circle outside Cayenne).

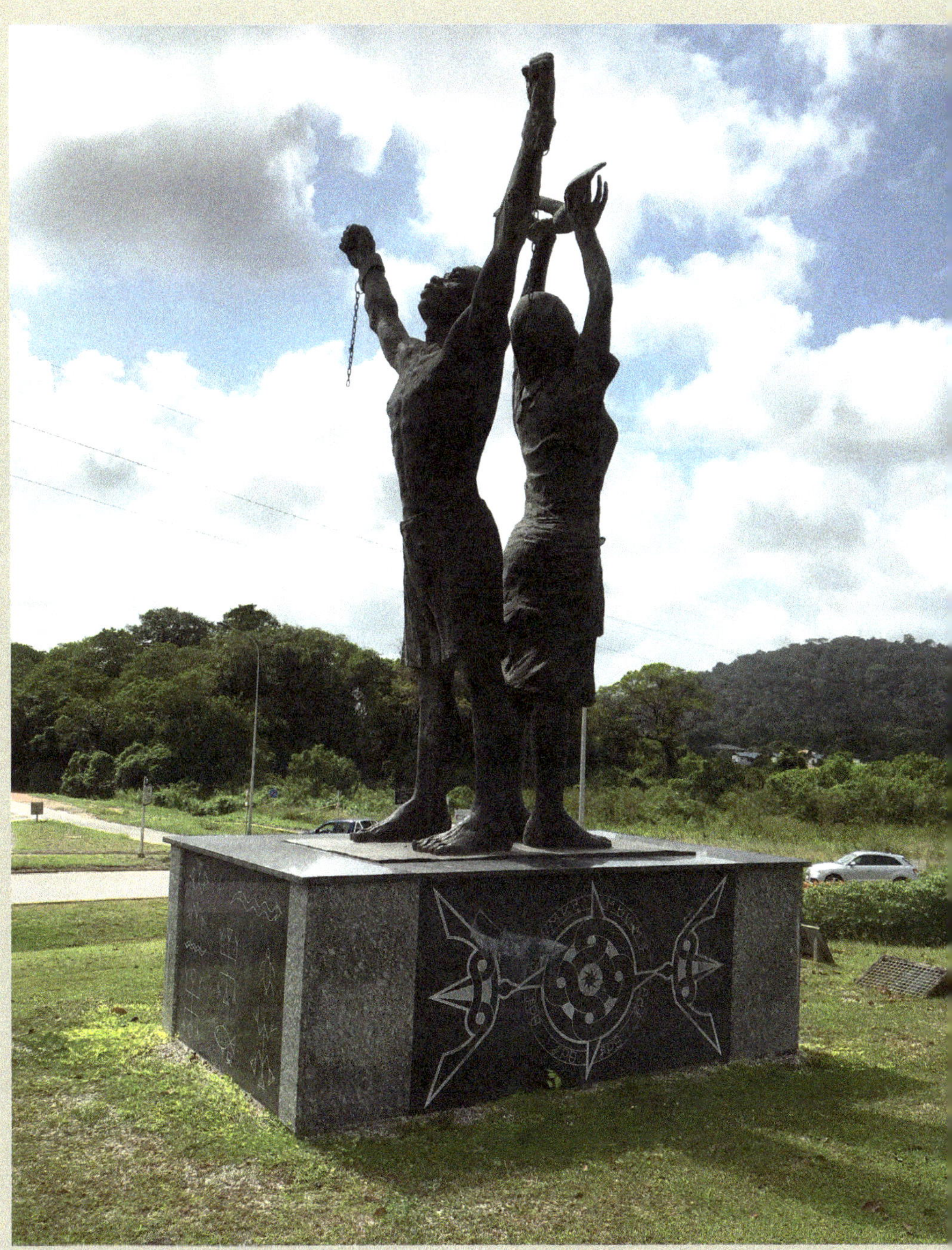

Lobie Cognac, *Les Marrons de la Liberté*, Remire.

The eclectic work of the Okanisi artist Marcel Pinas (based in Suriname, but a frequent visitor to Guyane) ranges from commemorative monuments, festivals, and open-air installations to oil paintings and even glass sculptures.

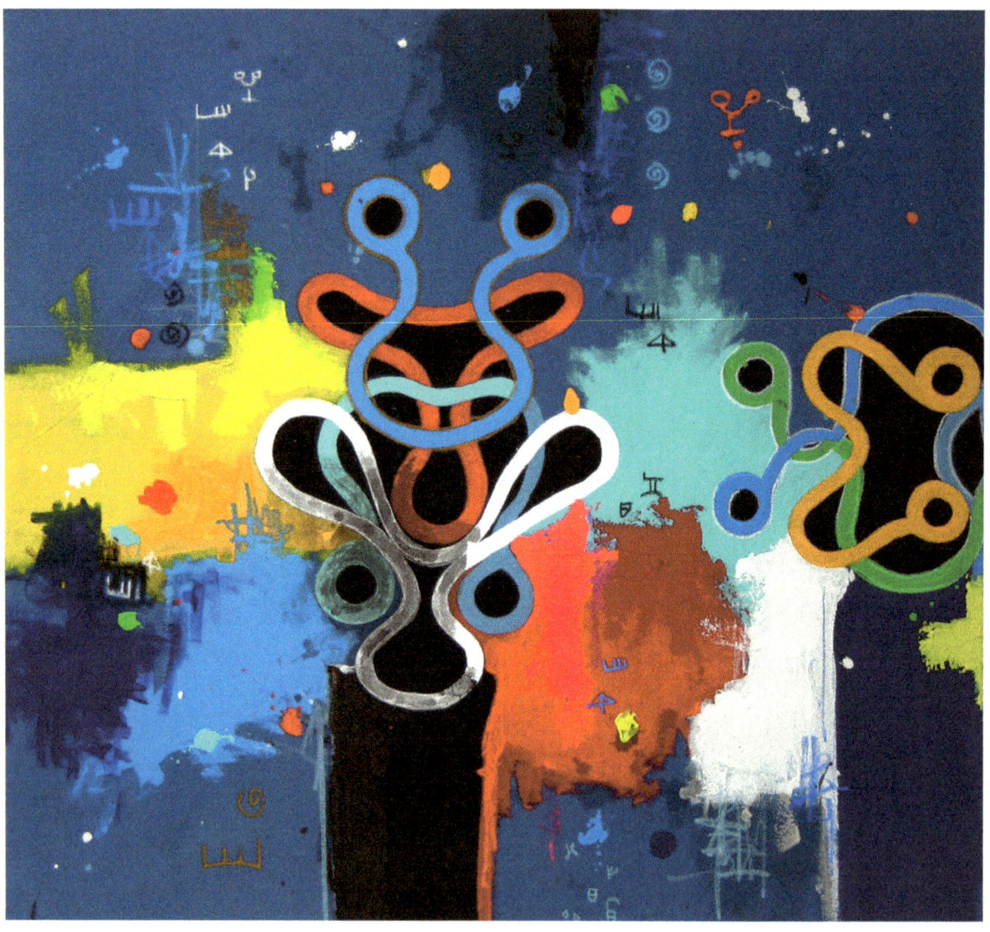

Marcel Pinas, *Baw tembe*, 2007, mixed media on canvas, 145 × 160 cm.

Maroon Women's Art

In the villages of the interior, when a woman received a woodcarving from a man, she would reciprocate the gift of love with artwork of her own. Cloth and thread imported from the coast have long provided materials for beautiful shoulder capes, breechcloths, and other men's garments in patchwork, appliqué, and embroidery. At the end of the nineteenth century, the main form of women's decorative sewing was embroidery, but patchwork was soon added.

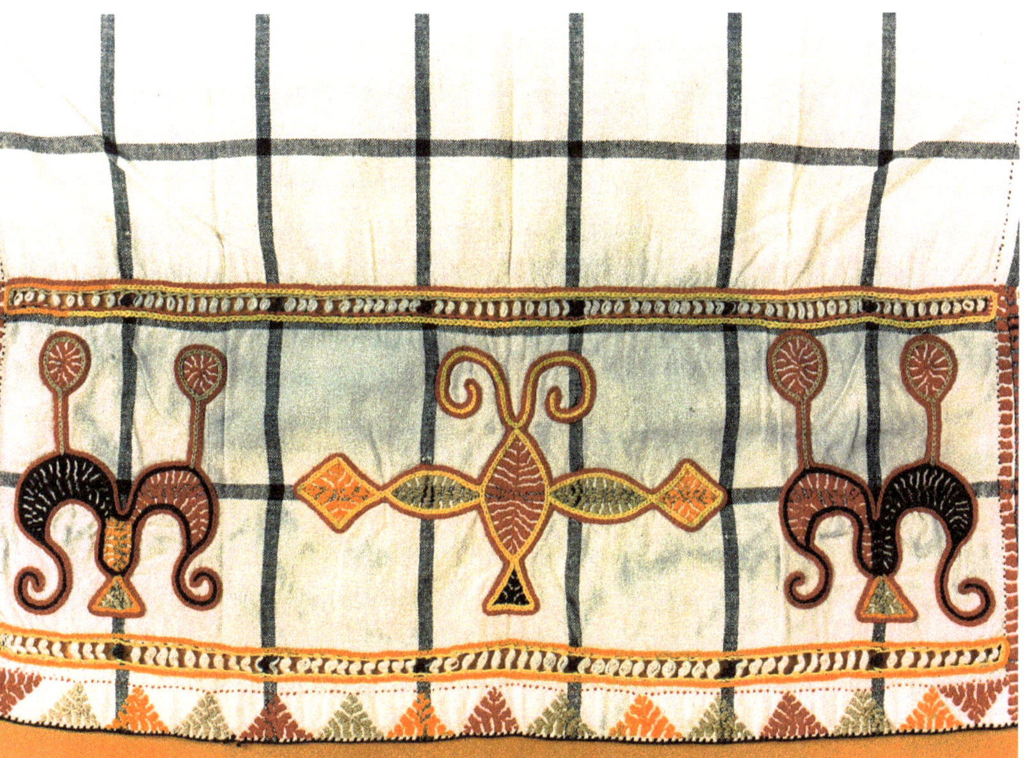

Embroidered breechcloth, sewn by Ma Diala, from the Okanisi village of Fandaaki, 1910–1915.

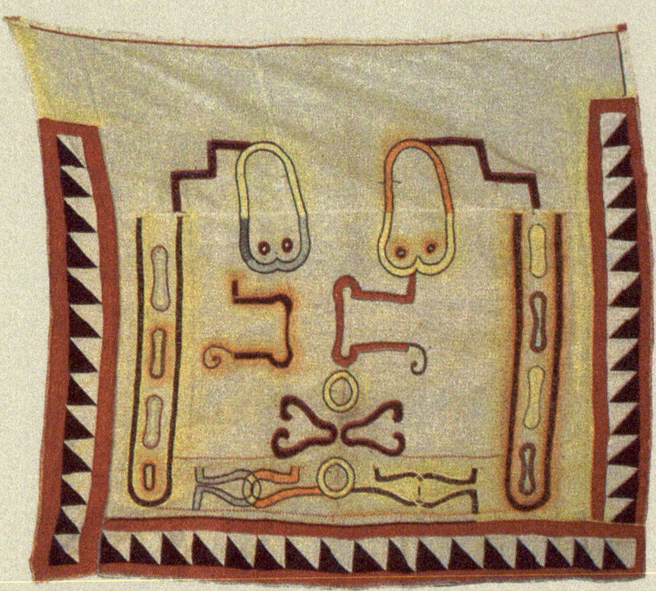

A shoulder cape sewn at the beginning of the twentieth century for Agbago Aboikoni, future paramount chief of the Saamaka. He told us that it was embroidered either by his mother, Boo, from the village of Dangogo, or by his first wife, Apumba, from the village of Pempe. He kept it to decorate his coffin—see the photos on pages 22 and 120.

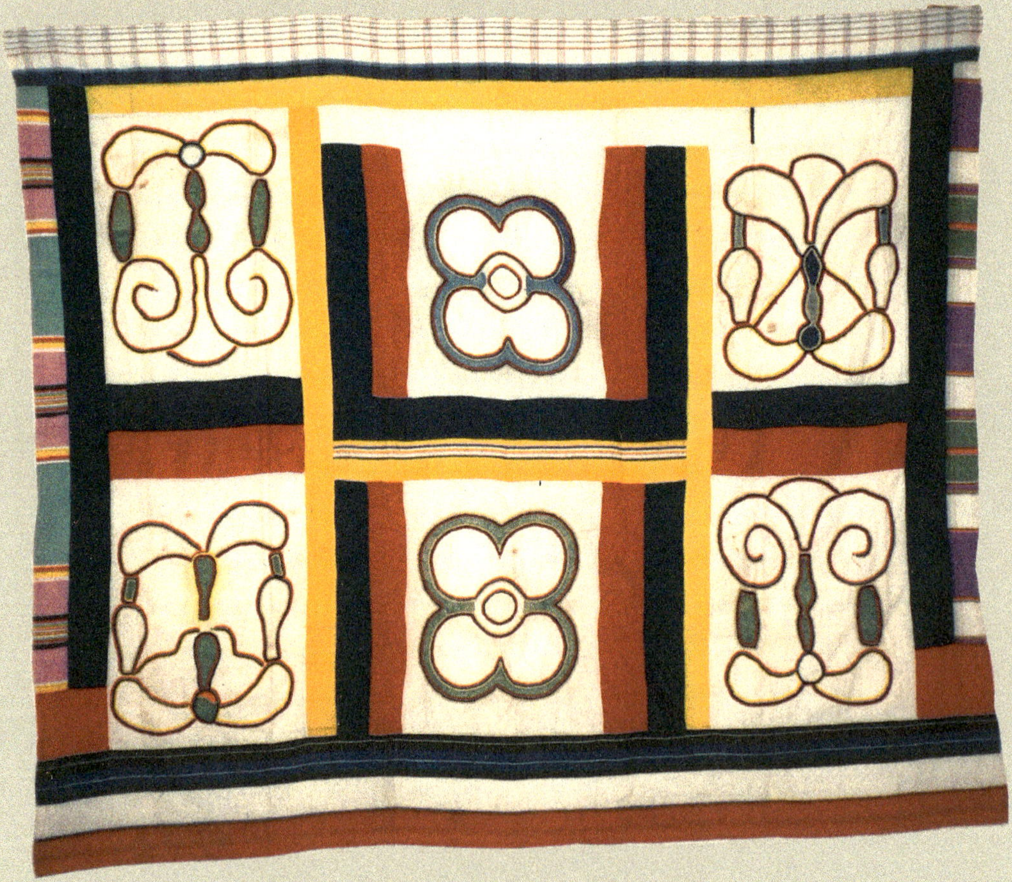

A shoulder cape sewn for Head Captain Faansisonu from the Saamaka village of Dangogo.

Compositions made from narrow strips of striped trade cotton were especially popular in the middle of the twentieth century.

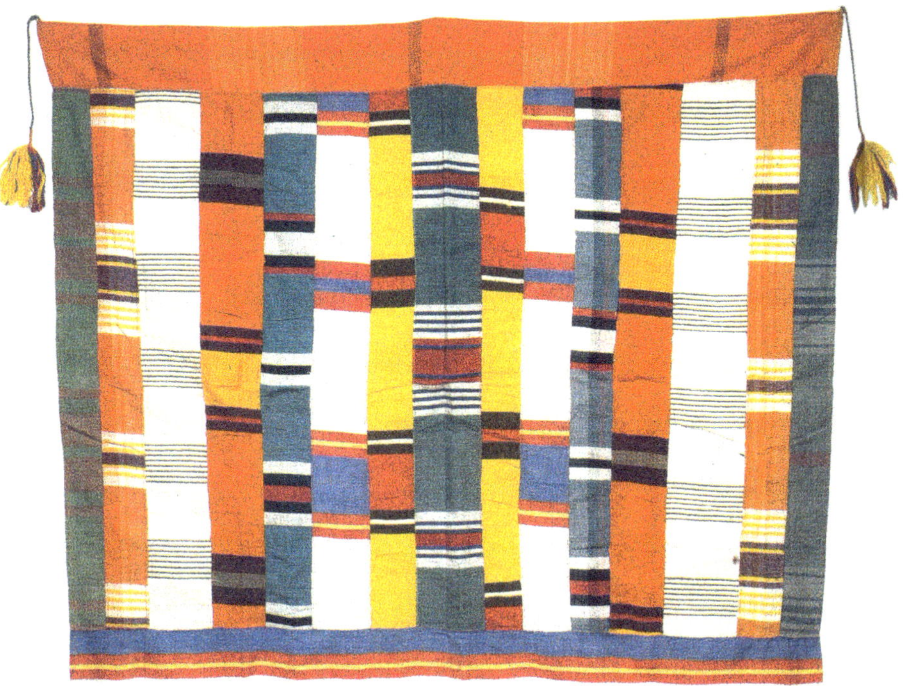

Narrow-strip Saamaka cape, 1940s–1950s.

By the 1970s, cross-stitch embroidery had become the height of fashion.

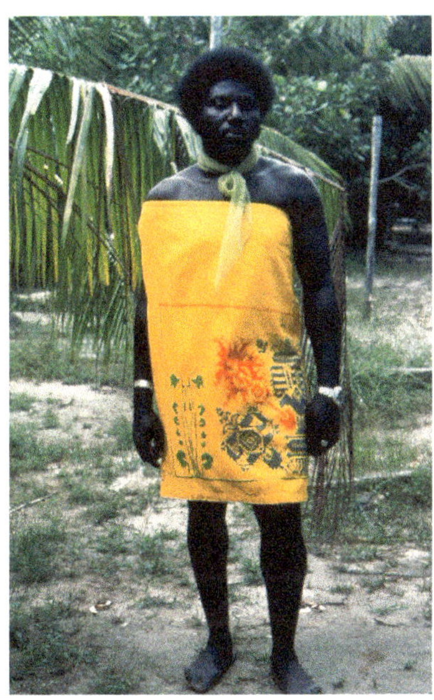

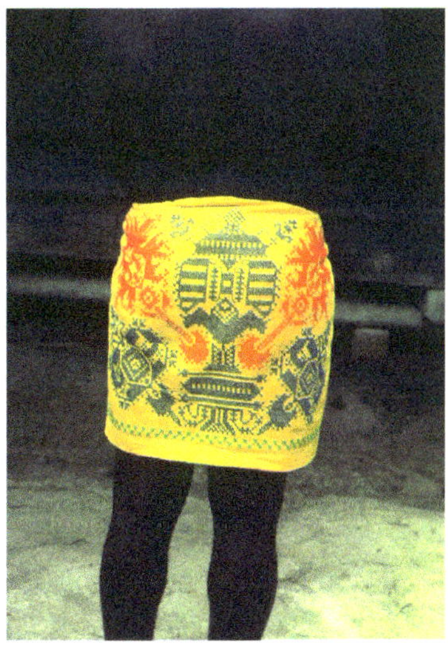

Breechcloth and cape in cross-stitch embroidery, made in the 1970s for Lamei, from the Saamaka village of Asindoopo.

Appliqué has been sewn in different styles at various times.

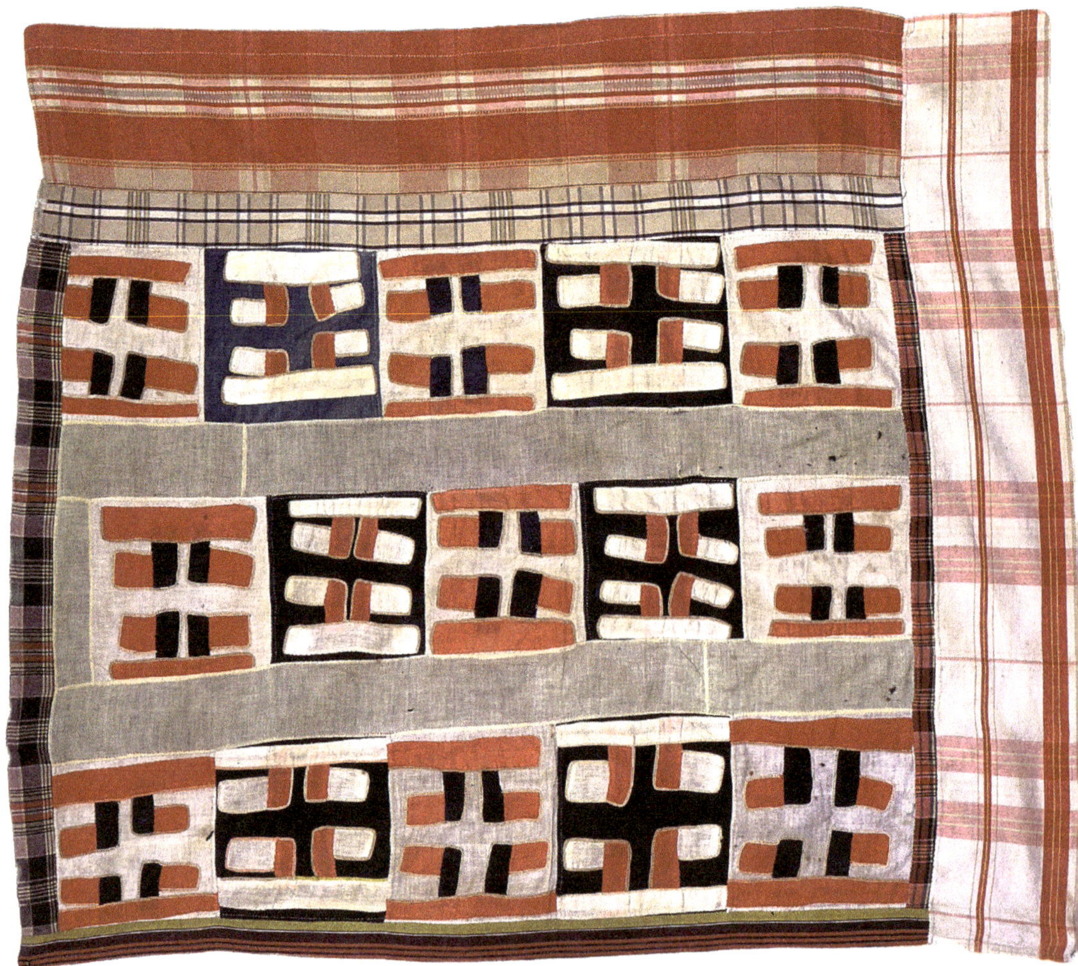

Cape in patchwork and appliqué, probably sewn at the beginning of the twentieth century.

Today, appliqué is more richly exploited than ever, thanks to the new availability to women of sewing machines.

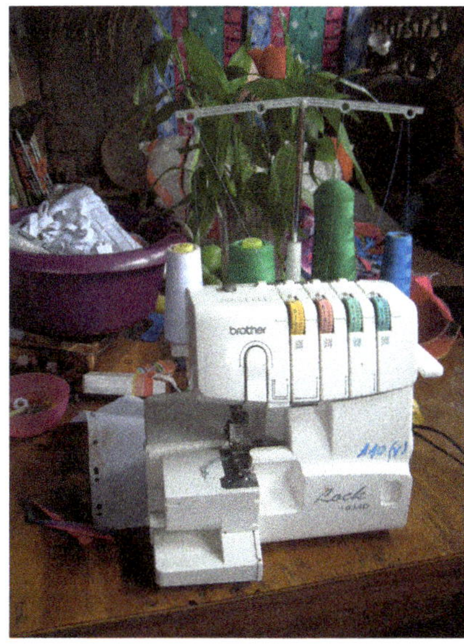

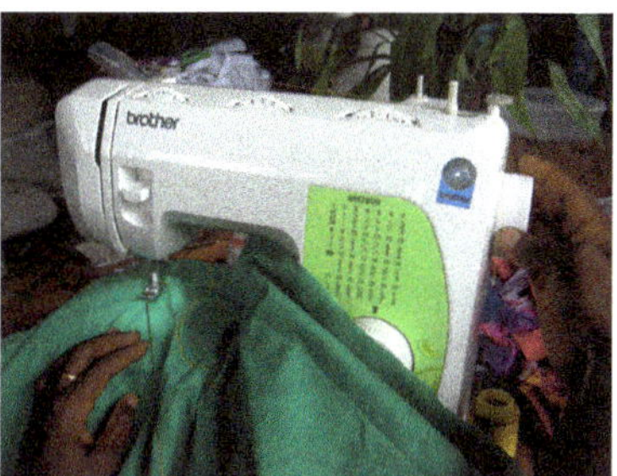

A sewing machine and a serger in the home of a Saamaka woman in Cayenne who makes appliqué textiles for sale, 2016.

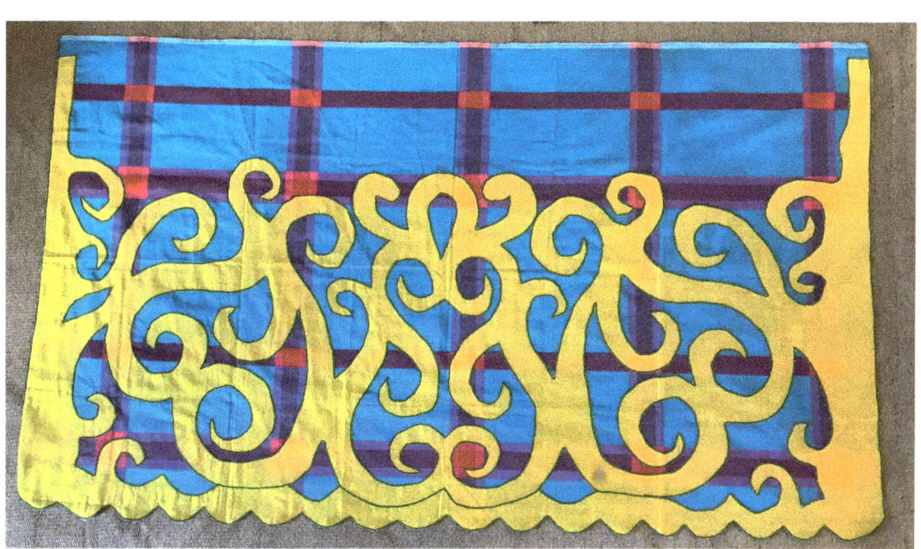

A wrap-skirt sold in 2018 in the market of Cayenne, made by a Saamaka woman from the village of Futunakaba.

But the most stunning development of recent decades is an art based on the painted designs that Eastern Maroon men make on both their own canoes and objects for sale to tourists. It uses colorful yarns to produce densely sewn cross-stitch embroidery.

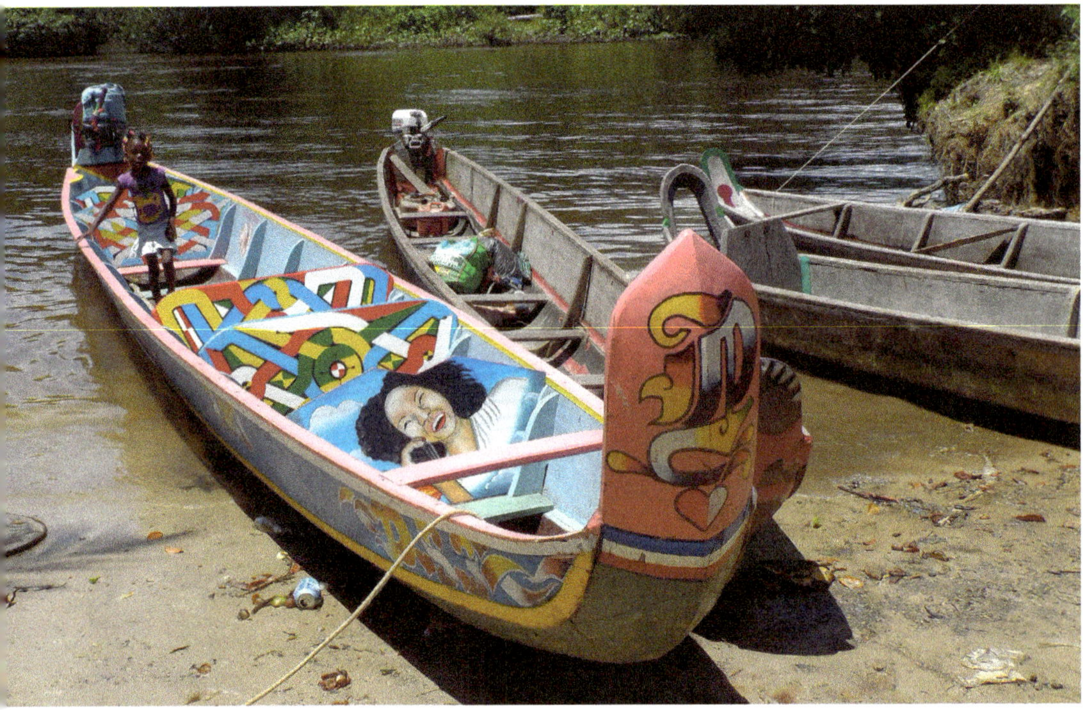

Okanisi canoes on the Tapanahoni, 2013.

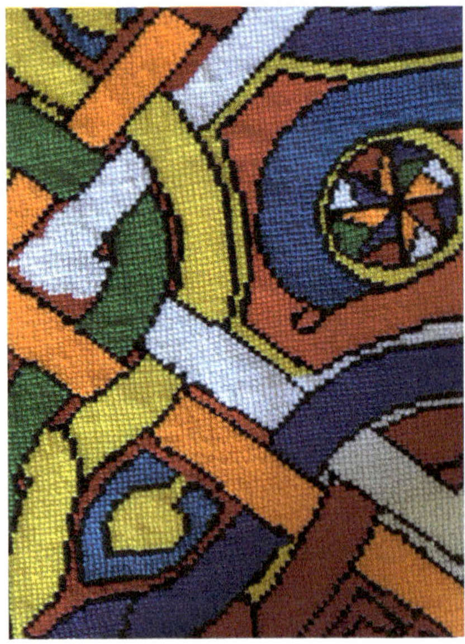

Detail of an Okanisi wrap-skirt embroidered in cross-stitch, 2017.

Threads are first extracted from the cloth to set up a grid. A design is then marked out with a pencil or pen and executed with yarn cross-stitch. Finally, a strip of cotton cloth is added along the top, and decorative borders (in crochet, eyelet, or cloth ruffles) are added on the bottom and sides.

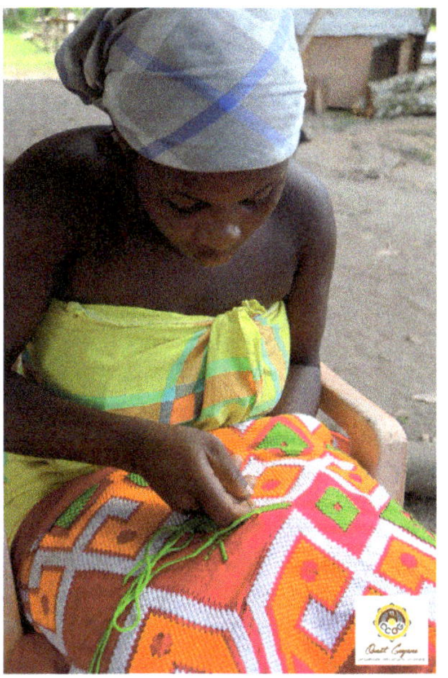

Papaïchton, 2016.

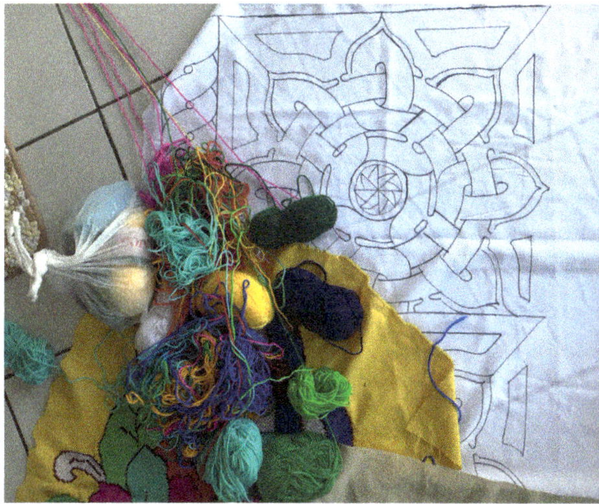

A design marked out for an Aluku wrap-skirt, with the multicolored cotton yarns that will be used to embroider it. At the home of Sa Loti, La Charbonnière, Saint-Laurent, 2018.

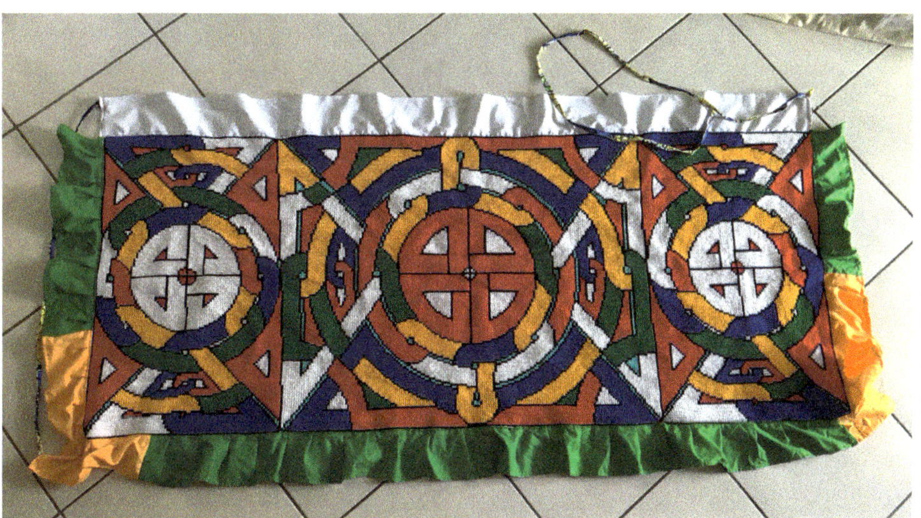

Okanisi wrap-skirt embroidered in Albina by Judith, for her sister Mea Adaina.

Unlike the textile arts of previous generations, destined mainly as gifts for men, this new art produces stylish clothing principally for the women themselves. And access to Facebook and other online sites has turned the women's sewing into a market commodity.[1]

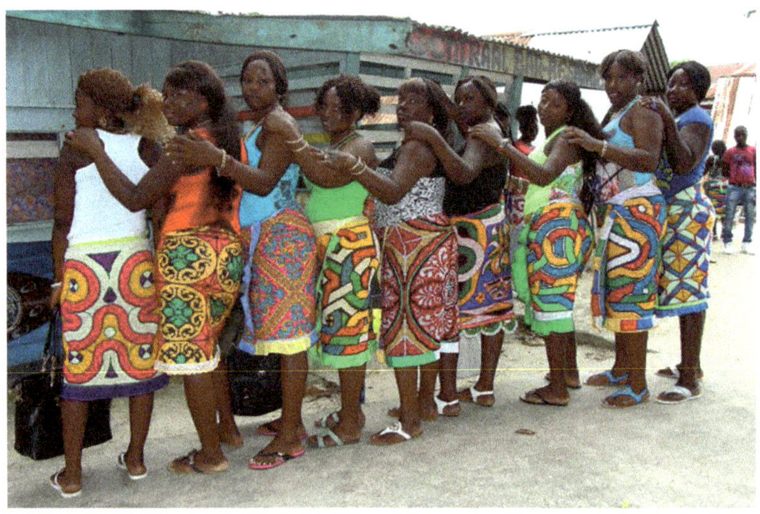

Women showing off the latest fashion in wrap-skirts.

Although some items of clothing have been abandoned in the new cosmopolitan setting of Guyane, others have been creatively turned into new artistic forms. For example, while frontal aprons were the standard item of clothing for teenage girls until the very late twentieth century, these are no longer used except as a ritual item in coming-of-age ceremonies. On the other hand, the calfbands that were worn frequently by men, women, and children have evolved from simple

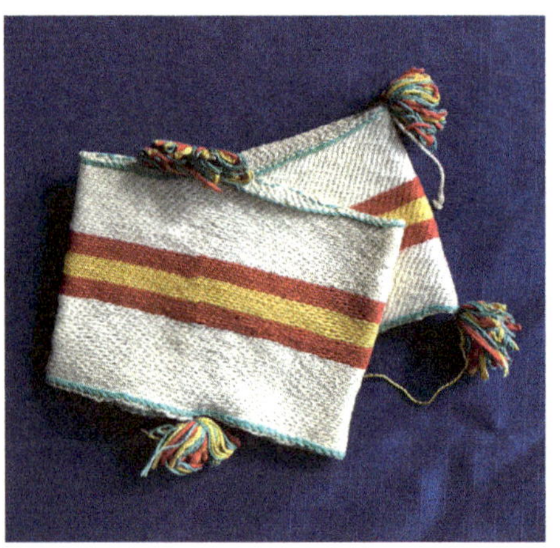

Saamaka calfbands, Suriname, 1968.

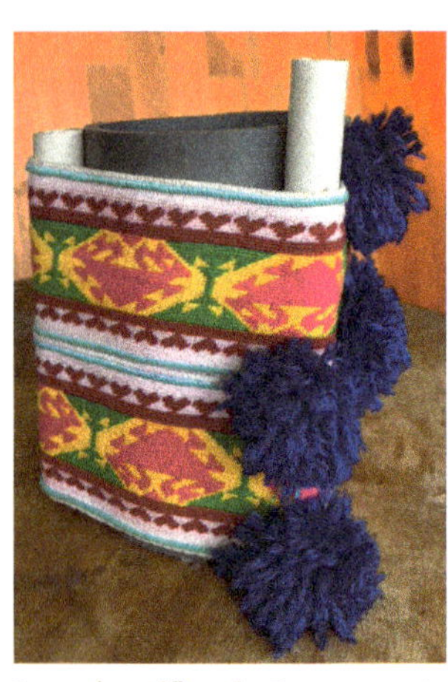

Saamaka calfbands, Guyane, 2018.

white bands with center stripes into complexly designed works of vibrant color for festive wear (and suitable for display as art objects in an urban apartment).

▶▶▶

The fruit of the calabash tree provides another artistic material. At first it was men who decorated the bowls and covered containers made from them, incising their designs on the fruit's exterior surface with woodcarving tools such as compasses and chisels. But soon women began experimenting with the interior surface of these same objects, carving designs with small pieces of broken glass. For over a century, their bowls were a ubiquitous part of Maroon material culture, adding elegance to the meals served to men and sometimes hung on walls as decoration. Today calabash carving is on its way to becoming an abandoned medium.

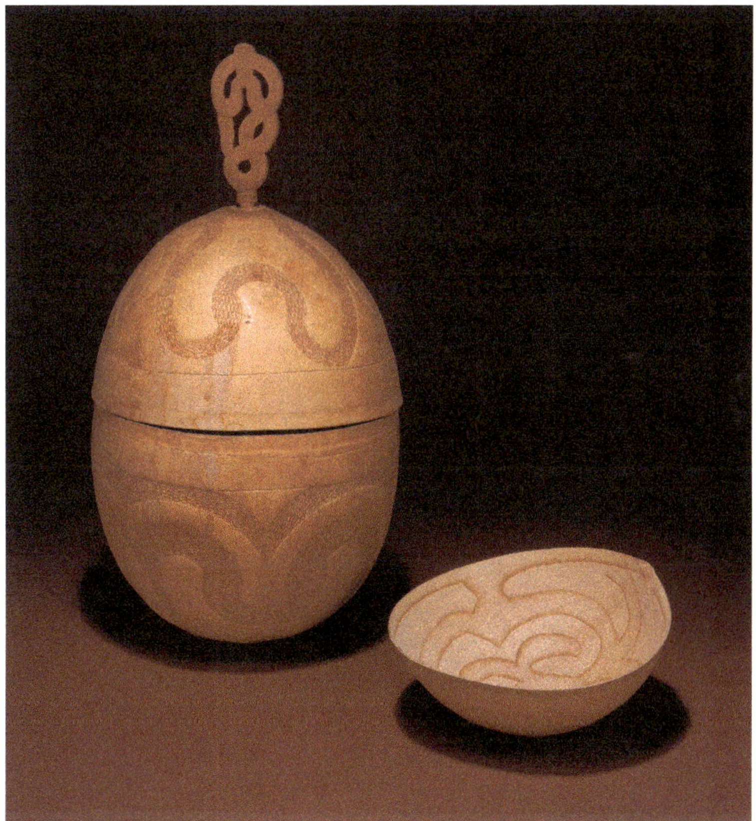

Covered container with a wooden handle, carved by an Aluku man, acquired by the Tropenmuseum, Amsterdam, 1932; calabash bowl carved by Keekete, a Saamaka woman from the village of Asindoopo, 1960s.

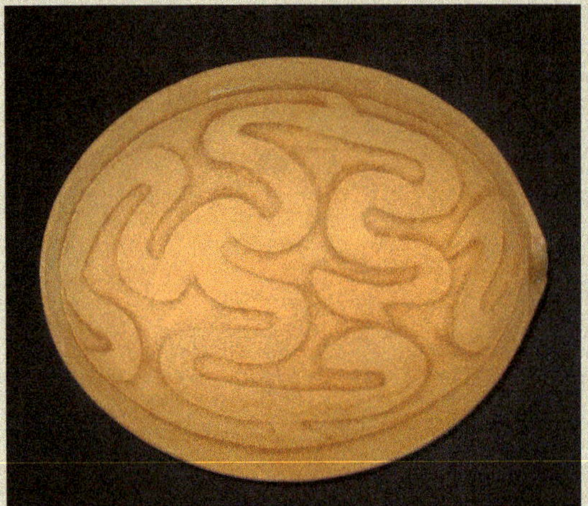

Bowl, carved by Anaaweli, from the Aluku village of Papai Siton, ca. 1960.

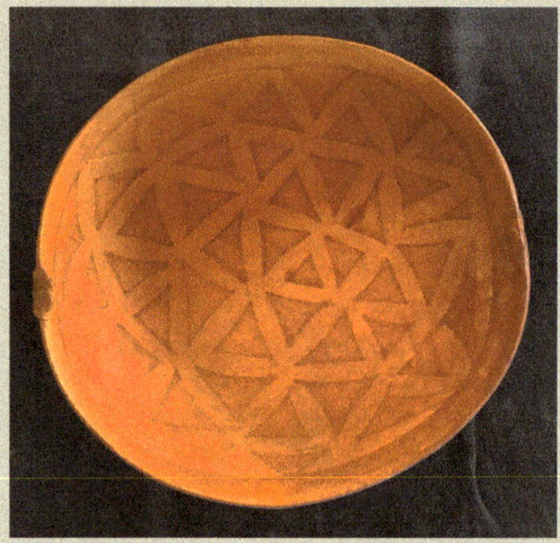

Bowl, carved in the Okanisi village of Fandaaki, collected in 1991.

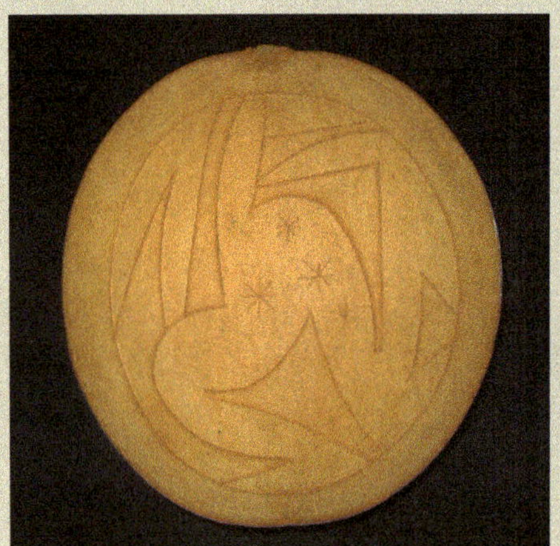

Bowl collected by John D. Lenoir in Pamaka at the beginning of the 1970s. For another Pamaka bowl, see p. 8.

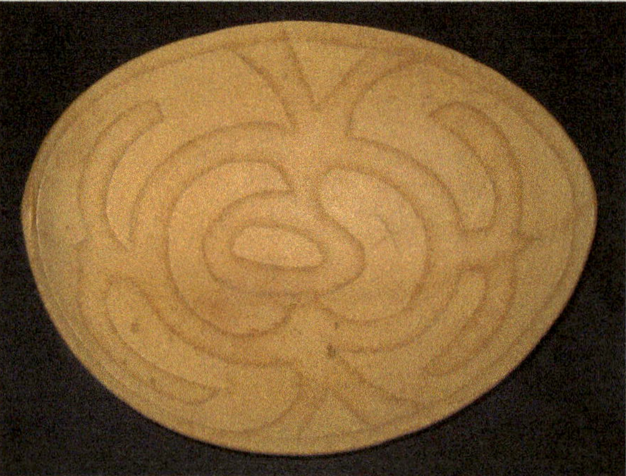

Bowl, carved by Keekete, from the Saamaka village of Asindoopo, 1950s or 1960s.

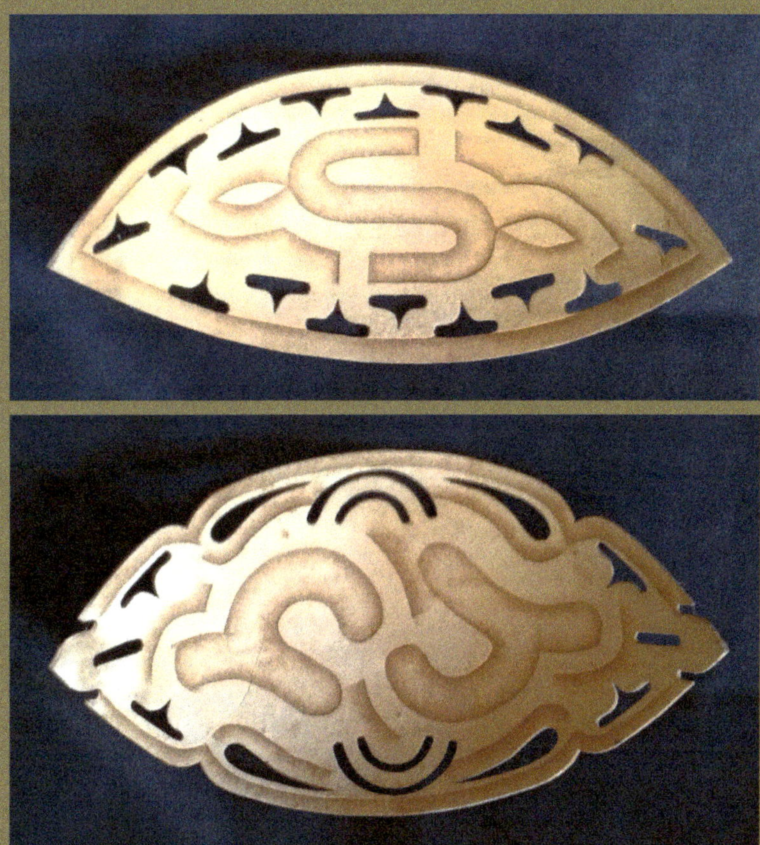

Two decorative calabashes carved by Yowensia Ngwete, from the Saamaka village of Soolan, 2002.

Notes

Preface

1. In 2010, the Saamaka People decided that their collective name should be written "Saamaka" rather than "Saramaka" (the spelling previously used in the literature), in order to reflect their own pronunciation—there is no *r* sound in their language. And the people previously known as "Ndyukas" often express a preference for being called "Okanisis," though those living on the Cottica River in Suriname generally prefer "Cottica Ndyuka."

Marronage: An Introduction

1. See José Juan Arrom, "Cimarrón: Apuntes sobre sus primeras documentaciones y su probable origen," in *Cimarrón*, by José Juan Arrom and Manuel A. García-Arévalo (Santo Domingo: Fundación García-Arévalo, 1986), 13–30.
2. Georg Friederici, *Amerikanistisches Wörterbuch und Hilfswörterbuch für den Amerikanisten* (Hamburg: Cram, De Gruyter, 1960), 191–192.
3. See Richard Price, *Travels with Tooy* (Chicago: University of Chicago Press, 2008).

The Origins of Maroons in Guyane

1. Two other groups, the Matawai and the Kwinti, settled to the west of the Saamaka. They have never been a significant presence in Guyane—though a small number of Matawai men worked at Mana at the beginning of the twentieth century.
2. Serge Mam Lam Fouck, *Histoire générale de la Guyane Française* (Cayenne: Ibis Rouge, 1996), 179–180. See also various contributions in Jean Moomou, ed., *Sociétés marronnes des Amériques: Mémoires, patrimoines, identités et histoire du XVII*^e^ *au XX*^e^ *siècles* (Matoury: Ibis Rouge, 2015).
3. Journal de Goupy des Marets, Bibliothèque de Rouen, manuscript, collection Montbret, c. 1675–1690, folio 31. (We thank Yannick Le Roux for this citation.)

4. Flávio dos Santos Gomes, "Les quilombos—lieux de marronnage—aux frontières entre Guyane française et l'Amérique portugaise (Amazonie XVIIIe siècle)," in Moomou, *Sociétés marronnes des Amériques*, 183–194.
5. David de Ishak Cohen Nassy, *Essai historique sur la colonie de Surinam* (Paramaribo, 1788), 1:87.
6. Jan Jacob Hartsinck, *Beschrijving van Guyana of de Wilde Kust in Zuid-Amerika* (Amsterdam: Gerrit Tielenburg, 1770), 759–765; Nassy, *Essai historique*, 93
7. Nassy, *Essai historique*, 92.
8. Hartsinck, *Beschrijving van Guyana*, 766–768.
9. Richard Price, *First-Time: The Historical Vision of an Afro-American People*, 2nd ed. (Chicago: University of Chicago Press, 2002), 157.

Cultural Similarities and Differences

1. These figures include the 24,000 Maroons who live in Europe and elsewhere in the world—see Richard Price, "The Maroon Population Explosion: Suriname and Guyane," *New West Indian Guide* 87 (2013): 323–327, and "Maroons in Guyane: Getting the Numbers Right," *New West Indian Guide* 92 (2018): 275–283.
2. The language spoken by the Kwinti has been little studied but appears to have more affinity with Okanisi than does Saamaka—that is, it can be placed somewhere between Saamaka and Okanisi. See George L. Huttar and Mary L. Huttar, *Ndyuka* (London: Routledge, 1994); and Bettina Migge, "Putting Matawai on the Surinamese Linguistic Map," *Journal of Pidgin and Creole Languages* 32 (2017): 233–262.
3. The lexicon of standard (everyday) Saamaka, for example, is about 35 percent English derived, 25 percent Portuguese derived, 5 percent derived from Amerindian, Dutch, or French, and 35 percent derived from one or another African language, though a complete dictionary of Saamaka (including esoteric languages) would raise the African contribution to 50 percent; see Richard Price, *Travels with Tooy: History, Memory, and the African American Imagination* (Chicago: University of Chicago Press, 2008), 309–389. Kenneth Bilby, who is finishing a large etymological dictionary of the closely related Aluku language (and has to date found etymons for over 5,300 items) suggests that words of African origin constitute *at least* 43 percent of the total lexicon of that language ("Reevaluating the African Lexical Component of the Surinamese Maroon Creoles: The Aluku Case," paper presented at 31st Annual Conference on African Linguistics, Boston University, March 3, 2000).

The Arrival of Maroons in Guyane

1. This section on Aluku history is drawn, with only minor additions and modifications, from Kenneth M. Bilby, "The Remaking of the Aluku: Culture, Politics, and Maroon Ethnicity in French South America" (PhD diss., Johns Hopkins University, 1990), 101–140. We are very grateful to Bilby for permission to use it here. See also Wim Hoogbergen, *De Boni-Oorlogen, 1757–1860: Marronage en guerrilla in Oost-Suriname* (Utrecht: Centrum voor Caraïbische Studies, 1985); Jean Moomou, *Les marrons Boni de Guyane: Luttes et survie en logique coloniale (1712–1880)* (Matoury: Ibis Rouge, 2013); and Yerri Urban, "Les conventions entre la France et les peuples Marrons du Surinam: Contribution à l'étude des *middle-grounds* post-esclavagistes," in *Justices en Guyane: À l'ombre du droit*, ed. Sylvie Humbert and Yerri Urban (Paris: Documentation Française, 2017), 203–222.
2. Silvia W. de Groot, *From Isolation towards Integration: The Surinam Maroons and Their Colonial Rulers; Official Documents Relating to the Djukas (1845–1863)* (The Hague: Martinus Nijhoff, 1977), 69.
3. Six hundred, according to de Groot, *From Isolation toward Integration*, 71), or 700–800, according to Frédéric Bouyer ("Voyage dans la Guyane Française," *Le Tour du Monde* 13 [1866]: 302).
4. Bouyer, "Voyage dans la Guyane Française," 352.
5. Silvia W. de Groot, "Migratiebewegingen der Djoeka's in Suriname van 1845 tot 1863," *Nieuwe West-Indische Gids* 45 (1965): 133–152; "Maroons of Surinam: Problems of integration into colonial labor systems," *Actes du XLIIe Congrès des Américanistes* (Paris: Société des américanistes, 1977), 1:331–339; H. U. E. Thoden van Velzen and W. van Wetering, *The Great Father and the Danger: Religious Cults, Material Forces and Collective Fantasies in the World of the Surinamese Maroons* (Dordrecht: Foris, 1988), 11–15.
6. Thoden van Velzen and van Wetering, *The Great Father and the Danger*, 141–142.
7. Cited in C. Taubira-Delannon, *L'or en Guyane: Éclats et artifices; Rapport à Monsieur le Premier Ministre* (2000), 88.
8. Jean Petot, *L'or en Guyane: Son histoire, ses hommes* (Paris: Editions Caribéennes, 1986), 121.
9. Jean Hurault, *La vie matérielle des Noirs Réfugiés Boni et des Indiens Wayana du Haut-Maroni* (Paris: ORSTOM, 1965), 100.
10. Henri Coudreau, *Chez nos Indiens: Quatre années dans la Guyane Française (1887–1891)* (Paris: Hachette, 1893), 49.
11. C. de Beet and H. U. E. Thoden van Velzen, "Bush Negro Prophetic Movements: Religions of Despair?," *Bijdragen tot de Taal-, Land- en Volkenkunde* 133 (1977): 126; see also Thoden van Velzen and van Wetering, *The Great Father and the Danger*, 25-29.

12. See Thoden van Velzen and van Wetering, *The Great Father and the Danger.*
13. For an excellent evocation of the life of Creole gold seekers from the Antilles, see Michèle Baj Strobel, *Les Gens de l'or: Mémoire des orpailleurs créoles du Maroni (Guyane)* (Paris: Plon, 2019).
14. Hurault, *La vie matérielle*, 102–103.
15. Ibid., 104.
16. Ibid., 100.
17. For the complete account, see Richard Price, *First-Time: The Historical Vision of an African American People*, 2nd ed. (Chicago: University of Chicago Press, 2002).
18. Serge Mam Lam Fouck, *Histoire de la société guyanaise: Les années cruciales, 1848–1946* (Paris: Éditions caribeéennes, 1987), 87–96, and Saamaka oral testimony.
19. Dossier benoeming Akrosoe, Landsarchief, Paramaribo.
20. Mam Lam Fouck, *Histoire de la société guyanaise*, 97–98. According to Thoden van Velzen and van Wetering, the Inini placers were 350 kilometers upstream from Saint-Laurent (*The Great Father and the Danger*, 142).
21. Mam Lam Fouck, *Histoire de la société guyanaise*, 111; Marie-José Jolivet, *La question créole: Essai de sociologie sur la Guyane française* (Paris: ORSTOM, 1982), 121.
22. Jean Hurault, *Français et Indiens en Guyane, 1604–1972* (Paris: Union Générale d'Editions, 1972), 196.
23. Territoire de l'Inini, cabinet du gouverneur, circulaire, 20 mars 1942, Archives Départementales, dossier "Saramacca."
24. Letter cited in Sophie François, *Les piroguiers de l'Approuague: Mutations sociales, techniques et culturelles d'un patrimoine fluvial peu étudié* (Rapport à la Mission du Patrimoine Ethnologique, 2001), 144–146.
25. Ibid., 148.
26. Ben Scholtens, *Bosnegers en overheid in Suriname: De ontwikkeling van de politieke verhouding 1651–1992* (Paramaribo: Afdeling Cultuurstudies / Minov, 1994), 194.
27. "Lettre du gendarme Senis, délégué du service local et chef de circonscription de la moyenne Mana à M. le gouverneur de la Guyane française et territoire de l'Inini, datée du 31 juillet 1947," in Archives départementales.
28. François, *Les piroguiers de l'Approuague*, 153.
29. Ibid., 147.
30. See, for example, the letter from Saamaka captain Fracas to the governor, dated 8 February 1934, which explains that there were 250 Saamaka men in Régina at the time (Archives départementales).
31. We are grateful to Marie-Paule Jean-Louis for this information.

32. Jolivet, *La question créole*, 233.
33. Mam Lam Fouck, *Histoire de la société guyanaise*, 75.
34. The mayor's mother, married to a Creole, speaks Saamaka. Her father was a Saamaka immigrant, and her mother (who also speaks Saamaka) is the daughter of a Saamaka immigrant. This pattern of Saamaka men marrying the daughters of a Saamaka man and a Creole (often half-Saamaka) woman was common throughout the twentieth century in St.-Georges and Tampaki.
35. Jean-Claude Michelot, *La guillotine sèche: Histoire du bagne de Cayenne* (Paris: Fayard, 1981), 192–193.
36. For stories of encounters between Saamakas and escaped prisoners, see Michelot, *La guillotine sèche*, 153–159, 193; Michel Pierre, *La terre de la grande punition: Histoire des bagnes de Guyane* (Paris: Ramsay, 1982), 223, 235; Richard Price, *The Convict and the Colonel* (Boston: Beacon, 1998), 107.
37. Richard Price, *Saramaka Social Structure: Analysis of a Maroon Society in Surinam* (Río Piedras, Puerto Rico: Institute of Caribbean Studies of the University of Puerto Rico, 1975), 71.
38. For archival citations, see Thoden van Velzen and van Wetering, *The Great Father and the Danger*, 421.
39. Scholtens, *Bosnegers en overheid in Suriname*, 84.
40. John D. Lenoir, "The Paramaka Maroons: A Study in Religious Acculturation" (PhD diss., New School for Social Research, 1973), 25–29.
41. Tristan Bellardie, "Les relations entre Français et Bonis en Guyane française, 1836–1893" (master's thesis, Université Toulouse-Le Mirail, 1994), 92. Until the 1920s, many Okanisi canoemen worked on the Inini, from which they reached the upper Mana.
42. Bellardie, "Les relations," 110.
43. Ibid., 122.
44. Scholtens, *Bosnegers en overheid in Suriname*, 81.
45. Bellardie, "Les relations," 123.
46. See also Thoden van Velzen and van Wetering, *The Great Father and the Danger*, 139.
47. Ibid., 233–235.
48. Scholtens, *Bosnegers en overheid in Suriname*, 81.
49. *L'Avenir de la Guyane Française*, 7 May 1921.
50. Scholtens, *Bosnegers en overheid in Suriname*, 81.
51. A. Franssen Herderschee, "Verslag van de Gonini-expeditie," *Tijdschrift van het Koninklijk Nederlandisch Aardrijkskundig Genootschap* 22 (1905): 127; J. A. Polak, *Historisch overzicht van de goudindustrie in Suriname* (The Hague: Martinus Nijhoff, 1908), 70; W. F. van Lier, *Diarum*, July–August 1925, cited in de Beet and Thoden van Velzen, "Bush Negro Prophetic Movements."
52. Scholtens, *Bosnegers en overheid in Suriname*, 80, 150.
53. L. C. van Panhuys, "Iets over de Marowijne rivier en hare geschiedenis,"

Bulletin van het Koloniaal Museum te Haarlem 12 (1908): 38; A. Franssen Herderschee, "Verslag van de Gonini-expeditie," *Tijdschrift van het Koninklijk Nederlandisch Aardrijkskundig Genootschap* 22 (1905): 53–54; see also de Beet and Thoden van Velzen, "Bush Negro Prophetic Movements."

Maroons in Guyane: 1970 to the Present

1. *Tableaux économiques régionaux de la Guyane* (Paris: INSEE, 2000), 30.
2. C. Taubira-Delannon, *L'or en Guyane: Éclats et artifices; Rapport à Monsieur le Premier Ministre* (2000), 41; "Une histoire. Les Noirs marrons: Sans-papiers français," *Libération* (Paris), 4 August 1999.
3. For a discussion of the demography of Maroons in Guyane (their numbers, birth rates, and distribution in the *département*), see Richard Price, "The Maroon Population Explosion: Suriname and Guyane," *New West Indian Guide* 87 (2013): 323–327, and "Maroons in Guyane: Getting the Numbers Right," *New West Indian Guide* 92 (2018): 275–283.
4. See Richard Price and Sally Price, *Saamaka Dreaming* (Durham, N.C.: Duke University Press, 2017).
5. T. S. Polimé and H. U. E. Thoden van Velzen, *Vluchtelingen, opstandelingen en andere Bosnegers van Oost-Suriname, 1986–1988* (Utrecht: Instituut voor Culturele Antropologie, 1988); H. U. E. Thoden van Velzen, "Priests, Mediums and Guerrillas in Suriname," in *Transactions: Essays in Honor of Jeremy F. Boissevain*, ed. J. Verrips (Amsterdam: Het Spinhuis, 1994), 209–228.
6. See Richard Price, *Rainforest Warriors: Human Rights on Trial* (Philadelphia: University of Pennsylvania Press, 2011), 83–103.
7. Richard Price, "Scrapping Maroon History: Brazil's Promise, Suriname's Shame," *New West Indian Guide* 72 (1998): 233–255.
8. See B. Rombouts, A. Meijknecht, and J. Asarfi, "The Implementation of IACtHR Judgments concerning Land Rights in Suriname—Saramaka People v. Suriname and Subsequent Cases," International Law Association (ILA), Committee on the implementation of the rights of indigenous peoples, case study, 2016.
9. Ellen-Rose Kambel and Fergus MacKay, *The Rights of Indigenous Peoples and Maroons in Suriname* (Moreton-in-Marsh, UK: The Forest Peoples Programme, 1999), 173.
10. Pieter Van Maele, "New Mine Brings Big Changes to Town in Suriname Rainforest," Associated Press, 31 October 2016.
11. Ibid.
12. It turns out that this refinery (the Kaloti Mint House), which has been given authority by the Suriname Central Bank to "assay, value, and collect taxes on gold exports," is a fiction. "Bouterse straw purchasers own 30%,"

but an international researcher "found no evidence that the refinery exists. . . . In addition to the lack of physical evidence of the refinery, interviews with gold dealers confirmed that there was no refinery and no gold refining taking place. Under these circumstances, the government can certify the exports of any amount of gold, real and fictitious, from a refinery that exists only on paper." Money laundering using gold as the vehicle is the modus operandi. See Douglas Farah and Kathryn Babineau, "Suriname: The New Paradigm of a Criminalized State," *Center for a Secure Free Society Global Dispatch*, issue 3 (March 2017).

13. Forest Peoples Programme, Suriname Information Update, 20 April 1998 (available online).
14. For details, see Kenneth M. Bilby, "The Remaking of the Aluku: Culture, Politics, and Maroon Ethnicity in French South America" (PhD diss., Johns Hopkins University, 1990).
15. Taubira-Delannon, *L'or en Guyane*, 82.
16. Bettina Migge and Isabelle Léglise, *Exploring Language in a Multilingual Context: Variation, Interaction and Ideology in Language Documentation* (Cambridge: Cambridge University Press, 2013), 65. We estimate that 3,500 Pamaka, 2,500 Okanisi, 600 Aluku, and 60 Saamaka live in the commune.
17. Bilby, "Remaking of the Aluku," 151–152.
18. See ibid., 173–174, 178–180.
19. Ibid.
20. For a detailed overview of the history of gold extraction and its environmental impact in Guyane, see Gabriel Melun and Mikaël Le Bihan, *Histoire et impacts environnementaux de l'orpaillage en Guyane: Clefs de compréhension des tensions actuelles*, Office français de la biodiversité, 2020, https://professionnels.ofb.fr/fr/recherche?search_api_fulltext=l%27orpaillage%2C+melun.
21. Taubira-Delannon, *L'or en Guyane*, 75.
22. Ibid., 94.
23. Ibid.
24. W. Hoogbergen, D. Kruijt, and T. Polimé, "Goud en Brazilianen," *Oso* 20 (2001): 109–127. See also Christel C. F. Antonius-Smits, "Gold and Commercial Sex: Exploring the Link between Small-Scale Gold Mining and Commercial Sex in the Rainforest of Suriname," in *Sun, Sex, and Gold: Tourism and Sex Work in the Caribbean*, ed. K. Kempadoo (Lanham, Md.: Rowman & Littlefield, 1999), 237–260.
25. Taubira-Delannon, *L'or en Guyane*, 74.
26. Hoogbergen, Kruijt, and Polimé, "Goud en Brazilianen."
27. In *Gowtu: Klopjacht op het Surinaamse goud* (Schoorl, Netherlands: Conserve, 2013), Jeroen Trommelen describes the system of corruption and provides useful information on the Lawa region.

28. Much of the information in the following two paragraphs comes from Marjo de Theije, "Small-Scale Gold Mining and Trans-Frontier Commerce on the Lawa River," in *In and Out of Suriname: Language, Mobility and Identity*, ed. Eithne Carlin, Isabelle Léglise, Bettina Migge, and Paul Tjon Sie Fat (Leiden: Brill, 2015), 58–75.
29. The information in this paragraph comes from Marieke Heemskerk, *Kleinschalige goudwinning in Suriname. Een overzicht van sociaaleconomische, politieke, en milieu aspecten* (Amsterdam: CEDLA, 2009), 35, and de Theije, "Small-Scale Gold Mining."
30. Marjo de Theije and Sabine Luning, "Small-Scale Mining and Cross-Border Movements of Gold from French Guiana," in *Mobilités, ethnicités, diversité culturelle: La Guyane entre Surinam et Brésil*, ed. Gérard Collomb and Serge Mam Lam Fouck (Matoury: Ibis Rouge, 2016), 141–161.
31. The information in this paragraph comes from Alex May, *Guyane française: L'or de la honte* (Paris: Calmann-Lévy, 2007), chaps. 4 and 5.
32. Ibid., chap. 4.
33. In 2015, 90 percent of the populations of the upper Maroni still had a level of mercury higher than the accepted norms; see Gabriel Serville et al., *Proposition de résolution tendant à la création d'une commission d'enquête sur la lutte contre l'orpaillage illégal en Guyane*, Enregistré à la Présidence de l'Assemblée Nationale, 16 July 2019. That same document reported that illegal gold mining accounted for 75 percent of the annual deforestation in Guyane.
34. "Guyane: Les mines d'or clandestines en hausse," *Le Figaro* (Paris), 14 January 2017.
35. Ibid.; see also David Gris, *Garimpeiros: La lutte contre l'orpaillage illégal racontée par un gendarme* (Saint-Denis, France: Edilivre, 2017).
36. François-Michel Le Tourneau, *Chercheurs d'or: L'orpaillage clandestin en Guyane française* (Paris: CNRS Éditions, 2020), 88, 90.
37. Alain Vasseur, "Lutte contre l'orpaillage illégal: Les autorités tirent un bilan positif pour le premier trimestre 2016," *GendXXI Agora*, 1 July 2016.
38. "Guyane," *Le Figaro*.
39. Marie-Claude Thébia, "L'opération Harpie se maintient," *Guyane 1ère*, 14 April 2020.
40. On the severe difficulty of obtaining residence papers (or French nationality) in Guyane, see Catherine Benoît, "*Pampila* et politique sur le Maroni: De l'état civil sur un fleuve frontière," in *Justices en Guyane: À l'ombre du droit*, ed. Sylvie Humbert and Yerri Urban (Paris: Documentation Française, 2017), 237–260; and Benoît, "'La carte n'est pas le territoire!': Coutume, droit et nationalité plurielle en Guyane," *Ethnologie française* 48 (2018): 121–130. On the production of "illegality" and the "deportation regime" in Guyane, see Benoît, "Fortress Europe's Far-Flung Borderlands: 'Illegality' and the 'Deportation Regime' in

France's Caribbean and Indian Ocean Territories," *Mobilities* 15, no. 2 (2020): 220–240.

41. Bilby, "Remaking of the Aluku," 290.
42. Ibid., 629, 632.
43. Ibid., 381–389.
44. See the letter reproduced in ibid., 678–679.
45. The population also includes Creoles, Amerindians, European French, Brazilians, Haitians, Chinese, and others.
46. For a description of life in a "ghetto" of Saint-Laurent, see Jessi Américain, *Nègre Marron: Itinéraire d'un enfant du ghetto* (Matoury: Ibis Rouge, 2016).
47. Bilby, "Remaking of the Aluku," 329, 335.
48. "The judicial authorities in Guyane estimate that the number of mules who make the trip annually is 4,000, with only 10% being caught. . . . Mules make up about half of the prisoners in the central penitentiary of Guyane" (*Le journal du soir*, TF1 [Cayenne], 25 April 2018). A mule normally receives 5,000 euros upon delivery. Last year, forty-four died when the cocaine-filled balloons or condoms ruptured before they were expelled. The standard sentence for mules arrested in France is eighteen months in prison—see *France-Guyane*, 26 April 2018. In 2018, France's most prestigious newspaper ran a three-part series on drug smuggling from Guyane: "In Saint-Laurent-du-Maroni, everyone knows someone who is involved in drug trafficking. . . . Samyna [a 27-year-old mother of two], now in prison in Fresnes [France] admits to having made five trips to smuggle cocaine, earning on average 5,000 euros per trip. 'I worked for three different groups,' she said, 'all friends from Saint-Laurent. They were my schoolmates.' . . . In the prison at Fresnes, the smugglers from Guyane are so numerous (40% of all inmates) that the rules of the prison are posted in Nengetongo, the language of the Maroon community that lives on the French and Suriname banks of the Maroni River, where the traffic originates" (Alexandre Kauffmann, "Les filières guyanaises de la cocaïne, une série en trois épisodes," *Le Monde*, 14–16 May 2019).
49. Sophie Bourgarel, "Migration sur le Maroni: Le cas des réfugiés surinamiens en Guyane" (master's thesis, Université Paul Valéry, Montpellier, 1988), 75–77.
50. *La Route de l'art: artistes de l'ouest Guyanais* (Guyane: Édition ONF, 2014), with photographs by David Damoison.
51. Carol Péaud, *Art et sculpture noirs marrons: Artisanat, mobilier, habitat* (Kourou: n.d. [1993?]), 31; see also Bilby, "Remaking of the Aluku," 393–396.
52. Since the 1940s, Maroon captains have received a salary that is 30 percent of the French minimum wage. In addition, they receive two official military-style uniforms.

53. See *France-Guyane*, 3 July 2001, 1, 8–9; Richard Price, *Travels with Tooy* (Chicago: University of Chicago Press, 2008).

Looking Back, Looking Ahead

1. Beginning in the 1970s, most Alukus had left their traditional villages for one of the new administrative centers (Papaïchton-Pompidouville or Maripasoula) or to live on the coast.
2. See Richard Price and Sally Price, *Saamaka Dreaming* (Durham, N.C.: Duke University Press, 2017), for a detailed picture of Maroon village life before the civil war.
3. Several names (*nengee, takitaki, businengetongo*) are used to refer to this urban lingua franca. See the excellent analysis in Bettina Migge and Isabelle Léglise, *Exploring Language in a Multilingual Context: Variation, Interaction and Ideology in Language Documentation* (Cambridge: Cambridge University Press, 2013).
4. Clémence Léobal, "'Osu,' 'baraques' et 'batiman': Redessiner les frontières de l'urbain à Soolan (Saint-Laurent-du-Maroni, Guyane)" (PhD diss., Université de Paris Déscartes, 2017), 316.
5. For a detailed discussion of a case in which the defendant was a Maroon, see Price, *Travels with Tooy*, 177–206.
6. Migge and Léglise, *Exploring Language*, 57.
7. Although he got only 50.7 percent of the total votes, this candidate received more than two-thirds of the votes in the communes of West Guyane and 98 percent in Grand-Santi, the only commune that is almost wholly Okanisi. And even if he didn't explicitly mention ethnicity, the spokesman for French president Emmanuel Macron acknowledged the origins of the new *député* in a tweet: "Bravo to @LenaickADAM . . . who proved his links to his territory, his river." See "Lénaïck Adam (LREM) reporte la legislative partielle en Guyane," France Info, 12 March 2018, https://la1ere.francetvinfo.fr/lenaick-adam-lrem-remporte-legislative-partielle-guyane-568033.html.
8. Later that year the mayor began a several-year-long prison term and was replaced by another member of his party.
9. See Richard Price, *Rainforest Warriors: Human Rights on Trial* (Philadelphia: University of Pennsylvania Press, 2011).
10. Nassira Belkacemi, "Les autochtones français: Populations ou peuples?," *Droits et Cultures*, 37, no. 1 (1999): 34–35.

Art Gallery

1. For a recent overview of women's textile arts, see Sally Price, "Maroon Fashion History: An Update," *New West Indian Guide* 94 (2020): 1–38.

Further Reading

Maroons in the Americas

The best general introduction remains Richard Price, ed., *Maroon Societies: Rebel Slave Communities in the Americas*, 3rd ed. (Baltimore: Johns Hopkins University Press, 1996 [orig. 1973]); see also Richard Price, "Maroons and their Communities in the Americas," Politika (EHESS), https://www.politikaio/en/notice/maroons-and-their-communities-in-the-americas. Other useful overviews include Rafael Duharte Jiménez, *Rebeldia esclava en el Caribe* (Xalapa, Mexico: Gobierno del Estado de Vera Cruz, 1992); Gad Heuman, ed., *Out of the House of Bondage: Runaways, Resistance and Marronage in Africa and the New World* (London: Frank Cass, 1982); and Jean Moomou, ed., *Sociétés marronnes des Amériques: Mémoires, patrimoines, identités et histoire du XVIIe au XXe siècles* (Matoury: Ibis Rouge, 2015).

Alukus

For Aluku history and culture, the basic sources on the Dutch-Aluku wars are Wim Hoogbergen, *De Boni-Oorlogen, 1757–1860: Marronage en guerrilla in Oost-Suriname* (Utrecht: Centrum voor Caraïbische Studies, 1985)—translated as *The Boni Maroon Wars in Suriname* (Leiden: Brill, 1990)—and John Gabriel Stedman, *Narrative of a Five Years Expedition against the Revolted Negroes of Surinam*, newly transcribed from the original 1790 manuscript, edited, and with an introduction and notes, by Richard Price and Sally Price (Baltimore: Johns Hopkins University Press, 1988). On Aluku relations with the French and Dutch administrations during the nineteenth century, see Silvia W. de Groot, *From Isolation towards Integration: The Suriname Maroons and their Colonial Rulers—Official Documents Relating to the Djukas (1845–1863)* (The Hague: Martinus Nijhoff, 1977); Ben Scholtens, *Bosnegers en overheid in Suriname: De ontwikkeling van de politieke verhouding, 1651–1992* (Paramaribo: Afdeling Cultuurstudies / Minov, 1994); Tristan Bellardie, "Les relations entre Français et Bonis en Guyane française, 1836–1893" (master's thesis, Université Toulouse-Le Mirail, 1994); and Jean Moomou, *Les marrons Boni de Guyane: Luttes et survie en logique coloniale (1712–1880)* (Matoury: Ibis Rouge, 2013).

For details about the life of Apatou, see Kenneth Bilby, "The Explorer as Hero: *Le fidèle Apatou* in the French Wilderness," *New West Indian Guide* 78 (2004): 197–227.

The most reliable general study of Aluku history and culture is Kenneth M. Bilby, "The Remaking of the Aluku: Culture, Politics, and Maroon Ethnicity in French South America" (PhD diss., Johns Hopkins University, 1990). See also the various works by the French geographer Jean Hurault: *Les Noirs Réfugiés Boni de la Guyane Française* (Dakar: Institut Français d'Afrique Noire, 1961), *La vie matérielle des Noirs Réfugiés Boni et des Indiens Wayana du Haut-Maroni (Guyane Française): Agriculture, économie et habitat* (Paris: ORSTOM, 1965), *Africains de Guyane: La vie matérielle et l'art des Noirs Réfugiés de Guyane* (Paris–The Hague: Mouton, 1970), and *Français et Indiens en Guyane* (Paris: Union Générale d'Éditions, 1972).

Okanisis (Ndyukas)

The basic sources on Okanisi history and culture, particularly their relations with the outside world, are Silvia W. de Groot, *From Isolation towards Integration: The Surinam Maroons and their Colonial Rulers—Official Documents Relating to the Djukas (1845–1863)* (The Hague: Martinus Nijhoff, 1977); Diane Vernon, *Money Magic in a Modernizing Maroon Society* (Tokyo: Institute for the Study of Languages and Cultures of Asia and Africa, 1985); and, particularly, H. U. E. Thoden van Velzen and W. van Wetering, *The Great Father and the Danger: Religious Cults, Material Forces and Collective Fantasies in the World of the Surinamese Maroons* (Dordrecht: Foris, 1988), and *In the Shadow of the Oracle: Religion as Politics in a Suriname Maroon Society* (Long Grove, Ill.: Waveland, 2004); H. U. E. Thoden van Velzen and Wim Hoogbergen, *Een zwarte vrijstaat in Suriname: De Okaanse samenleving in de 18ᵉ eeuw* (Leiden: KITLV, 2011); H. U. E. Thoden van Velzen and Wilhelmina van Wetering, *Een zwarte vrijstaat in Suriname: De Okaanse samenleving in de 19ᵉ en 20ᵉ eeuw* (Leiden: Brill, 2013); H. U. E. Thoden van Velzen, *Prophets of Doom: A History of the Okanisi Maroons* (Leiden: Brill, 2022).

The traditional sources on the great strike of 1921 are G. J. Staal, "Overeenkomst met de Aucaner Boschnegers," *De West-Indische Gids* 4 (1922): 48–52; and Willem F. van Lier, "Bij de Aucaners. II," *De West-Indische Gids* 4 (1922): 205–230. See also Ben Scholtens, *Bosnegers en overheid in Suriname: De ontwikkeling van de politieke verhouding 1651–1992* (Paramaribo: Afdeling Cultuurstudies/Minov, 1994), 72–73, 76–80. A fuller study is found in H. U. E. Thoden van Velzen, *Een koloniaal drama: De grote staking van de Marron vrachtvaarders, 1921* (Amsterdam: Rozenberg, 2003).

Saamakas

Following the pioneering report of Melville Herskovits and Frances Herskovits, *Rebel Destiny: Among the Bush Negroes of Dutch Guiana* (New York: McGraw-Hill, 1934), the basic works on Saamaka life and history date from the second half of the twentieth century: Richard Price, *Saramaka Social Structure: Analysis of a Maroon Society in Surinam* (Río Piedras: Institute of Caribbean Studies of the University of Puerto Rico, 1975), *To Slay the Hydra: Dutch Colonial Perspectives on the Saramaka Wars* (Ann Arbor, Mich.: Karoma, 1983), *First-Time: The Historical Vision of an African American People*, 2nd ed. (Chicago: University of Chicago Press, 2002 [orig. 1983]) and an edition in the Saamaka language, *Fesiten* (La Roque d'Anthéron: Vents d'ailleurs, 2013), *Alabi's World* (Baltimore: Johns Hopkins University Press, 1990), and *Travels with Tooy: History, Memory, and the African American Imagination* (Chicago: University of Chicago Press, 2008); Sally Price, *Co-Wives and Calabashes* (Ann Arbor: University of Michigan Press, 1984); Richard Price and Sally Price, *Two Evenings in Saramaka* (Chicago: University of Chicago Press, 1991) and an edition in the Saamaka language, *Boo go a Kontukonde* (La Roque d'Anthéron, France: Vents d'ailleurs, 2016), *The Root of Roots: Or, How Afro-American Anthropology Got Its Start* (Chicago: Prickly Paradigm, 2003), and *Saamaka Dreaming* (Durham, N.C.: Duke University Press, 2017).

The Other Groups

Much less has been published about the Matawai, Pamaka, and Kwinti. The best studies for the Matawai are Chris de Beet and Miriam Sterman, *People in Between: The Matawai Maroons of Suriname* (Utrecht: Krips Repro Meppel, 1981), and Edward Green, "The Matawai Maroons: An Acculturating Afro-American Society" (PhD diss., Catholic University of America, 1974). For the Pamaka, John D. Lenoir, "The Paramaka Maroons: A Study in Religious Acculturation" (PhD diss., New School for Social Research, 1973). For the Kwinti, see Dirk van der Elst, "The Coppename Kwinti: Notes on an Afro-American tribe in Surinam," *Nieuwe West-Indische Gids* 50 (1975): 7–17, 107–122, 200–211.

Maroon Art

Books about Maroon art include Sally Price and Richard Price, *Afro-American Arts of the Suriname Rain Forest* (Berkeley: University of California Press, 1980), *Maroon Arts: Cultural Vitality in the African Diaspora* (Boston: Beacon, 1999), and, for an expanded and updated version with many color plates, *Les Arts des Marrons* (La Roque d'Anthéron, France: Vents d'ailleurs, 2005). See also Richard Price and Sally Price, *Equatoria* (New York: Routledge, 1992), and *Enigma Variations: A Novel* (Cambridge,

Mass.: Harvard University Press, 1995), as well as Ben Scholtens, Gloria Wekker, Laddy van Putten, and Stanley Dieko, *Gaama Duumi, Buta Gaama: Overlijden en opvolging van Aboikoni, grootopperhoofd van de Saramaka Bosnegers* (Paramaribo: Afdeling Cultuurstudies / Minov, 1992).

The Current Crisis

On the current, threatening human rights situation of Maroons in Suriname and Guyane, see Ellen-Rose Kambel and Fergus MacKay, *The Rights of Indigenous Peoples and Maroons in Suriname* (Moreton-in-Marsh, UK: Forest Peoples Programme, 1999); C. Taubira-Delannon, *L'or en Guyane: Éclats et artifices; Rapport à Monsieur le Premier Ministre* (2000); and Richard Price, *Rainforest Warriors: Human Rights on Trial* (Philadelphia: University of Pennsylvania Press, 2011).

Photo Credits

p. iv: Photo Martha Cooper, 1989.

p. xiv: Surinaams Museum, Paramaribo; photo A. Graeber, 1980.

p. 2 left: Photo Albert Mangonès.

p. 2 right: Photo Museo de América, Madrid.

p. 3 top: Photo Walker Art Gallery, Liverpool.

p. 3 bottom: From R. C. Dallas, *The History of the Maroons* (London: Longman & Rees, 1803).

pp. 4–5: Private Collection / Bridgeman Images.

p. 6 top: Herskovits Collection, 1930, Hamburgisches Museum für Völkerkunde; photo A. Graeber, 1980.

p. 6 bottom: American Museum of Natural History, New York; photo A. Graeber, 1980.

p. 7: From Bryan Edwards, *Observations on the Maroons* (London, 1796).

p. 8: R. and S. Price Collection; photo P. Buirette, 1997.

p. 11: Photo Danish Royal Museum of Fine Arts, Copenhagen.

p. 13 top: From John Gabriel Stedman, *Narrative of a Five Years Expedition against the Revolted Negroes of Surinam*, newly transcribed from the original manuscript of 1790, edited, and with an introduction and notes by Richard Price and Sally Price (Baltimore: Johns Hopkins University Press, 1988), 105.

p. 13 bottom: From Stedman, *Narrative of a Five Years Expedition*, 548.

p. 15: Archieven van de Sociëteit van Suriname, Algemeen Rijksarchief, The Hague, 320, p. 333, 16/9/1763.

p. 16: Richard and Sally Price Collection, Schomburg Center for Research in Black Culture, New York; photo A. Graeber, 1980.

p. 18: Map by Ici et ailleurs.

p. 19: Map by Erin Kirk.

p. 20: Photo Dr. J. B. Ch. Wekker, Centraal Bureau Luchtkartering, Paramaribo.

p. 21: Photo Wilhelmina van Wetering.

p. 22 top: From Jean Hurault, *Africains de Guyane* (The Hague–Paris: Mouton, 1970), pl. 44.

p. 22 bottom: From Ben Scholtens, Gloria Wekker, Laddy van Putten, and Stanley Dieko, *Gaama Duumi, Buta Gaama: Overlijden en Opvolging van Aboikoni, grootopperhoofd van de Saramaka Bosnegers* (Paramaribo, Minov/Cultuurstudies, 1992). Photo Robert Lo Asioe.

p. 24: Photo Chris de Beet.

p. 25 top: Photo Wilhelmina van Wetering.

p. 25 bottom left: Photo R. Price.

p. 25 bottom right: From Hurault, *Africains de Guyane*, pl. 14.

p. 27 left: Photo R. Price.

p. 27 right: Photo Wilhelmina van Wetering.

p. 29 top: From Hurault, *Africains de Guyane*, pl. 11.

p. 29 bottom: Photo R. Price.

p. 30: Photo Wilhelmina van Wetering, 1962.

p. 34 left: From Stedman, *Narrative of a Five Years Expedition*, 403.

p. 34 right: From Stedman, *Narrative of a Five Years Expedition*, 391.

p. 38: From Jules Crevaux, "Voyage d'exploration dans l'intérieur des Guyanes, 1876–1877," *Le Tour du monde* 20 (1879): 373.

p. 43: From Hurault, *Africains de Guyane*, pl. 30.

p. 44 left: From Hassoldt Davis, *The Jungle and the Damned* (New York: Duell, Sloan and Pearce, 1952), between 128 and 129.

p. 44 right: From J. Tripot, *La Guyane: Au pays de l'or, des forçats et des peaux-rouges* (Paris: Plon-Nourrit, 1910), facing 136.

p. 46: From Crevaux, "Voyage d'exploration."

p. 47: Photo Mme. Georges Evrard.

p. 48: From Hurault, *Africains de Guyane*, pl. 6.

p. 49: From Hurault, *Africains de Guyane*, pl. 25.

p. 50: From Hurault, *Africains de Guyane*, pl. 12.

p. 53: Anonymous engraving in the Atlas van Stolk, Rotterdam, after a drawing by J. H. Hottinger based on a painting by J. A. Kaldebach.

p. 54: From Willem van de Poll, *Suriname* (Paramaribo: Varekamp, 1959), 83.

p. 58: From Hurault, *Africains de Guyane*, fig. 20.

p. 62: Photo S. Price, 2002.

p. 63: Archives départementales de Guyane.

p. 64: Photo S. Price.

p. 66: From Henri Coudreau, *Chez nos Indiens: Quatre années dans la Guyane française (1887–1891)* (Paris: Hachette, 1893), 57.

p. 74 left to right: Fowler Museum of Cultural History, Los Angeles; Fowler Museum of Cultural History, Los Angeles; American Museum of Natural History, New York; Surinaams Museum, Paramaribo; Fowler Museum of Cultural History, Los Angeles; photo A. Graeber.

p. 77 left: From John Walsh, *Time Is Short and the Water Rises* (New York: Dutton, 1967), 30; photo Patricia Caulfield.

p. 77 right: From Gerard van Westerloo and Willem Diepraam, *Frimangron* (Amsterdam: De Arbeiderspers, 1975), 158; photo Willem Diepraam.
p. 78: Photo S. Price, 2001.
p. 81 top: Photo Vicente Franco (Goldman Environmental Prize).
p. 81 bottom: Photo Michael Swerdlyk.
p. 83: Photo Ranu Abhelakh.
p. 85 top: Photo Kenneth Bilby.
p. 85 bottom: Photo Kenneth Bilby.
p. 87: Photo R. Price.
p. 88: Photo R. or S. Price.
p. 89 top: Ouest Guyane.
p. 89 middle: Photo R. or S. Price, 2018.
p. 89 bottom: Photo R. or S. Price, 2018.
p. 90: Photo S. Price.
p. 91 top: Photo R. Price.
p. 91 bottom: Photo S. Price.
p. 96 top left: Photo Marieke Heemskerk.
p. 96 top right: Photo Marieke Heemskerk.
p. 96 bottom: Photo Marieke Heemskerk.
pp. 96–97: Photo Marieke Heemskerk.
p. 104: Photo S. Price.
p. 105: We thank the late Angèle Gilormini for giving us this drawing. Photo S. Price.
p. 106: Photo R. Price.
p. 107: Photo Jean-Pierre Wieczorek.
p. 108 top: Photo Clémence Léobal.
p. 108 bottom: Photo Clémence Léobal.
p. 110: Photo Hatt Eaton.
p. 112: Photo R. Price, 2018.
p. 113 all: Photos S. Price.
p. 115 top: Photo R. Price.
p. 115 bottom: Kenneth M. Bilby, "The Remaking of the Aluku: Culture, Politics, and Maroon Ethnicity in French South America" (PhD diss., Johns Hopkins University, 1990), 395.
p. 116 top: Photo S. Price.
p. 116 bottom: Photo S. Price.
p. 117: Photo R. Price.
p. 119: Photo Jody Amiel, *France-Guyane*.
p. 120: Photo Martha Cooper, Asindoopo.
p. 124 top left: Photo S. Price.
p. 124 top right: Photo S. Price.
p. 124 middle left: Photo Clémence Léobal.

p. 124 middle right: Photo R. Price.
p. 124 bottom left: Photo S. Price.
p. 124 bottom right: Photo S. Price.
p. 133 left: Photo R. Price, 2000.
p. 133 middle: Photo R. Price, 2000.
p. 133 right: Photo R. Price, 2000.
p. 135: Postcard, 1990s, Éditions G. Delabergerie.
p. 139: S. W. de Groot Collection; photo A. Graeber.
p. 140 top: Musée des Cultures guyanaises, Cayenne; photo P. Buirette.
p. 140 middle: Musée des Cultures guyanaises, Cayenne; photo P. Buirette.
p. 140 bottom: Musée des Cultures guyanaises, Cayenne; photo P. Buirette.
p. 141: Photo David Damoison.
p. 142 top left: Photo A. Graeber.
p. 142 top middle: American Museum of Natural History, New York; photo A. Graeber.
p. 142 top right: American Museum of Natural History, New York; photo A. Graeber.
p. 142 bottom: Collection Jean Hurault, Musée du Quai Branly–Jacques Chirac; photo Jean Hurault.
p. 143 top left: R. and S. Price Collection; photo A. Graeber.
p. 143 bottom left: American Museum of Natural History, New York; photo A. Graeber.
p. 143 right: Fowler Museum of Cultural History, Los Angeles; photo A. Graeber.
p. 144 top left: Photo R. Price, Dangogo, 1968.
p. 144 top right: Photo P. Buirette.
p. 144 bottom: Photo R. Price, Dangogo, 1968.
p. 145: S. W. de Groot Collection; photo A. Graeber.
p. 146: Musée des cultures guyanaises, Cayenne; photo P. Buirette.
p. 147 top: Photo R. Price, 2018.
p. 147 middle: Bibliothèque municipale de Maripasoula; photo R. Price, 2018.
p. 147 bottom: R. and S. Price Collection; photo S. Price.
p. 148 top: Photo S. Price.
p. 148 bottom: Photo S. Price, 2001.
p. 149 top: Photo S. Price.
p. 149 bottom left: Musée des Cultures guyanaises, Cayenne; photo P. Buirette.
p. 149 middle right: Musée des Cultures guyanaises, Cayenne; photo P. Buirette.
p. 149 bottom right: R. and S. Price Collection; photo S. Price.
p. 150 top: Photo S. Price, 2001.
p. 150 bottom: Photo S. Price.
p. 151 top: Patrick and Setti Lacaisse Collection, Mana; photo S. Price, 2018.

p. 151 bottom left: Photo S. Price, 2018.
p. 151 bottom right: Photo S. Price, 2018.
p. 152 left: R. and S. Price Collection; photo R. or S. Price.
p. 152 right: *Left*: R. and S. Price Collection; *Right:* Musée des Cultures guyanaises, Cayenne; photo P. Buirette.
p. 153: Photo S. Price, 2018.
p. 154: Photo kindly provided by Marcel Pinas.
p. 155: Musée des Cultures guyanaises, Cayenne; photo P. Buirette.
p. 156 top: Photo R. Price, 1978.
p. 156 bottom: R. and S. Price Collection, Schomburg Center for Research in Black Culture, New York; photo H. Lorenz.
p. 157 top: R. and S. Price Collection, Schomburg Center for Research in Black Culture, New York; photo A. Vonk.
p. 157 bottom left: Photo R. Price.
p. 157 bottom right: Photo R. Price.
p. 158: Tropenmuseum, Amsterdam; photo A. Graeber.
p. 159 top left: Photo S. Price.
p. 159 top right: Photo S. Price.
p. 159 bottom: R. and S. Price Collection; photo S. Price.
p. 160 top: Photo Clémence Léobal.
p. 160 bottom: R. and S. Price Collection, Schomburg Center for Research in Black Culture, New York; photo R. Price.
p. 161 top left: Photo kindly provided by the Photothèque de Ouest-Guyane.
p. 161 top right: Photo S. Price.
p. 161 bottom: R. and S. Price Collection, Schomburg Center for Research in Black Culture, New York; photo S. Price.
p. 162 top: Photo Steven Alfaisi.
p. 162 bottom left: R. and S. Price Collection, Schomburg Center for Research in Black Culture, New York; photo S. Price.
p. 162 bottom right: Photo S. Price.
p. 163: *Left:* Tropenmuseum, Amsterdam; *Right*: R. and S. Price Collection, Schomburg Center for Research in Black Culture, New York; photo A. Graeber.
p. 164 all: R. and S. Price Collection; photo S. Price.
p. 165 top: R. and S. Price Collection; photo S. Price, 2002.
p. 165 bottom: R. and S. Price Collection; photo S. Price, 2002.

Race in the Atlantic World, 1700–1900

The Hanging of Angélique: The Untold Story of Canadian Slavery and the Burning of Old Montréal
by Afua Cooper

Christian Ritual and the Creation of British Slave Societies, 1650–1780
by Nicholas M. Beasley

African American Life in the Georgia Lowcountry: The Atlantic World and the Gullah Geechee
edited by Philip Morgan

The Horrible Gift of Freedom: Atlantic Slavery and the Representation of Emancipation
by Marcus Wood

The Life and Letters of Philip Quaque, the First African Anglican Missionary
edited by Vincent Carretta and Ty M. Reese

In Search of Brightest Africa: Reimagining the Dark Continent in American Culture, 1884–1936
by Jeannette Eileen Jones

Contentious Liberties: American Abolitionists in Post-emancipation Jamaica, 1834–1866
by Gale L. Kenny

We Are the Revolutionists: German-Speaking Immigrants and American Abolitionists after 1848
by Mischa Honeck

The American Dreams of John B. Prentis, Slave Trader
by Kari J. Winter

Missing Links: The African and American Worlds of R. L. Garner, Primate Collector
by Jeremy Rich

Almost Free: A Story about Family and Race in Antebellum Virginia
by Eva Sheppard Wolf

To Live an Antislavery Life: Personal Politics and the Antebellum Black Middle Class
by Erica L. Ball

Flush Times and Fever Dreams: A Story of Capitalism and Slavery in the Age of Jackson
by Joshua D. Rothman

Diplomacy in Black and White: John Adams, Toussaint Louverture, and Their Atlantic World Alliance
by Ronald Angelo Johnson

Enterprising Women: Gender, Race, and Power in the Revolutionary Atlantic
by Kit Candlin and Cassandra Pybus

Eighty-Eight Years: The Long Death of Slavery in the United States, 1777–1865
by Patrick Rael

Finding Charity's Folk: Enslaved and Free Black Women in Maryland
by Jessica Millward

The Mulatta Concubine: Terror, Intimacy, Freedom, and Desire in the Black Transatlantic
by Lisa Ze Winters

The Politics of Black Citizenship: Free African Americans in the Mid-Atlantic Borderland, 1817–1863
by Andrew K. Diemer

Punishing the Black Body: Marking Social and Racial Structures in Barbados and Jamaica
by Dawn P. Harris

Race and Nation in the Age of Emancipations
edited by Whitney Nell Stewart and John Garrison Marks

Vénus Noire: Black Women and Colonial Fantasies in Nineteenth-Century France
by Robin Mitchell

City of Refuge: Slavery and Petit Marronage in the Great Dismal Swamp, 1763–1856
by Marcus P. Nevius

In Search of Liberty: African American Internationalism in the Nineteenth-Century Atlantic World
Edited by Ronald Angelo Johnson and Ousmane K. Power-Greene

An American Color: Race and Identity in New Orleans and the Atlantic World
by Andrew N. Wegmann

Maroons in Guyane: Past, Present, Future
by Richard Price and Sally Price

For more than four centuries, communities of maroons (men and women who escaped slavery) dotted the fringes of plantation America, from Brazil through the Caribbean to the United States. Today their descendants still form semi-independent enclaves—in Jamaica, Brazil, Colombia, Belize, Suriname, Guyane, and elsewhere—remaining proud of their maroon origins and, in some cases, faithful to unique cultural traditions forged during the earliest days of Afro-American history.

In 1986, after two decades working with Maroons in Suriname, anthropologists Richard and Sally Price were suddenly expelled by the military regime and began research in neighboring Guyane (French Guiana), where thousands of Maroons were taking refuge from the Suriname civil war. Over the next fifteen years, their conversations with local people convinced them of the need to replace the pervasive stereotypes about Maroons in Guyane with accurate information. In 2003, *Les Marrons* became a local best seller. In 2020, after a series of further visits, the Prices wrote a new edition taking into account the many rapid changes.

Available for the first time in English, *Maroons in Guyane* reviews the history of Maroon peoples in Guyane, explains how these groups differ from one another, and analyzes their current situations in the bustling, multicultural world of this far-flung outpost of the French Republic. A gallery of the magnificent arts of the Maroons completes the volume.

"Based on decades of research, *Maroons in Guyane* pays close attention to Maroon communities on their own terms—from African customs that survived the Middle Passage to ecological principles undergirding Maroon life—while also illuminating the wider world of Marronage and thus Black resistance throughout Atlantic society. It is a wonderful and ramifying book."—RICHARD S. NEWMAN, author of *Abolitionism: A Very Short Introduction*

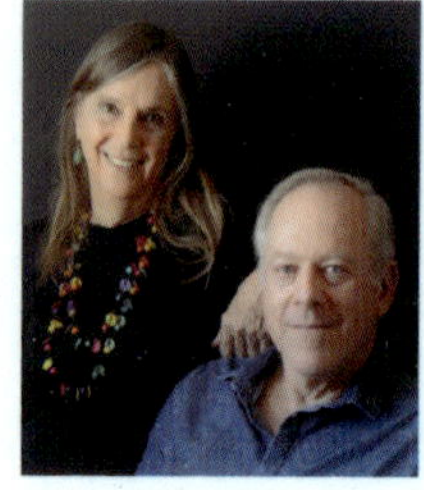

RICHARD and SALLY PRICE have written extensively on the history and culture of African Americans throughout the hemisphere. Richard Price's books include *First-Time, Alabi's World, The Convict and the Colonel, Travels with Tooy*, and *Rainforest Warriors*. Sally Price is the author of *Co-Wives and Calabashes, Primitive Art in Civilized Places*, and *Paris Primitive: Jacques Chirac's Museum on the Quai Branly*. Their most recent coauthored book is *Saamaka Dreaming*.

COVER DESIGN: Erin Kirk

COVER: Cottica Ndyukas from the village of Ovia Olo arriving at Poolo Boto Festival, Moengo, Suriname, close to the border with Guyane, 2015. (Photo: Olívia Gomes da Cunha)

A Sarah Mills Hodge Fund Publication

The University of Georgia Press
Athens, Georgia 30602 *www.ugapress.org*

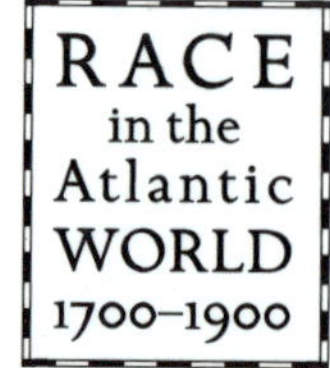